Taxing Ourselves

A Citizen's Guide to the
Great Debate Over Tax
Reform

Taxing Ourselves

A Citizen's Guide to the
Great Debate Over Tax
Reform

Joel Slemrod and Jon Bakija

The MIT Press
Cambridge, Massachusetts
London, England

This book was set in Palatino by Graphic Composition, Inc., and was printed and bound in the United States of America.

Library of Congress Cataloging-in-Publication Data
Slemrod, Joel.
    Taxing ourselves: a citizen's guide to the great debate over tax reform / Joel Slemrod and Jon Bakija
        p. cm.
    Includes bibliographical references and index.
    ISBN 0-262-19375-2 (alk. paper)
        1. Income tax—United States.   I. Bakija, Jon M.   II. Title.
HJ4652.S528 1996   96–15005
336.2'05'0973—dc20   CIP

To the memory of my father, Saul Slemrod
—J.S.

To Rebeccah
—J.B.

Contents

Tables

Note: Numbers in text, tables, and figures may not add to totals because of rounding.

Figures

Foreword

Albert Einstein once said that the hardest thing in the world to understand was the income tax. But understand it we must, because it is a critical part of how government affects the lives of Americans. Unfortunately, though, when tax reform enters the political arena, the subtleties of the key issues are usually lost in the midst of self-serving arguments and misleading simplifications. Academic treatments of the subject are of little help to the vast majority of citizens not familiar with the jargon and methods of economics.

This book is our attempt to bridge the gap between sound bites and treatises. It lays out what is known, and not known, about how taxes affect the economy, offers guidelines for evaluating tax systems, and provides enough information to evaluate the current income tax system against the leading proposals to replace or reform it. We have attempted to present this information in a clear, nontechnical way, while not misleading the reader by oversimplifying. We do not conclude with our own pet plan for the U.S. tax system; any such conclusion would require applying not only our judgments on the economics of taxation, but our values as well. However, if our book is successful, it will provide to readers enough background so that they can make an informed choice about how we should tax ourselves.

While working on the book, we were fortunate to have at our disposal the resources of the Office of Tax Policy Research (OTPR) at the University of Michigan Business School. We also owe a special debt to those colleagues who read and made extensive comments on an early draft of the book—Gerard Brannon, Leonard Burman, Don Fullerton, Louis Kaplow, and three anonymous reviewers. Mary Ceccanese, administrative assistant of OTPR, typed or reprocessed the entire manuscript, and provided encouragement and advice from start to finish. Monica Young and Brent Smith helped to track down vital information. Finally, Joel would like to thank Ava, Anna, and Jonathan for putting up with a sometimes absent and often distracted husband and father.

1   Introduction

As never before, the U.S. income tax system is under attack. Almost no one seems satisfied with the way it works, complaining that it is overly complex, unfair, and inhibits economic growth. In spite of this widespread dissatisfaction, what exactly should be done about it commands much less agreement. Although some argue that changes around the edge are sufficient, a growing chorus calls for a fundamental overhaul—even complete abolition of the income tax and the Internal Revenue Service (IRS).

While this idea certainly sounds appealing to many people, Americans also have a right to be apprehensive about big changes in the tax system. After all, this is the aspect of government that directly affects more people than any other. Many Americans recall the promises made about the last big change in the tax system, the Tax Reform Act of 1986, and have noticed little, if any, improvement since then. Others are concerned that tax reform will trade the deductions they have come to rely on for lower tax rates, only to see these rates climb back up to where they were. Some are worried that big changes in the distribution of the tax burden will shift more of it their way. Despite these concerns, there's plenty of frustration with the existing tax system, and little doubt that we ought to be able to do better.

Complaints About the Current Income Tax System

The most common complaint about taxes is straightforward enough—they are too high. Some of this attitude reflects simple self-interest; no one likes to pay taxes, just as no one enjoys paying utility bills. However, we all benefit in some way from the government activities those taxes finance. As Chief Justice Oliver Wendell Holmes, Jr., once noted, "taxes are what we pay for civilized society." For a given level of government expenditure, the alternative to taxes is to run large budget deficits, financed either by borrowing or the printing of money. This strategy runs the risk of causing high interest rates and high inflation, hurting private investment, and damaging our long-term prospects for economic growth.

Dissatisfaction with the overall level of taxes also arises from philosophical differences regarding the appropriate role for government in society, or fears that the government is wasting money. Many voters want to see a smaller government, with a correspondingly smaller tax bill.[1] Such questions are naturally controversial and difficult to resolve. But even agreement on this point would not resolve how taxes should be raised.[2] Similarly, people who disagree vehemently about the proper extent of government might well find agreement on how our tax system ought to be designed. Aside from the level of taxes, the major complaints about our current tax system are that it is too complicated and difficult to enforce, is excessively harmful to the economy, and is unfair. These latter issues are the ones we are concerned with when we discuss tax "reform."

It Is Too Complicated

One of the most common grievances taxpayers have with the design of the U.S. tax system is that it is too complicated. For many, complying with our labyrinthine tax regulations is an incredibly frustrating, costly, and intrusive process. Literally billions of hours are spent every year in the United States on fundamentally unproductive tax activities such as recordkeeping, wading through instructions, hunting for deductions and credits, and arranging one's financial affairs to take advantage of tax preferences. Of course, the taxpaying process is not that difficult for everyone. Millions of poor households have income below the filing threshold, and need not submit a return at all. Of the 115 million taxpayers who do file, 18 percent are able to use the very simple form 1040EZ; furthermore, survey evidence indicates that 45 percent of all taxpayers spend less than 10 hours per year on their taxes.[3] But for businesses and individuals with more complicated finances, the burden of compliance can be onerous indeed.

The cost of this complexity is staggering. Individual taxpayers spend as much as three *billion* hours of their own time on tax matters, or about 27 hours per taxpayer on average.[4] That is the equivalent of over one-and-a-half million hidden, unpaid IRS employees! Many buy books or computer software such as Turbotax® to help them through tax season. On top of that, about half of all individual taxpayers purchase professional assistance from an accountant, lawyer, or other advisor to prepare their tax returns.[5] Businesses also face a heavy compliance burden, with a typical Fortune 500 firm spending over $2 million per year on tax matters.

The total cost of collecting income tax, including the value of those billions of hours that taxpayers might have used more productively, probably comes to about $75 billion per year, which amounts to about 10 cents for every dollar of revenue raised. Politicians as diverse as House Ways and Means Committee Chairman Bill Archer (R-TX) and House Minority Leader Richard Gephardt (D-MO) have been citing annual compliance cost figures as high as $300 billion.[6] While $300 billion is almost certainly an overestimate,[7] there's little doubt that the tax compliance burden is large and wasteful, and that it angers many people from across the political spectrum.

It Is Difficult to Enforce

Administering and enforcing almost any tax code is a difficult and costly enterprise. Some argue that the U.S. tax code is harder to enforce than it has to be, in part because legislators have made it so complex. The annual budget for the IRS is now approaching $8 billion.[8] In a single year, the IRS processes over 200 million returns, including 115 million individual returns. It audits over one million tax returns and sends out over five million computer-generated notices to taxpayers. The IRS compares the information from over one billion documents, such as reports from banks, stockbrokers, and mortgage lenders, to the numbers taxpayers report on their returns.

In spite of the significant expenditures on IRS enforcement, the massive compliance costs borne by the public, and all the misery suffered by those who are investigated by the IRS, there is still a great deal of cheating on taxes. Although it is hard to measure such things accurately, the IRS estimates that in 1992 it lost $119 billion to noncompliance with the individual and corporate income taxes, or about 17 percent of total tax liability.[9] Other things being equal, this means higher tax rates and a heavier burden for the many people who are honest or who have little opportunity to cheat.

It Is Bad for the Economy

For most people, the thought of taxes conjures up the pain of figuring out and paying what they owe. However, the political debates about taxes are rarely about the process itself. Instead, these debates often center on how taxes affect the economy. Sometimes the debates are about short-term questions such as whether a tax increase will snuff out a boom, or prolong a recession, or whether a tax cut will get an underperforming economy moving. Other times, the deficit-reducing benefits of a tax increase are pitted against the costs of such an approach. Occasionally, the focus is on how the design of the tax code, or some aspect of it, affects the long-term prosperity of the economy. It is this last issue that is most relevant to the debate over tax reform.

The sheer size of taxes—in 1994, federal taxes consumed 20.5 percent of the gross domestic product, while state and local taxes took up another 11.1 percent[10]—suggests that they can have a very important effect on the way our economy operates. Taxes affect the terms of almost every economic decision. They have an impact on the size of the rewards we can get from saving, working hard, taking a second job, and investing in education or training. The income tax changes how much it costs to contribute to charity, buy a home, or put children in day care. Business decisions such as whether and how much to invest in a new technology, or whether to locate a factory in the United States or Mexico, can all hinge on the tax consequences.

A wide variety of complaints have been leveled against the current income tax regarding its effects on the long-term prosperity of the economy. One charge is that high tax rates on the well-to-do discourage the hard work, innovation, and entrepreneurship necessary for a vibrant economy. A second claim is that the tax system is biased against saving and investment, which are essential for maintaining and improving our long-run standard of living, and is at least partly responsible for a U.S. national saving rate that is very low by both international and historical standards. Another grievance is that the preferences and penalties that are littered throughout the individual and corporate tax codes can significantly distort economic choices. By capriciously changing the relative costs and benefits of various activities and investments from what they would be in the free market, goes this argument, the tax system causes us to put our money in the wrong places. This misallocation hampers the efficiency of the economy and shackles long-term growth prospects.

It Is Unfair

In an April 1995 *Wall Street Journal*/NBC News poll, two-thirds of respondents agreed that "the current income tax is unfair."[11] Another
poll, which has followed public opinion on different types of taxes for
20 years, found that in 1993, 36 percent viewed the federal income tax
as "the worst tax—that is, the least fair," compared with 26 percent for
property taxes, 16 percent for state sales taxes, and 10 percent for the
state income tax.[12] The federal income tax had briefly improved in relative popularity following the 1986 tax reform, but has recently fallen
on harder times.

What is it about income taxes that people think is unfair? There is
certainly disagreement about how the burden should be shared across
families with different incomes. The current personal income tax is
"progressive," meaning that higher-income people typically pay a
larger percentage of their incomes in taxes than those with lower incomes. This progressivity is achieved mainly by exempting the first
several thousand dollars of income from taxation ($16,550 for a family
of four in 1995), and then imposing a set of "graduated" tax rates,
which ranged from 15 percent to 39.6 percent in 1995, on successive
brackets of income above that level. For some, a "fair" tax system
means maintaining graduated rates and perhaps increasing the burden on those with high incomes. But others dismiss this as "soaking
the rich" or "class warfare," and would prefer a less progressive
system.

While these kinds of issues are a perpetual source of controversy,
there does seem to be more room for agreement on some other aspects
of "unfairness." For example, there is a widely held perception that
those with good lobbyists, lawyers, and accountants are able to manipulate the tax code and take advantage of numerous loopholes and preferences, so as to avoid paying their "fair share" of the tax burden.
Those who believe this often favor a streamlined tax system, stripped
of opportunities for tax avoidance.

Haven't We Heard This Before?

These complaints are not new. In 1977 President Jimmy Carter called
the income tax "a disgrace to the human race," and offered a plan to
reform it. The plan went nowhere.[13] In 1986, following two years of
intensive debate, the Congress passed and President Reagan signed a

tax reform bill designed to make the tax system fairer and simpler, and to reduce its negative impact on the economy. This act eliminated or curtailed many deductions, credits, and other tax preferences in exchange for significantly reduced tax rates. The top rate in the personal income tax fell from 50 percent to 28 percent, while the top rate in the corporate income tax dropped from 46 percent to 34 percent. The tax shelter industry was devastated, and special tax preferences in the individual code were reduced in value by an estimated $200 billion.[14] Despite the lower rates, the tax system continued to raise roughly the same level of revenue, and the distribution of tax burdens across different income classes was not substantially altered.[15]

While this hard-won set of reforms arguably produced an improvement in the efficiency and fairness of the tax system, complaints persisted and the public seemed largely unimpressed. In a 1990 poll, 31 percent of taxpayers said they thought the Tax Reform Act of 1986 made taxes more complicated, while only 12 percent thought they had become less complicated. Moreover, 37 percent thought the distribution of tax burdens had become less fair as a result of the 1986 reforms, compared to just 9 percent who said it had become more fair.[16]

In the years following the 1986 reforms, concerns about fairness and the budget deficit led to increases in the top tax rate, which was restored to just short of 40 percent by 1994. Discussion of any major tax reform was put on the back burner, perhaps in part because the exhausting fight over the 1986 reforms seemed to bring few political rewards. But since the election of a Republican majority in Congress in 1994, talk of tax reform has been in the air again.

What makes the recent debate different is the serious consideration being paid to *fundamental* changes in the way we tax ourselves. The key word is overhaul, not reform. Several congressional leaders and Republican presidential candidates have advocated abolishing the existing personal and corporate income tax systems, and replacing them with something quite different. Consider, for example, this quote from Representative William Archer (R-TX), chairman of the powerful House Ways and Means Committee, from which all tax bills originate: "We've got to tear the income-tax system out by its roots. We have to remove the Internal Revenue Service from the lives of Americans totally."[17]

Representative Archer and others would like to replace the personal and corporate income taxes entirely with some form of tax on consumption, that is, on the portion of income that people spend instead of saving. Included among these proposals are a national sales tax, a value-added tax (or VAT), a flat tax, and a personal consumption tax. Yet another set of proposed reforms would retain the basic framework of the existing income tax, but make sweeping changes to it. While these reforms may be less dramatic than moving to a consumption tax, some of them still would represent changes as profound as anything we've seen in decades. Chapters 7 and 8 offer a careful examination of all the major options for reform. For now, let's have a brief look at the radical tax alternatives that have been attracting so much interest, and see what their proponents are saying about them.

Promises About Alternative Tax Systems

Advocates claim that their tax plans address each of the four complaints about the income tax discussed above, with varying emphasis. A major goal of all of these proposals is to remove any disincentives that the current system creates for saving and investing, and to improve the incentives to work hard, innovate, and create new businesses. They are also intended to remove many or all of the deductions, special preferences, and other features that distort economic choices and complicate the tax code. Some stress the possibility of eliminating the IRS from our lives.[18] And, of course, all of the would-be reformers promise that their plans will be "fair."

The most familiar tax alternative is probably the retail sales tax, since it is already used by all but five states. One adherent of this approach is a former Republican presidential candidate, Senator Richard Lugar, who supported a plan to replace the corporate and personal income taxes with a 17 percent national retail sales tax.[19] Lugar argues that "the national sales tax would allow for the dismantling of the current IRS and the intrusive, inefficient and costly enforcement of the current tax code." He also contends that, upon adoption of the sales tax, "Americans will enjoy a capital formation boom with strongly increased productivity, higher paying jobs, and new investment from around the world. . . ."[20]

Another kind of national sales tax is the VAT, which already serves as a major source of revenue in many countries throughout the world. Instead of collecting tax only from retailers, as in a sales tax, the VAT collects a little bit of the tax at each stage of the production and distribution process. Each firm pays tax on its "value-added," which is simply its total sales minus the costs of the goods and services (except for labor) that the firm had to buy to produce its output. For example, a furniture-building company would pay tax on its sales of furniture, but would get to deduct the cost of the wood, nails, tools, and machinery that it had purchased.

Supporters of the VAT believe it has many of the same advantages as the retail sales tax, but is much easier to administer equitably and efficiently. The VAT can be designed so that each firm has an incentive to make sure that any other firm it buys from has paid its tax. One long-time political backer of the VAT is Representative Sam Gibbons (D-FL), as of 1996 the ranking Democrat on the House of Representatives Ways and Means Committee. He has proposed using the VAT to replace not only the personal and corporate income taxes, but also the Social Security payroll tax.

Of all the radical alternatives to the income tax, recently most attention has focused on the "flat tax" developed by Robert Hall and Alvin Rabushka. Steve Forbes championed a 17 percent flat tax in his run at the Republican presidential sweepstakes in early 1996, and the 1996 report of a tax reform commission headed by former Republican presidential hopeful Jack Kemp endorsed many elements of this approach. House Majority Leader Richard Armey (R-TX) has been touting the flat tax since 1994.

Under the flat tax, all businesses and individuals would be taxed at a single, flat rate. The business tax base would be the same as that for a VAT, except that labor costs would be deductible. At the personal level, individuals would still file a tax return every year, but this return would only require them to pay taxes on their wages, salaries, and pension benefits. All other kinds of income, such as interest, dividends, and capital gains, would be completely excluded from taxation at the personal level, so there would be no need to report them. The personal tax would have a large tax-free "allowance," or exempt level of income, based on family size. But there would be no itemized deductions or other special preferences of any kind. As a result, proponents emphasize, the entire personal flat tax form could be made to fit on a postcard.

Although it looks like a simpler version of our current tax system, the Hall-Rabushka flat tax is not an income tax at all; rather, it is essentially a modified VAT or consumption tax. The only significant difference is that the flat tax takes wages and salaries out of the VAT's business tax base (by making them deductible), and then taxes them separately, and at the same rate, at the individual level. Taxing labor income at the personal level, with a generous personal exemption level, means that the flat tax can impose a much smaller burden on low-income people than a broad-based VAT or retail sales tax would, while retaining much of their simplicity and potential economic advantages.

Advocates of the flat tax express great confidence in its potential benefits. Hall and Rabushka promise their flat tax "would give an enormous boost to the U.S. economy by dramatically improving incentives to work, save, invest, and take entrepreneurial risks."[21] Moreover, they contend, it would raise "the same revenue as does the current system," yet "everyone's after-tax income would rise."[22] Representative Armey says the flat tax is "fair" precisely because "it treats everyone the same."[23] Hall and Rabushka add that it is "fair to ordinary Americans because it would provide a tax-free allowance."[24] Finally, they pledge that the flat tax "would save taxpayers hundreds of billions in direct and indirect compliance costs."[25]

A fourth option, which we'll call the "personal consumption tax," offers a somewhat different approach to consumption taxation. Unlike the first three proposals discussed above, which are all essentially variations on a sales tax, the personal consumption tax attempts to measure how much each family actually consumes during the year. Each year the taxpayer would report income and net saving; the difference, income minus saving, is the base on which tax liability depends.

Senators Pete Domenici (R-NM) and Sam Nunn (D-GA) recently proposed a version of this approach called the "Unlimited Savings Allowance," or USA Tax. In this plan, the individual income tax would be replaced by a personal consumption tax with graduated rates of 8, 19, and 40 percent. Their proposal would also allow deductions for charitable contributions, home mortgage interest, and postsecondary education expenses, and a credit for Social Security payroll taxes paid. Meanwhile, the corporate tax would be replaced by an 11.5 percent VAT (with no deduction for labor income).[26]

Like other consumption tax sponsors, Senator Domenici contends his proposal would "simplify and eliminate many of the economic distortions inherent in the current code," and would "unshackle our productive power, encouraging international trade and economic growth that will benefit all Americans."[27] Moreover, he asserts, the USA Tax would "retain the progressivity of the current federal income tax."[28]

Objections to Radical Reform

Most people would probably like to change some parts of our tax system, but not everyone favors a complete overhaul. Back in 1984, President Reagan's Treasury Department seriously considered the idea of replacing the income tax with some kind of consumption tax, but counseled against it on the grounds that the American people would perceive it as unfair.[29] A 1994 survey of the members of the National Tax Association, the leading professional group of tax experts from academia, government, and business, suggests that they are also quite skeptical. Just 36 percent favored replacing "much or all" of the current income tax with a VAT, while 80 percent expressed support for retaining a personal income tax with rates that rise with income.[30] The National Association of Homebuilders and the National Retail Federation, representing industries that comprise major portions of the U.S. economy, have expressed strong reservations about the reform proposals.[31] About the flat tax, journalist Robert Kuttner cautions that, "behind the promise of simplicity and tax reduction are higher deficits and a more regressive tax system." "The supply-siders are back," he says. "Check your wallet."[32]

The most commonly expressed objection to radical reform proposals concerns their distributional consequences. Robert McIntyre of Citizens for Tax Justice says "there is little or no disagreement among serious analysts that replacing the current, progressive income tax with a flat rate tax would dramatically shift the tax burden away from the wealthy—and onto the middle class and the poor."[33] A 1996 U.S. Treasury Department study of a flat tax proposed by Representative Armey and Senator Richard Shelby (R-AL) concluded that the total federal tax bill for people with incomes below $200,000 would increase by an average of 11.8 percent, while the tax bill for those with incomes above $200,000 would fall by 28.3 percent.[34] A federal retail sales tax or VAT would shift even more of the tax burden toward people at the low end of the income distribution, as these taxes have no way of exempting a minimum level of income.

Are we willing to accept a big change in who bears the tax burden, in exchange for the promised benefits of the reforms? The public seems ambivalent. In a September 1995 *Wall Street Journal*/NBC News poll, a graduated income tax was preferred to a flat tax by a 57 to 38 percent margin.[35] In a 1993 Gallup poll, three-quarters of respondents said that "upper income people" pay "too little" in taxes.[36] In apparent contradiction to these survey results, an April 1995 *Newsweek* poll found that 61 percent of respondents said they favored some form of "flat tax" over "the current system."[37] What could account for the mixed signals? Perhaps people will say they prefer almost anything over the current tax system. Many skeptical Americans probably also believe that loopholes destroy most of the progressivity or fairness in the current income tax anyway. Some people may be equating a flat tax with a cut in the overall level of taxes. In any event, it seems that many people haven't yet developed well-considered or consistent opinions on these matters.

A second common critique of the radical reform proposals is that their promised economic and simplification benefits are overstated. Although proponents have heavily emphasized their potential for improving long-run economic growth and simplifying the taxpaying process, the degree to which they would actually accomplish these goals is subject to much debate among economists. For example, advocates often claim that consumption taxes would cause a dramatic boost in saving and investment by improving the financial reward to saving. Moreover, some contend that because a low, flat tax rate would increase the reward for working (the after-tax wage), it would lead Americans to work considerably harder. But the conventional wisdom among economists, based on evidence from recent U.S. history, is that the financial reward to saving has little discernible effect on aggregate saving rates, while after-tax wages have little or no effect on hours of work for adult males. At the very least, there is far less certainty about the economic consequences of tax reform than advocates usually admit.

As for simplification, many analysts believe that while either the flat tax or VAT would be significantly simpler than the current system, a personal consumption tax such as the USA Tax would actually make the taxpaying process for many people more complicated and harder to enforce, and a federal retail sales tax would be impossible to administer equitably at the rates necessary to replace income taxation. Moreover, much of the simplification that radical tax reform offers comes only at the cost of foregoing progressivity and the kind of personalized tax system that many Americans seem to favor.

A third set of objections concerns the all-important transition to a radically different system—how to get from here to there. Changing to a new tax code inevitably causes many "winners" and "losers," and the losers will likely perceive the changes as arbitrary and unfair. For example, many reform proposals would wipe out most or all tax deductions and preferences, such as those for home mortgage interest, state and local government bonds, and so forth, in exchange for lower tax rates. Reformers might be able to get most people to agree that this is more efficient and fair in the long run. But is it fair to people who already made decisions based on the old law? Many people take out bigger mortgages than they would otherwise, because they expect to be able to deduct the interest on the mortgage indefinitely. They would feel unfairly penalized by the removal of that deduction, since it's too late to change their decisions. Moreover, the resale value of their homes would probably fall. Depending on how it is implemented, a switch to a consumption tax could also impose a one-time tax on existing wealth; for elderly families who had paid income tax on their earnings all their working life, this tax on wealth could show up as a sharp increase in the price level, which reduces the buying power of their accumulated savings. While the impact of these problems could be softened by special transitional provisions, such provisions can get very complex very quickly.

The transition to a radically new tax system raises concerns not only about fairness, but also about the possibility of short-run economic disruptions. Different businesses will be affected in very different ways by tax reform, and it will take a while for workers and other resources to shift to new uses. Moreover, replacing the government's main revenue source with something completely different and untested strikes some people as risky, to say the least. It is difficult enough to project how much revenue the existing income tax system will bring in; estimating the revenues from a newly adopted system would be even trickier. Taxpayers, along with their lawyers and accountants, have demonstrated that they can come up with very sophisticated ways of avoiding taxes, so it's hard to predict how they would respond to an entirely new system. Some fear that we could end up raising much less revenue than we expect, causing the deficit to explode.

Critics also object to specific proposals that would sharply reduce revenues. For example, many are concerned by Treasury Department estimates that the Armey-Shelby 17 percent flat tax would lose $138 billion per year in revenue compared to the current system.[38] Sponsors of these plans often offer unspecified spending cuts to offset some of the cost, and promise improved economic growth will take care of the rest. But others worry that the result would instead be greatly increased budget deficits. Moreover, even some conservatives are uneasy about confusing the debate over the design of the tax system with the debate over the appropriate size of government.

Finally, some skeptics are afraid that we're opening quite a can of worms. A free-for-all over tax policy, with special interests thrown into the mix, could conceivably end up producing legislation that is even more of a mess than what we have now. Veterans of the perpetual struggle over taxes remember a similar effort at reform under President Ford in the mid-seventies, which ended up adding so many complications and preferences to the code that it was nicknamed "The Tax Practitioners Act of 1976." Similarly, some critics and advocates of reform are united by the concern that once we overhaul the system, there may be nothing to keep it from gradually getting messed up again. They argue that any one-time tax change ought to be accompanied by reforms in the policy process itself to prevent a gradual drift back to complexity, inefficiency, and unfairness.

Fixing the Existing Income Tax

Although proposals to scrap the income tax entirely have recently been the focus of attention, others would like to see the existing system fixed rather than replaced. Several political leaders are working on reforms that would take the approach of the Tax Reform Act of 1986 further, attempting to simplify and streamline the income tax as much as possible. Many of these plans are called flat taxes, or modified flat taxes, as that seems to be the buzzword of the moment. Some of the "flat" taxes are not noticeably flat in the sense that they maintain some of the key deductions of the current tax system.

House Minority Leader Richard Gephardt (D-MO) has offered a plan that would eliminate almost all itemized deductions and, in exchange, would enable "the vast majority (75 percent) of all taxpayers to pay their federal income taxes at no more than a 10 percent rate." Unlike most consumption tax proposals mentioned above, interest, dividends, and capital gains would continue to be taxed at the personal level, and higher marginal tax rates would be retained on high-income people. The existing corporate income tax system would also be retained, but many special preferences in this code would be eliminated. Gephardt argues that his approach "would make the tax system fairer and simpler" and that "average taxpayers will know that everyone else is paying their fair share: high-priced lawyers and accountants won't help the privileged reduce their tax bill."[39]

Naturally, these plans have drawn plenty of criticism of their own. For example, Representative Archer calls Gephardt's plan a "faulty proposal that increases taxes, pounds people who save, and leaves the IRS directly involved in the lives of the American people," and goes on to charge that it "continues the liberal doctrine of class warfare against all those who are successful in America."[40]

Whether or not any particular income tax reform plan is the right fix for the problems that ail it, it is important to keep in mind that the policy choices are not simply to keep the system as it is, or abandon it entirely for a completely different one. Even if the schemes for radical reform are ultimately rejected, the impetus to streamline and simplify the tax system need not be abandoned. The Tax Reform Act of 1986 made strides in this direction, and it may be that further change along these lines is the best of the available options. This approach will be examined in more detail in Chapter 8.

The Need for "Objective" Analysis

The odds are that we're in for a tremendous battle over our tax system, maybe not in 1996 or even 1997, but at some time in the near future. The outcome of this battle could have a profound effect on the lives of all Americans. Sorting out the pros and cons of the many competing reform proposals will be a difficult task even for the most informed and interested citizens. There will be quite a clash among those with differing values regarding what is "fair" and differing beliefs about the economic effects of taxation.

As if this weren't enough to confuse matters, the concerned citizen will have to wade through a sea of self-serving arguments. Those groups that have the most to gain or lose from tax reform will produce arguments that buttress their point of view. The potential losers will seldom say they are opposing a policy simply because it skins their own hides. Much more often the argument is couched in terms of how the national interest is hurt, how many jobs will be lost, and how unfair it is. The potential winners won't trumpet the money they stand to make, but will have their own arguments about growth, productivity, and achieving the American dream.

Making an intelligent judgment about tax policy requires seeing through the self-serving arguments to a clear understanding of the issues involved. Unfortunately, decisions must be made without the luxury of having definitive answers to many of the critical questions.

Some issues, such as what is "fair," ultimately rely on individual value judgments. Moreover, even many questions about fact may be impossible to resolve before we have to make a decision. In his 1990 book *The Growth Experiment*, current Federal Reserve Board member Lawrence Lindsey asserts that the argument over the economic effects of taxes "has persisted for lack of the data or methods of analysis to settle important disputes of fact," and promises that his book "will remedy that deficit," noting that "the computer technology to do all this has not been available until this decade, and our analytic methods have only recently caught up to the technology."[41] However, the problems are much deeper than that. Contrary to what he says, many of the important disputes in the economics of taxation have not even come close to being settled by "better technology and analytical methods." We do know some things, and can make good educated guesses about others, but definitive answers to many key questions remain elusive.

What's Ahead

In this book, we offer a guide to the coming debate over tax reform, designed to help the concerned citizen make intelligent decisions. Our goal is to cut through the academic jargon, the Washingtonspeak, and the self-serving arguments, to explore the fundamental choices and questions inherent in tax policymaking.

Chapter 2 offers some historical and international perspective on taxation in America, and a concise description of our existing federal income tax system. Chapters 3 through 5 examine the basic principles that must serve as guides for tax policy: fairness, the promotion of economic prosperity, simplicity, and enforceability. In addition to laying out the basic principles, we explore the controversies and difficulties that arise. Moreover, these chapters examine the evidence on crucial questions such as how the burden of our tax system is distributed and what is known about the economic effects of taxation. Such evidence is critical for evaluating the claims of various reform proposals, and for weighing the inevitable trade-offs among principles in any tax system. Chapter 6 goes over the key elements of many tax reform proposals: a clean base (removal of all the deductions and exceptions of the current code), a single rate, and a consumption rather than an income base. While reform proposals often contain more than one of these elements, it's important to recognize that they are indeed separable issues; in principle, we could adopt any combination of these elements without accepting the whole package. We'll explore the importance and implications of each of these elements in detail. Chapter 7 provides a thorough examination of the major alternatives to the income tax, and Chapter 8 addresses options that would keep the income tax but reform it. Chapter 9 closes with a voter's guide to the coming debate over tax reform, for the concerned citizen to keep handy when the rhetoric heats up, to help sort out fact from fiction and promises from reality.

2

An Overview of the U.S. Tax System

Before discussing whether we need to change the way we tax ourselves, it will be useful to consider the history and basic features of the system we already have. First, we'll take a glance at the overall tax picture for the United States, surveying how much revenue governments at all levels take in, what kinds of taxes they use, and how these compare to other countries. Next, we offer a bit of historical background on American taxation, in order to put the current debate in perspective. Finally, we lay out the basic frameworks of the federal government's personal and corporate income taxes, the two main targets for reform or replacement in the present political environment. Here, we'll explain the essentials of how these taxes work and clarify some of the terminology that you'll be hearing repeatedly whenever tax reform is discussed.

How Governments in the United States Get Their Money

Table 2.1 lists the major taxes used by federal, state, and local governments in the United States, illustrating the relative importance of each. Altogether, governments in our country raised over $2.1 *trillion* in taxes and other revenues during 1994. One way to put such a large number in perspective is to compare it with the size of the economy, which is usually represented by the gross domestic product (GDP). GDP is a measure of the total dollar value of all goods and services produced within the United States in a single year for sale in the market. In 1994, total federal, state, and local government revenues amounted to a bit less than one-third, or 31.5 percent, of our 6.7 trillion dollar GDP. Federal revenues were 20.5 percent of GDP, while state and local revenues accounted for 11.1 percent of GDP.[1]

Table 2.1
Sources of revenue for U.S. governments, 1994

	Billions of 1994 dollars	Percentage of revenues at that level of government	Percentage of GDP
Total federal revenues	**1,379**	**100.0**	**20.5**
Contributions for social insurance	555	40.3	8.2
Personal income taxes	549	39.8	8.1
Corporate income taxes	167	12.1	2.5
Excise taxes and customs duties	75	5.4	1.1
Estate and gift taxes	15	1.1	0.2
Other federal revenues	18	1.3	0.3
Total state and local revenues	**746**	**100.0**	**11.1**
Sales taxes	226	30.3	3.4
Property taxes	191	25.6	2.8
Personal income taxes	132	17.6	2.0
Contributions for social insurance	71	9.5	1.1
Corporate income taxes	35	4.7	0.5
Other state and local revenues	91	12.2	1.3
Total federal, state, and local revenues	**2,125**	**100.0**	**31.5**

Source: U.S. Bureau of Economic Analysis, *Survey of Current Business* (August 1995).

At the federal level, "contributions to social insurance" are now the largest source of receipts, providing just over 40 percent of total federal revenues. The Social Security payroll tax, which finances retirement and health benefits for the elderly and disabled, accounts for the vast majority of these contributions.[2] Some of the smaller items in this category include the unemployment insurance payroll tax and federal employee pension contributions.

The distinguishing characteristic of most social insurance programs is that the benefits received are determined in part by the amount of taxes, or "contributions," paid. For example, people who pay large amounts of taxes into Social Security over their lifetimes typically receive larger retirement benefits from the system than those who contribute less, although the relationship is far from proportional. Most current tax reform proposals do not include major changes in the system of social insurance taxes, in part because of a reluctance to upset this relationship between contributions and benefits.[3] While the financing of the Social Security system is clearly an important question, and is itself the subject of major reform proposals, it will not be the focus of this book.

The second biggest source of federal revenue is the personal income tax, which raised $549 billion in 1994, or just under 40 percent of federal revenues. The corporate income tax takes in another $167 billion. Together, they accounted for over half of all federal revenues in 1994, at $716 billion. Because of the vast amount of money raised by these two taxes, replacing them, as many critics hope to do, is clearly a tall order. This chapter will explain the basics of how these two taxes work.

A few other small items round out the federal list. Excise taxes on commodities such as cigarettes, alcohol, and gasoline, together with customs duties on imported goods, produced 5.4 percent of federal revenues in 1994. A tax on large estates and gifts (those exceeding $600,000) accounted for an additional 1.1 percent.

State and local governments rely very heavily on taxes not levied by the federal government—sales and property taxes. In 1994, retail sales taxes accounted for 30.3 percent of state and local revenues, while property taxes provided another 25.6 percent. Income taxation plays a smaller role for states and localities; 17.6 percent of their revenues came from personal income taxes, while just 4.7 percent came from corporate income taxes.

International Comparisons

Table 2.2 shows how our nation's tax system stacks up against those of other economically advanced countries. You may be surprised to learn that, relative to the size of our economy, the United States has *lower* taxes than the vast majority of other comparable nations. In 1993, the United States had the fourth-lowest tax-to-GDP ratio of the 24 countries in the Organisation for Economic Co-operation and Development (OECD), a group of industrialized nations from North America, Europe, and the Pacific. On average, OECD countries raised taxes equal to 38.7 percent of their GDPs in 1993, compared to just 29.7 percent for the U.S.[4] Japan was slightly below the U.S. level, with taxes at 29.1 percent of GDP. Sweden, on the other hand, had taxes amounting to 49.9 percent of GDP, tying it with Denmark for the OECD lead.

What sets the United States apart from most other advanced nations is not how much we raise through either income taxes or social insurance taxes; for these two, our tax-to-GDP ratio is only a bit below the

Table 2.2
International comparison of taxes as a percentage of GDP, 1993

	United States	OECD average[a]	Japan	United Kingdom	Canada	Germany	Sweden
Total taxes	29.7	38.7	29.1	33.6	35.6	39.0	49.9
Income taxes	12.6	14.1	11.8	11.8	15.7	12.0	20.6
Personal income taxes	10.2	11.3	7.5	9.3	13.5	10.6	18.4
Corporate income taxes	2.3	2.6	4.3	2.4	2.0	1.4	2.2
Consumption taxes[b]	4.5	11.0	3.7	11.3	8.7	10.4	13.2
Value-added taxes	–	6.1	1.5	6.6	2.6	6.8	8.5
Sales taxes	2.3	0.4	–	–	2.7	–	–
Social insurance taxes	8.7	10.2	9.8	6.0	5.9	15.1	13.8
Other taxes	3.9	3.4	3.8	4.5	5.3	1.5	2.3

Notes: Dash (–) indicates tax not used by country in question. Includes taxes at all levels of government. Total revenue figure is slightly lower than in Table 2.1 because certain nontax revenues, such as fees and fines, are excluded by OECD here.
[a]Unweighted average of all 24 nations in the Organisation for Economic Co-operation and Development.
[b]Includes value-added taxes, sales taxes, excise taxes, import and customs duties, and other consumption taxes.
Source: OECD (1995a).

mean. The big difference is in consumption taxes; we collect 4.5 percent of GDP in consumption taxes, compared to an 11.0 percent OECD average. Moreover, the United States is unusual in the kinds of consumption taxes it uses. Retail sales taxes are now rare outside the United States; only 5 of the other 23 OECD member countries still had them in 1993. The value-added tax (VAT), a close cousin to the retail sales tax that we discuss at length in Chapter 7, is the most common variety of consumption tax. As of 1993, all OECD nations except the United States, Australia, and Switzerland had VATs, which on average raised 6.1 percent of GDP.

Completely replacing personal and corporate income taxation with a VAT, as some hope to do in the United States, would be an unprecedented move among major industrialized nations. All of the OECD countries have very large income taxes in addition to their large consumption taxes. However, the VAT that would be required to replace income taxation in the United States would not be that much larger

than VATs already used successfully in some other countries. Retail
sales taxes of that size, though, have never been attempted in any of
these nations.

Historical Perspective on the U.S. Tax System

Taxes Overall

Figure 2.1 illustrates how government revenues have changed in the
United States since 1900. Perhaps the most striking feature is the tremendous growth in total revenues, from 7 percent of GDP at the beginning of the century to 30 percent by 1969. But even more striking to
some may be the fact that, since the late 1960s, the overall tax-to-GDP
ratio has hardly changed, hovering around that 30 percent mark for
most of the past twenty-five years. Of course, the U.S. economy has
grown enormously during this time, so taxes take in a much larger

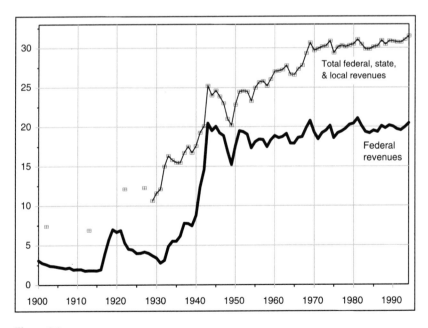

Figure 2.1
Government revenues as a percentage of GDP in the United States for the period
1900–1994
Note: Before 1929, data on state and local revenues is available only for selected years.
Sources: U.S. Bureau of the Census (1975); U.S. Bureau of Economic Analysis *National
Income and Product Accounts* (1992) and *Survey of Current Business* (various years).

dollar amount than they used to, even after adjusting for inflation. Thirty percent of our GDP can buy a lot more today than it could twenty-five years ago, in fact nearly twice as much.[5] Still, there's been little change during that time in the slice of our economic pie that goes to taxes.

Federal taxes have been steady relative to GDP for an even longer time—over fifty years. Their level in 1994, 20.5 percent of GDP, is the same as it was in 1943. Except for a temporary dip during the late 1940s, total federal revenues have remained remarkably stable over this period, never straying more than two percentage points in either direction from their 19.2 percent average since 1943. For all the talk of the expanding federal government, and attempts to downsize it, its size as a share of the economy has hardly budged for half a century.

For really big changes in the level of federal revenues related to GDP, we need to go back to the first half of the century. Clearly, World War II was the critical juncture for federal taxes; they jumped to 20.5 percent of GDP in 1943 from just 7.5 percent in 1939. The New Deal years of the 1930s were also important. Not only did federal revenues grow significantly relative to GDP during the 1930s, but many programs that would require high taxes in later years, such as the Social Security system, were born in this period.

State and local revenues have followed a somewhat more complicated pattern. In the early part of the century, state and local governments generally played a larger role than the federal government. At their peak in 1932, they were raising taxes equal to 12 percent of GDP, compared to only 3 percent at the federal level. As the federal role expanded, state and local revenues began to shrink relative to GDP, hitting a low of just 4 percent by 1948. They then grew back toward their former prominence throughout the fifties and sixties, and reached 10 percent of GDP by 1970. Since then, they have consistently remained in the 10 to 11 percent range.

History of the Personal Income Tax

Our nation's first income tax was a temporary emergency measure used during the Civil War; it was enacted in 1861 and expired in 1871. In the late 1800s and early 1900s, popular opposition began to mount against what were then the major sources of federal revenues: tariffs, excise taxes, and property taxes. Some viewed a personal income tax as an appealing alternative, because it could be made progressive, imposing a heavier proportional burden on the rich than on the poor.

Congress first enacted income taxation on a permanent basis in 1894, but the Supreme Court declared it unconstitutional one year later.[6] This obstacle to an income tax was eliminated by the Sixteenth Amendment to the U.S. Constitution, which was ratified in February 1913. President Woodrow Wilson signed the modern personal income tax into law shortly thereafter, in October 1913.[7]

The basic structure of the 1913 personal income tax was similar to today's, with some important differences. It had graduated rates, like the current system, but they only ranged from 1 to 7 percent. Many of today's most important deductions and exclusions were already there in 1913; examples include deductions for home mortgage interest and tax payments to state and local governments, and the exclusion of interest on state and local bonds. Deductions for charitable contributions were added just four years later, in 1917.[8] The biggest difference from today was that personal exemptions were so large, relative to typical incomes of the day, that only those with extremely high incomes had to pay any income tax at all. In 1914, the total number of personal tax returns filed amounted to less than 0.5 percent of the total U.S. population;[9] these days the figure is over 40 percent!

Figure 2.2 illustrates how two aspects of the U.S. personal income tax—revenues as a percentage of GDP, and the tax rate in the top bracket—have changed since 1913. The historical revenue pattern for the personal income tax is very similar to that for the overall federal government. Until World War II, receipts were quite small, staying well below 2 percent of GDP. This was true even when top rates were very high, sometimes exceeding 70 percent, because these rates continued to apply to only a very small number of high-income people. The number of returns filed never exceeded 7 percent of the total population between 1913 and 1939.

Because of the need for a lot of revenue fast, personal income taxation was expanded dramatically during World War II. The exempt level of income was reduced greatly, transforming what had been a "class tax" into a "mass tax." In the five years between 1939 and 1944 alone, the number of returns filed rose sharply from 6 percent of the population to 34 percent, and revenues surged from 1 percent to 8 percent of GDP. To facilitate the collection of taxes from so many people, employer withholding of income taxes on wages and salaries was introduced in 1943.

Ever since rising to 8 percent of GDP during World War II, the personal income tax has generally stayed close to that level, again excluding a brief drop during the late 1940s. It has remained a "mass" tax,

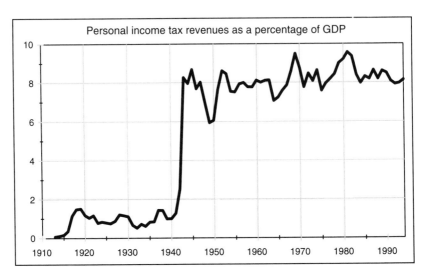

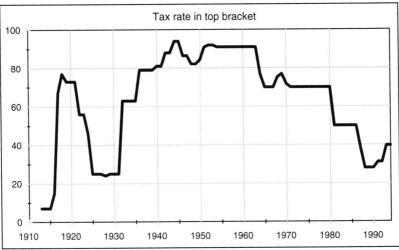

Figure 2.2
The U.S. personal income tax: Revenues and top rate for the period 1913–1994
Sources: U.S. Bureau of the Census (1975); U.S. Bureau of Economic Analysis *National Income and Product Accounts* (1992) and *Survey of Current Business* (various years); and IRS *Statistics of Income: Individual Income Tax Returns* (various years).

with the number of returns amounting to 44 percent of the total population in 1994.

One very striking feature of Figure 2.2 is that, while revenues as a fraction of GDP have changed little since World War II, the top tax rate has fallen dramatically. The top rate hit a peak of 94 percent in 1944–1945, stayed at 91 percent or higher from 1951 until the Kennedy-Johnson tax cut of 1964, and remained as high as 70 percent until 1981. By 1988, it had fallen all the way to 28 percent, and was still at a historically low 39.6 percent as of 1994.

This top tax rate has played a central role in the public debate over taxes, especially in recent years. There has been a good deal of controversy over the exact relationship between tax rates and revenues, a question that will be addressed later in this book. But note that the top rate, by itself, can give a seriously misleading impression of the personal income tax. During the years when the top rate was very high, it typically affected only a small fraction of 1 percent of taxpayers; almost everyone else was in a significantly lower tax bracket. And even among those who did face the top rate, it just applied to the portion of their incomes that exceeded the top bracket amount; all income below that fell into lower tax brackets, and hence was taxed at lower rates. Moreover, historically there have been significant changes not only in tax *rates*, but also in the tax *base*—that is, the portion of income that is taxable, after subtracting out all the deductions, exemptions, and other preferences allowed by the tax code. Both tax rates and the tax base are critical determinants of the level of revenues. Despite these caveats, the decline in the top rate has been a truly important part of the story of taxes over the past few decades.

History of the Corporate Income Tax

As with the personal income tax, the first special tax on corporations in the United States was a temporary emergency levy during the Civil War. Corporate income taxation was first adopted on a permanent basis in 1909. Its support also arose from opposition to the prevailing taxes of the day, and a belief that its burden would fall disproportionately on the wealthy. Unlike the personal tax, however, the corporate tax was able to escape constitutional problems, as Congress packaged it as an "excise" tax.[10]

Corporate income tax revenues followed a pattern similar to that of the personal income tax up through World War II (see Figure 2.3).

Figure 2.3
The U.S. corporate income tax: Revenues and top rate for the period 1909–1994
Sources: U.S. Bureau of the Census (1975); U.S. Bureau of Economic Analysis *National Income and Product Accounts* (1992) and *Survey of Current Business* (various years); Pechman (1987); and Gravelle (1994).

Revenues leaped from 1.4 percent of GDP in 1939 to a peak of 7.1 percent in 1943. However, since 1950 there has been a major decline in corporate tax revenues relative to GDP, falling to just 2.5 percent of GDP by 1994. The overall level of federal revenues remained steady over this period, in spite of the shrinking corporate tax, because Social Security payroll taxes took up much of the slack.

It appears that changes in the tax law itself explain little of the decline in corporate tax revenues. The tax rate on profits of large corporations, pictured in Figure 2.3, is imposed on the vast majority of corporate income. This rate hardly changed at all between 1950 and 1986, while revenues dropped sharply. Rather, most of the decline reflects a drop in taxable corporate profits, which fell from 13.5 percent of GDP in 1950 to just 4.6 percent by 1993.[11] Some of this may reflect statutory changes in the tax base, as features such as allowances for depreciation and investment tax credits (which will be explained in more detail later in this chapter) were altered over time. Still, most of the decline is probably unrelated to specific changes in the tax law. For example, corporations over this period increased the share of their incomes paid out as interest, which has always been deductible from the corporate tax base, as opposed to dividends and capital gains, which are not deductible. Net interest payments by corporations rose from .3 percent of GDP in 1950 to 2.3 percent in 1993.[12]

Recent Changes

Dissatisfaction with the income tax is by no means a new phenomenon. Throughout its life, there has been great controversy over both its level and its structure, and it has often been "reformed" in an attempt to reassign the tax burden or to ameliorate its impact on the economy.

Two of the most dramatic changes in the U.S. income tax system since its inception both occurred in the 1980s. Although both happened during the Reagan Administration, their underlying philosophies were vastly different, and in some ways contradictory. The impacts of these changes, and their implications for future reform efforts, are still being argued about by economists and politicians today. The differing philosophies still resonate in the current debate over tax reform.

In 1981, President Reagan and Congress collaborated to produce the Economic Recovery Tax Act (ERTA). Reagan had just won the presidency on a campaign that emphasized what he believed to be the negative economic effects of high tax rates, and he had promised an across-the-board cut in personal rates of 30 percent. As of 1980, the top personal income tax rate was 70 percent, but even people who did not have very large incomes had recently begun to face unusually high rates, because inflation was gradually pushing people into higher and higher tax brackets—"bracket creep." Unchecked bracket creep from 1976 through 1981 had caused an upward blip in revenues that is clear from Figure 2.2.

The defining feature of ERTA was tax rate cuts; only minor changes were made in the structure of the tax system. At the personal level, ERTA reduced the top rate from 70 percent to 50 percent immediately in 1981, and cut rates in all other brackets by approximately 23 percent of their former levels over three years.[13] It also provided for automatic adjustments of tax brackets for inflation beginning in 1984, to prevent further bracket creep. Savings incentives such as Individual Retirement Arrangements (IRAs) were expanded, and a special deduction for two-earner couples was introduced. At the corporate level, ERTA made deductions for depreciation (the wearing out of plant and equipment) considerably more generous, allowing firms to significantly reduce their taxable incomes.

No sooner had the ink dried on ERTA when projections of large federal deficits grabbed public attention. One response was to scale back some of the revenue-losing aspects of ERTA. In 1982 and 1984, some of the deductions and credits in the corporate income tax were scaled back a bit, and modest efforts were made to curb the burgeoning market for "tax shelters." A 1983 act accelerated the implementation of scheduled increases in the Social Security payroll tax, and for the first time subjected to income taxation a small portion of Social Security benefits received by high-income people.

In spite of these measures, revenues did decline relative to GDP following the tax cuts adopted in 1981, falling from levels that were historically high to levels close to the average for the postwar era. Between 1981 and 1984, the personal income tax dropped from an all-time peak of 9.6 percent of GDP back to 8 percent, while overall federal revenues fell from 21.1 percent of GDP down to 19.2 percent (see Figures 2.1 and 2.2).

By the mid-1980s, another debate about taxes had begun, this time centered not solely on lowering tax rates but instead on simplifying the tax system, making it fairer, and reducing its harmful effects on the economy. A tax reform plan introduced in 1983 by Democrats Bill Bradley and Richard Gephardt, which broadened the tax base and further lowered tax rates, had attracted attention, and in the election year of 1984, President Reagan instructed his Treasury Department to produce its own plan to improve the tax system. This idea eventually worked its way through Congress and, in October 1986, was signed by Ronald Reagan as the Tax Reform Act of 1986 (TRA). This reform resulted from the unusual coalition of a Republican president determined to lower the top rate yet further, and a Democratic Congress committed to improving the fairness of the system by ending apparent loopholes in the law such as tax shelters. It represented a surprising departure for tax legislation in the United States. Traditionally, changes in tax law, and especially those in 1981, had always added more and more special preferences and exceptions to the tax code. TRA took the opposite tack, opting to clean up the tax base.

Unlike the 1981 changes, the 1986 act was explicitly designed to maintain the existing level of revenues and the existing distribution of the tax burden across annual income classes. The top personal income tax rate was reduced from 50 percent to 28 percent, when fully phased in by 1988. But while the rate reductions in TRA primarily benefited upper-income people, the act also curtailed several deductions and exclusions that were used most heavily by those same people. Deductions for state and local sales taxes, two-earner couples, and consumer interest were eliminated. Limitations were placed on eligibility for IRAs, medical expense deductions, deductions for business meals and entertainment, and certain business losses. Moreover, the effective top rate on long-term capital gains, largely received by high-income taxpayers, increased from 20 to 28 percent. At the same time, features that benefit low- and moderate-income people, such as personal exemptions and the standard deduction, were increased.

At the corporate level, TRA broadened the tax base considerably by limiting depreciation deductions, eliminating the investment tax credit, and strengthening an "alternative minimum tax" provision. In exchange, the top corporate rate was reduced from 46 percent to 34 percent.

There have not been any tax reforms of the magnitude of either 1981 or 1986 since then. Nevertheless, two recent changes in tax law have garnered a great deal of attention. A deficit reduction plan enacted in 1990 raised the top personal rate to 31 percent. This act was famous for President Bush's abandonment of his "read my lips—no new taxes" pledge. In the deficit reduction act passed in 1993 under President Clinton, the top personal rate was increased again to 39.6 percent, the top corporate rate edged up to 35 percent, and an "earned income tax credit" that benefits the working poor was expanded. Although the top rates of tax have increased quite a bit since 1986, the vast majority of taxpayers were unaffected by these changes. It is also fair to say that most of the base-broadening structural reforms of TRA have stood up well in the past decade.

There is still a heated dispute over the effects of the tax changes that have occurred since 1980. For example, it is clear that personal income tax revenues declined relative to GDP following the 1981 tax cut, but some contend that the rate reductions spurred an increase in economic growth, causing revenues to fall by much less than they would have otherwise. Many others are skeptical that the tax cut had much effect on economic growth at all. The impacts of TRA, as well as the two more recent deficit-reduction acts, are also a subject of much debate among economists and politicians. These are critical issues that we will take up in more depth in Chapters 3 through 5, where we discuss the impact of taxation on fairness, simplicity, and economic prosperity.

Now that our brief history of American taxation has brought us up to the present, let's take a closer look at the basic features of the personal and corporate income taxes as they are today.

Basic Features of the U.S. Personal Income Tax

Rate Structure

At this point, you might be wondering why, if personal income tax collections amount to 8 percent of total national income, your own taxes are so much higher than that. Indeed, most taxpayers do face tax rates considerably higher than 8 percent, at least on part of their incomes. Table 2.3 illustrates the rate structure of the U.S. personal income tax for 1995. There are five official tax brackets, with rates ranging from 15 percent at the low end all the way up to 39.6 percent for taxable income above $256,500. Note that taxable income is considerably lower than total income, because it represents income after subtracting out all of the exemptions, deductions, and exclusions allowed by the tax code. We'll discuss these later in the chapter.

How does this rate structure work? Once you've figured out your "taxable income," it's usually pretty straightforward. Most people just look up how much they owe using the table in the instruction booklet, in which the calculations implied by Table 2.3 are already done. To

Table 2.3
Statutory rates in the personal income tax, 1995

Marginal tax rate	Taxable Income Range		
	Single return	Head-of-household return	Married couple, joint return
15%	0–23,350	0–31,250	0–39,000
28%	23,351–56,550	31,251–80,750	39,001–94,250
31%	56,551–117,950	80,751–130,800	94,251–143,600
36%	117,951–256,500	130,801–256,500	143,601–256,500
39.6%	above 256,500	above 256,500	above 256,500

Note: The tax brackets shown are for tax year 1995, and are indexed annually for inflation.

illustrate the underlying calculation, consider the example of a married couple, filing a joint return, with $50,000 of taxable income in 1995. Although this family is "in" the 28 percent bracket, they don't pay 28 percent of their entire income in taxes. Rather, they pay 15 percent of their first $39,000 of taxable income, and 28 percent on the remaining $11,000, for a total tax bill of $8,930. Here, we can introduce a bit of useful terminology. The *marginal* tax rate is the rate you pay on your next dollar of income; in the case of the family in this example, it is 28 percent. The *average* tax rate is your total tax bill expressed as a percentage of your income. As a share of taxable income, this family's average tax rate is (8,930 / 50,000), or 17.9 percent. As a share of total income, it is even lower.

The graduated rate structure is one reason why marginal income tax rates are generally so much higher than 8 percent. Our income tax has been designed to be progressive, meaning that average tax rates (tax divided by income) are higher for those with higher incomes. This result is accomplished in part by having marginal rates that rise with higher tax brackets, like those depicted in Table 2.3. As will be discussed later, the personal exemption, standard deduction, and earned income credit are the other key sources of progressivity in the tax system. The personal income tax's graduated rate structure is almost unique among American taxes. Most other taxes charge the same percentage rate regardless of one's income level. Some, like the Social Security tax, even charge a *lower* average rate for those with higher incomes, because only the Medicare portion of the tax is charged on wages and salaries above a certain level.

There is, however, another very important reason why personal tax rates are higher than 8 percent: a lot of income in the United States isn't counted as "taxable income" at all. Not only does this lead to higher tax rates on what is counted as taxable income, but as any taxpayer knows, the main difficulty of the taxpaying process is figuring out and keeping track of exactly what to add and subtract in order to *get* to taxable income.

What Is Income?—The Economist's Definition

To operate an income tax, it is necessary to define precisely what is meant by "income." This may, at first glance, seem easy, and for some taxpayers it is easy. But in many situations defining annual income turns out to be rather tricky. Ideally, what we're after is a measure of money and other gains received in a given period of time, from all sources, which can be used, either now or later, to purchase goods and services. This reasoning leads to the economist's definition of income—"the increase in an individual's ability to consume during a given period of time."[14] In other words, your annual income is the value of the goods and services you consume during a year, plus the net change in your wealth (saving) that occurs in that year. The latter reflects that part of annual income you choose not to spend this year, but which increases your ability to consume goods and services in the future.

Clearly, cash wages and salaries increase one's ability to consume, and are part of income. Noncash benefits that your employer provides to you, such as health insurance, are also a kind of income. Most people probably don't think of health insurance as income, but it certainly does increase one's ability to consume services, in this case services provided by doctors and hospitals. Someone whose health insurance is provided by an employer is clearly better off than someone with equal cash income but no insurance. Similarly, benefits provided by the government, such as Social Security, Medicare, or unemployment insurance benefits, also increase one's ability to consume and are considered part of income.

Returns to the ownership of capital add to your ability to consume as well, and thus count as income. Common examples would be interest and dividends that you accumulate on your savings, or rent received on a building you own. Another example is a capital gain, which is the increase in value over time of an asset such as a house, or shares in a corporation. Symmetrically, capital losses would be subtracted from income. Ideally, only *real* capital income and losses, as opposed to those due to inflation, would be counted. If you earn interest of 4 percent this year, but inflation is also 4 percent, your ability to consume hasn't really increased at all.

The costs of earning income reduce one's ability to consume, and so would be subtracted from the idealized definition of income. For example, if a farmer earns $50,000 from selling crops, but had to pay $20,000 for nondurable materials such as seeds, fertilizer, and so forth, then net income is only $30,000. On the other hand, the cost of durable goods, such as a tractor or a barn, would not be deducted in full right away. Durable goods still have value at the end of the year, so subtracting their full purchase price immediately would not accurately capture the change in your ability to consume. Rather, the idealized definition of income would each year subtract out the amount of *depreciation* that had occurred, that is, the amount by which goods or equipment had declined in value because they had worn out or become obsolete. Finally, if you had to borrow money to purchase the materials and equipment necessary to earn your income, the interest payments on that borrowing would be counted as a deductible expense.

Some durable goods, such as a home or a car, provide consumption services to their owners over multiple years, and these services are another form of income according to the economist's definition. For example, a home provides its owner with shelter every year, a service equal in value to the amount of rent that could be charged on that home. So according to the economist's conception, this rental value counts as income—owning the house certainly reflects a greater ability to consume housing services. As with durable productive goods, depreciation and interest payments on durable consumption goods would be subtracted to obtain net income.

The idealized definition of income refers to individuals, so that all income earned by businesses must ultimately be assigned in some way to individuals. As a step toward making that assignment, we can calculate net income for a business as total sales minus the costs of labor, material inputs, depreciation, and interest payments. This net income can either be paid out to owners of the firm, or can be reinvested back into the company. In the former case, it is fairly clear that the money paid out is income to the earners. What is less clear, but equally true, is that the earnings retained in the firm also represent income for the owners of the firm because they increase the value of the firm.

The Tax System's Definition of Income

So much for an idealized notion of what a person's, or family's, true annual income is. For a host of reasons, the definition of income on which we assess tax liability differs considerably from this idealized notion. In some cases, income is difficult to measure in the ideal fashion, so our tax system settles for an approximation. In many cases, special treatment has been intentionally granted to income that comes from certain sources, or which is used for certain purposes. Whether each of these deviations from economic income is justified will be explored in later chapters; for now, we'll just describe some of the major deviations from the economist's notion of income.

To begin, consider what items are included in the tax system's definition of income. The process of paying personal income taxes begins with the computation of adjusted gross income (AGI). Of all the items that are included in AGI, wages and salaries are by far the largest. They account for a little more than three-fourths of all AGI reported to the IRS. Most other items in AGI represent returns to the ownership of capital—dividends, interest, capital gains, rents, royalties, and profits from farms and small businesses. Some types of income, such as most wages and salaries, can be included in AGI in a very straightforward fashion, and require little elaboration. But others involve special complications, which deserve some mention here.

Consider capital gains. Counting them according to the economist's ideal notion of income would require measuring and reporting the increase (or decrease) in value of all assets, including houses and real estate, every year. In practice, capital gains are counted in AGI only when they are "realized," generally when the asset is sold. Capital gains on assets that are held until the owner's death, moreover, are completely absolved from taxation. The top tax rate on capital gain realizations was limited to 28 percent as of 1995, while regular income could be taxed at a rate as high as 39.6 percent. Capital gains on sales of owner-occupied housing are not taxed as long as you buy another home of equal or greater value. Even if you don't, there's a one-time exclusion of up to $125,000 of capital gains from the sale of a home by people over age 55. On the other hand, deductions for capital losses (on any type of asset) are limited to just $3,000 beyond the amount of realized capital gains in any one year, although the unused portion may be carried forward into future years.

Another major divergence from the idealized measure of income is that our tax system counts all interest, dividends, and capital gains/ losses at their *nominal* values, rather than at their real, inflation-adjusted, values. This is true both for income received and for deductions, such as those for capital losses and interest paid on durable productive goods and homes. Ideally, all of these items would be adjusted for inflation, but this could make the taxpaying process considerably more complicated.

Some of the most difficult problems in defining income in the personal code arise from the taxation of business income. Medium- and large-sized businesses typically must pay tax under the separate corporate system described at the end of this chapter. But most smaller businesses, amounting to about 91 percent of all firms in the United States, are taxed under the personal income tax rules.[15] Examples include sole proprietorships (small businesses with only one owner), partnerships, and S corporations (a kind of corporation that is limited to 35 or fewer shareholders). For these types of firms, all net income is allocated directly to owners and included in their AGIs. Net income is computed roughly in accordance with the economic principles described above, allowing deductibility of depreciation, interest payments, and other costs of doing business. Many of the problems involved in defining taxable business income, such as determining appropriate allowances for depreciation, are common to all businesses. We will deal with these issues later when we describe the corporation income tax.

What Gets Left Out of the Personal Tax Base?

Now that we've considered the items that *are* counted as income under the personal tax code, let's examine which items are left out or subtracted. The pie chart in Figure 2.4 illustrates, for the latest year available (1993), the vast difference between the total dollar value of what the Department of Commerce measures as *personal* income and what the IRS calls *taxable* income. Personal income, which is somewhat smaller than GDP ($5.5 trillion versus $6.6 trillion in 1993), is a reasonable approximation of the broadest possible income base that the government could attempt to tax.[16] It is not exactly the same as the economist's idealized definition of income, but it is close. Going step-by-step through which items are included in personal income, but are

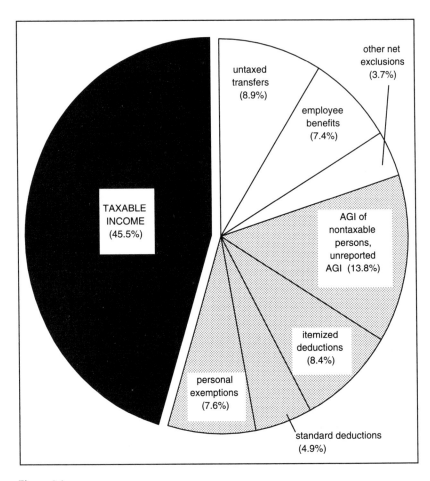

Figure 2.4
Taxable and tax-free components of personal income, 1993
Note: Pie represents total personal income.
Deductions and exemptions are for taxable returns only.
Source: IRS *Statistics of Income Bulletin* (Spring and Fall 1995).

not part of taxable income will provide a good overview of the most basic features of our personal tax code.

As the chart indicates, only 45.5 percent of personal income ends up counted as taxable income, mainly because of various exclusions, deductions, and exemptions. Consequently, the average tax rate on what is counted as taxable income is closer to 20 percent than 8 percent.[17]

Exclusions from Adjusted Gross Income

By the time we get to AGI on the tax form, we've already left out several major items of personal income, which we'll group under the heading of *exclusions*. These exclusions are depicted as the white slices of the pie in Figure 2.4. Altogether, about one-fifth of personal income is excluded from AGI.

The largest category of exclusions is *untaxed transfers* received by beneficiaries of government programs. For example, workers and their employers pay a large Social Security tax, the money from which is transferred directly into cash benefits and Medicare for retired and disabled people. The part of employee compensation labeled the "employer" contribution is not counted as taxable income under the income tax, nor are the Medicare benefits or most of the cash Social Security benefits that the contributions finance; it is true that some portion of Social Security benefits is taxable for high-income people, but the vast majority remains tax-free. In all, untaxed transfers removed about 8.9 percent of personal income from the tax base in 1993.

A second important category of excluded income is *employee benefits.* Employer contributions to private health insurance plans, pensions, life insurance, and many other fringe benefits are all excluded from taxation. In addition, pension and life insurance plans are allowed to accumulate interest every year tax-free. Retirement benefits from a pension plan, on the other hand, are subject to tax when they are paid out. On balance, the tax treatment of employee benefits ends up excluding about 7.4 percent of personal income from the tax base.[18]

Several other statutory exclusions and accounting differences explain another 3.7 percentage points of the gap between personal income and AGI. An important example is the full statutory exclusion of interest on state and local government bonds. IRAs are another. IRAs receive tax-deferred treatment similar to other pensions; contributions and interest accumulations are tax-free, but withdrawals are taxable. As of 1995, up to $2,000 of contributions to an IRA could be excluded from AGI per year, but only for workers who have no other pension plan or who have AGIs below a certain threshold ($40,000 for married couples).[19] Unlike most other exclusions, IRA contributions are reported directly on your tax form and then subtracted from your other income in order to calculate AGI.

The imputed rental value of owner-occupied homes is also excluded from AGI. Our tax system makes no attempt to measure the value of services provided by homes or other durable goods, although an estimate of the former is counted in personal income. Some other items that are counted as AGI but not personal income, such as capital gains realizations, are subtracted from this category.[20]

From AGI to Taxable Income

A very large gap, equal to over one-third (34.7 percent) of personal income, remains between AGI and taxable income; these are indicated by the shaded slices of the pie in Figure 2.4. Most of this gap arises from exemptions and deductions that are subtracted directly from AGI in order to determine taxable income.

First of all, a *personal exemption* is allowed for each family member in a taxpayer's household. This exemption is $2,500 per family member for the tax year 1995. Taxpayers are then given a choice of either taking a *standard deduction*, or of totaling their *itemized deductions*, the most important of which are for home mortgage interest payments, most state and local taxes, and charitable contributions. The standard deduction for tax year 1995 is $6,550 for married taxpayers filing joint returns, $5,750 for a single-parent head-of-household, and $3,900 for a single person. These deduction levels are somewhat higher if the taxpayer is elderly or blind. Taxpayers can use either the standard deduction or the total of itemized deductions, whichever is larger.

The personal exemption and standard deduction are very different in character from the numerous other exclusions and deductions in the tax code. Unlike these other features, they do not favor any particular sources or uses of income over others (except to the extent that exemptions favor families who prefer a large number of children), nor do they significantly complicate the taxpaying process. In a sense, the personal exemption and standard deduction simply create an extra tax bracket at the bottom of the income scale, in which the tax rate is zero. This "zero bracket," or "tax-exempt threshold," amounts to $16,550 for a married couple with two children for tax year 1995 (see Table 2.4); the $16,550 figure comes from having four exemption allowances worth $2,500 each, plus the standard deduction of $6,550. A tax-exempt threshold of this size helps remove many low-income people from the income tax rolls, and makes the system more progressive by reducing average tax rates on low- and moderate-income people.

Table 2.4
Personal exemption and standard deductions, 1995

	Single person	Head-of-household with 2 children	Married couple (joint return) with 2 children
Personal exemption (per family member)	2,500	2,500	2,500
Standard deduction	3,900	5,750	6,550
Tax-exempt threshold (standard deduction + personal exemptions)	6,400	13,250	16,550

Note: Amounts shown are for tax year 1995, and are indexed annually for inflation.

To see how this system works, consider two families, each consisting of a married couple with two children. Both are in the 15 percent tax bracket, and both do not itemize their deductions. The first family has an AGI of $20,000, so its average tax rate, as a percent of AGI, is: [(20,000 − 16,550) x 0.15] / (20,000) = 2.6 percent. The second family, with an AGI of $50,000, faces an average tax rate on AGI of: [(50,000 − 16,550) x 0.15] / (50,000) = 10.0 percent. So the personal exemption and standard deduction by themselves introduce some degree of progressivity, in the sense of having average tax rates that rise with income. Even if there were only a single flat tax rate, the system could still be progressive as long as there was a tax-exempt level of income.

Itemized deductions, on the other hand, do favor particular uses of income, and make the taxpaying process more complicated. Moreover, they tend to benefit higher-income taxpayers most of all; only people with high incomes are likely to accumulate enough itemized deductions to make them larger than the standard deduction. About 29 percent of taxpayers used itemized deductions in 1993. However, only 14 percent of those with AGI below $40,000 chose to itemize, compared to 95 percent of those with AGI above $100,000.[21]

Although there are numerous types of itemized deductions, 89 percent of their total value comes from three main categories: interest paid, state and local taxes paid, and charitable contributions. The largest category, *interest paid deductions*, totaled $200 billion in 1993, or 41 percent of the value of all itemized deductions. Most of this is due to the deductibility of interest paid on home mortgages. A taxpayer can deduct interest on up to two homes with a total value of up to $1 million. One can also deduct up to $100,000 in interest on home equity loans ("second mortgages"), the money from which can be used for any purpose. However, interest payments on credit cards and other consumer debt such as automobile loans are no longer deductible, as a result of the TRA. Interest used to finance investments can be deducted, but only to the extent that it offsets investment income.

The second largest kind of itemized deduction is for *state and local taxes paid*. Taxpayers may deduct the full amount of state and local income and property taxes paid, but deductions for sales taxes were eliminated in 1986. As of 1993, the taxes paid deduction accounted for $170 billion, or 35 percent of the value of all itemized deductions. *Charitable contribution deductions* totaled $68 billion, or 14 percent of all itemized deductions. *Medical and dental expenses* are deductible to the extent that they exceed 7.5 percent of AGI. This accounts for another 5 percent of deductions, or $27 billion. The remaining 5 percent comes from a variety of deductions, including unreimbursed employee expenses (such as travel costs), casualty and theft losses, gambling losses, and tax preparation fees.[22]

In recent years, phase-outs of the personal exemption and of some itemized deductions have been introduced for those with AGI above very high thresholds. The real effect of these phase-outs is essentially to raise marginal tax rates by a few percentage points in certain high-income ranges.[23] The phase-out of itemized deductions eliminated about 3 percent of their total value in 1993.[24]

Credits

Credits offer one more opportunity for reducing taxes, which in this case is not reflected in Figure 2.4. Unlike exemptions and deductions, which reduce your taxable income, credits reduce your tax *bill* dollar-for-dollar. Some examples of credits in the personal tax code include one for child-care expenses, another for elderly or disabled poor people, and one for taxes paid to foreign governments.

By far, the largest of credits is the *earned income tax credit* (EITC), which was originally designed to offset Social Security tax payments for low-income families, and has since been expanded to become a program intended to improve work incentives and well-being for the working poor. The basic idea is to subsidize earnings from work by offering a credit for every dollar earned up to a certain level. Unlike the other credits in the personal tax system, the EITC is refundable, meaning that if it is larger than your total tax bill, you get a check for the difference. In 1992, the total dollar value of the EITC was $13.4 billion, with $11.3 billion of that representing the refundable portion.[25] An expansion of the EITC enacted in 1993 would increase its value to an estimated $25 billion when fully implemented in 1996.[26]

At its 1996 level, for families with two children, the EITC is worth 40 cents for every dollar earned up to $8,890 in income. The credit is then phased out gradually, at a rate of 21 cents per additional dollar earned between $11,610 and $28,495. In the phase-in range, the EITC amounts to a 40 percent subsidy to working for these families. But in the phase-out range, the EITC adds 21 percent to the actual marginal tax rate on working; thus, some taxpayers in the 15 percent tax bracket actually face a 36 percent marginal tax rate, because every additional dollar earned generates both an additional 15 cents of tax liability and also a cutback of 21 cents in the EITC.[27] The credit and phase-out rates are both lower for individuals and smaller families. When considered in conjunction with the personal exemption and the standard deduction, the EITC increases the tax-exempt threshold considerably, to $22,672 for a married couple with two children in 1996.

The Alternative Minimum Tax

As a backstop to the erosion of the tax base caused by deductions and other preferences, Congress has established an "alternative minimum tax" (AMT) for those with high incomes. The AMT requires upper-income taxpayers to calculate an alternative definition of taxable income, which adds back in a few exclusions and most itemized deductions, and then subtracts a large exemption ($45,000 for a joint return).[28] An alternative tax of 26 percent of the first $175,000 and 28 percent of income above that is then calculated. The individual's final tax is the greater of its "regular" tax and the AMT liability, so that tax liability is not allowed to fall below the alternative minimum tax. As it turns out, only a very small, mostly affluent portion of taxpayers— fewer than .3 percent in 1993—end up having to pay higher taxes because of the AMT. But about ten times as many people fill out and submit the form to the IRS, most of them unnecessarily.[29]

Basic Features of the U.S. Corporate Income Tax

The majority of businesses in the United States are relatively small, and their incomes are taxed directly under the personal tax code. But if owners of a business want both the full protection from legal liability that a corporation offers and the ability to raise funds by selling stock in the company to an unlimited number of shareholders, then they must form a traditional "C corporation" and become subject to the corporate income tax. In 1992, C corporations accounted for only 9 percent of the total number of businesses in the United States, but 58 percent of all business income.[30]

Corporate Rate Structure

The U.S. corporate income tax operates according to principles similar to the personal income tax. It applies a straightforward graduated rate structure to a measure of "taxable income" to determine tax liability. In 1995, rates started at 15 percent, and reached a maximum of 35 percent for net income above $10 million. Most corporate income ends up getting taxed at the 35 percent rate.[31]

Defining the Tax Base

A corporation's net income for tax purposes is, in the most general sense, the proceeds from the firm's sales less the costs of doing business. The costs of many inputs to production are deductible in the year of purchase, or when the items they produce are sold. These include wages, salaries, and benefits for employees; the costs of material inputs; taxes paid to state and local governments; employer contributions to Social Security; costs of repairs; advertising costs; and many other miscellaneous expenses. Deducting the costs of investment in durable equipment and buildings, however, is a bit more complicated.

Depreciation Allowances

The costs of investing in capital assets, such as productive machinery and buildings, are *not* deducted in full at the time of purchase. Instead, in accordance with the economic income concept described earlier, a depreciation deduction is allowed. Recall that depreciation is the decline in value of an asset, such as a factory or a machine, which occurs as the asset wears out or becomes obsolete. A firm can deduct a portion of the capital asset's purchase price every year for several years, until eventually the full purchase price is deducted. Spreading the deduction out over time is less favorable to the firm than allowing a full deduction at the time of purchase, because the tax savings from an immediate deduction can be invested and accumulate interest.

Measuring true depreciation is very difficult and would be feasible only in cases where there are active markets for used capital goods. The depreciation allowances provided in the tax code are rough approximations for broad categories of capital equipment and structures. For instance, all equipment is assigned to one of six categories of useful life: three, five, seven, ten, fifteen, or twenty years. As an example of how the rules work in one of these categories, consider a piece of equipment assigned a ten-year life. For each of the first five years, a firm can deduct 20 percent of the previous year's undepreciated cost of the asset, known as its "basis"; thus, for a machine that cost $1,000, it can deduct $200 in the first year, $160 in the second year (20 percent of the basis of $800), $128 in the third year, and so on. In each of years six through ten, the firm deducts a flat amount equal to one-fifth of the basis that remained at the end of year five.

TRA moved tax depreciation allowances closer to true economic depreciation than they had been in the early 1980s. But the allowances still bear only a loose resemblance to true depreciation. In some cases, especially generous depreciation rules have been created for politically favored industries, such as oil, gas, and mineral-extracting operations.

Deductibility of Interest and Double Taxation

As would be suggested by an economic definition of income, if a firm raises money for an investment by borrowing, the interest payments are generally deductible from the corporate tax base in the year they are made. So business proceeds that are paid out in the form of interest escape taxation at the corporate level, and are taxed only once, at the personal level. On the other hand, when a firm raises money by issuing shares, returns to the shareholders—in the form of dividends and capital gains—are *not* deductible from the corporate tax base. So corporate income that is distributed as dividends or capital gains is taxed *twice:* once at the corporate level and then again at the personal level when distributed to shareholders or realized in the form of a capital gain.

Recall, though, that at the personal level, capital gains income is taxed much more generously than other income. Tax is due not when the gain is made, but when the stock is sold, a valuable postponement of tax liability. Moreover, the top rate on capital gains is lower than that for other income, and gains held until death are excluded entirely from taxation. Dividends, on the other hand, receive no special treatment.

Double taxation of corporate income, particularly of dividends, represents a troublesome divergence from the principles of economic income. It can produce a very high combined tax rate, and creates an incentive to finance investment through debt (the selling of bonds) rather than equity (the selling of shares). It is also one of the most important differences between the tax treatment of C corporations and other businesses. Most of the rules regarding definition of the tax base, depreciation, credits, and deductibility of interest apply across all businesses, regardless of whether they are chartered under the personal or corporate codes. But firms taxed solely at the personal level—such as partnerships, S corporations, and sole proprietorships—avoid double taxation altogether. The tax design issues raised by the double taxation of corporate income are addressed in Chapter 8.

Business Credits

A tax credit is currently allowed for certain expenditures on research and experimentation. (This provision expired in July of 1995, but is likely to be restored.) It reduces a corporation's tax bill by 20 percent of the amount by which qualified research expenditures exceed an average base level for that firm. A credit is also allowed for taxes paid to foreign governments by U.S. corporations. The principle here is to have U.S. companies pay U.S. tax, and only U.S. tax, on all of their income, regardless of the country in which the income was earned. Most foreign governments offer symmetric treatment. Investment tax credits have been in effect numerous times since 1962, although there is no longer one now, the latest version having been repealed by the TRA. These credits reduced tax liability by a certain percentage for every dollar of new investment spending on capital equipment.

Corporate Alternative Minimum Tax and Treatment of Losses

Like the personal tax code, the corporate tax system has its own alternative minimum tax (AMT), which is intended to prevent apparently profitable corporations from reducing their taxes "too much." The AMT applies a lower tax rate (20 percent) to a broader definition of net income, involving less generous depreciation and accounting rules. Firms then pay the larger of the AMT or the regular tax. This provision, which was strengthened by the TRA, affects a sizable minority of corporations, and requires many firms to do a good deal of extra accounting.

If, after subtracting out all the deductions and allowances, a corporation has a net loss, the firm can carry that loss either forward or backward to other years, so as to offset positive taxable income earned in those years. Losses from particular investments are also deductible against taxable income, although there are some restrictions.[32]

Conclusion

The first two chapters have presented some basic background information that should be helpful as an introduction to the debate over tax reform. Chapter 1 looked at the complaints about the current system, outlined the suggested replacements, and laid out some of the key issues in the debate over the future of the income tax. This chapter explained the essentials of how the current personal and corporate income taxes work, discussed their role in the overall tax system, and placed them in their historical and international contexts. Along the way, we've become familiar with many of the aspects of the system that bother would-be reformers. For example, exclusions and deductions remove a great deal of income from the tax base, meaning that we must have higher rates to raise a given amount of revenue. The next three chapters will explore the principles that ought to guide any tax system, and will address to what extent our current system adheres to these principles.

3   Fairness

The worst riots seen in London for decades occurred on March 31, 1990. More than 400 demonstrators and police officers were injured, and 341 people were arrested for assault, looting, and arson. Rioters set fire to parked Porsches and Jaguars, smashed restaurant and store windows, and demolished a Renault showroom. The reason? A new tax proposed by the Thatcher government was scheduled to take effect the next day. The new tax, called a community charge or poll tax, was to be a flat charge on all adults living in a jurisdiction, the same amount for rich and poor alike, and was to replace a system of real estate taxes remitted only by property owners or people who rented from them. The public outcry, which included not only civil unrest but also widespread nonviolent protest and noncompliance, is widely credited as the principal reason for the challenge to Margaret Thatcher's party leadership, and her eventual replacement by John Major. The Conservative party has since abandoned the poll tax.[1]

Although the political repercussions were enormous, the public reaction to the Thatcher poll tax was exceedingly mild compared to the previous time such a tax was attempted by a British government, in 1381. In that year, mobs roamed from town to town, sacking the houses of prominent citizens and tax officials, and beheading several. One unfortunate soul dispatched to collect taxes was not only "tortured and wounded so that he was half killed, [but] the miscreants then turned to his horse, cut off its tail and ears and affixed them to the pillory there to be subjected to public opprobrium and derision."[2]

Why all the uproar over the Thatcher government's poll tax? There were mistakes made in its implementation, to be sure, but the overriding reason for the outcry was that people thought it was unfair. The poll tax was to replace a property tax under which tax payments varied with the value of one's property. Under the poll tax, every adult in a given local jurisdiction paid the same annual tax, *period.* The duke with his estate paid the same tax as the butcher in his three-room flat. That the affluent should pay more tax than everyone else struck many as a first principle of fair taxation, one that was violated by the "community charge."

In the United States, it has been a long time since controversy over fair taxation has erupted into violence, although of course our nation's origins are strongly tied to colonial indignation over the duties imposed by England on imports of tea and other goods. An excise tax on distilled spirits spurred the Whiskey Rebellion of 1794, which caused several deaths and much property damage; to quell the rebellion, President Washington nationalized 13,000 militiamen, an army three times as big as the one he commanded at Valley Forge.[3]

Although violence over the fairness of taxation has largely subsided, the oratorical skirmishing certainly continues; efforts to raise taxes on the well-to-do are decried by some Republicans as "class warfare." Usually the first question anyone asks about a proposed new tax is "who pays?" For tax bills discussed in Congress, the Joint Committee on Taxation, the Congressional Budget Office (CBO), and/or the Treasury Department will publish "distributional tables" that purport to show how the burden of the proposed tax will be "distributed," or shared, among various income groups. Sometimes private organizations produce their own distributional tables. In recent years, the distributional tables have themselves become political footballs, and the economic assumptions underlying the assignment of tax burden to income classes have been challenged.

The appearance of these tables produces a predictable response. If the extra tax burden is shown to effect the poor disproportionately, it is derided by some as unfair. If the extra tax burden is disproportionately high on the middle-income classes, others will denounce that as unfair. If the rich are the relative losers, some will criticize it as "soaking the rich."

Sometimes the group allegedly wronged is defined by something other than income or wealth. It could be defined by region, such as residents of the Northeast if the tax considered is on heating oil, or on westerners if a gasoline tax increase is considered. The aggrieved group could be defined by age, as would be the case for a tax on Social Security benefits, or by some other characteristic, such as being a smoker, if cigarette taxes are the issue.

The fairness or unfairness of tax changes has become such a divisive issue that, in the last major overhaul of the tax system in 1986, the issue was to some extent sidestepped by putting together a package of tax provisions that could be characterized as "distributionally neutral," meaning that no one income group was to gain or lose, compared to any other. In the Treasury Department's supporting documents, distributional neutrality was defended not because the current sharing of the tax burden was deemed to be exactly right, and therefore no adjustment was appropriate, but rather because the tax reform's objectives were unrelated to reassigning the tax burden across income classes. However, an important objective of the 1986 reform was to make the tax burden fairer *within* each income group, by eliminating tax preferences available to people because they had the willingness or opportunity to exploit loopholes in the tax structure, or happened to engage in an activity afforded favorable tax treatment. This is a separate aspect of fairness, which will carefully be distinguished below.

The prominence of fairness in tax policy debates makes it essential that the issues involved are understood. Fairness also deserves close scrutiny because much of the bewildering complexity of the tax law is justified in its name. Recall that it is because of its evident unfairness that what is arguably the simplest tax system of all—the poll tax—is rejected by most everyone. Slightly more complicated systems—but still much simpler than our current system—such as the "flat tax," do not allow the tax burden to be fine-tuned for personal circumstances and also permit limited flexibility in assigning the tax burden across income groups. Before we resign ourselves to the bewildering complexity of taxation for the sake of fairness, it behooves us to think carefully about what we mean by fairness and how much citizens are willing to sacrifice to achieve it.

Vertical Equity

There are two distinct aspects to the fairness of a tax system. The first, called "vertical equity" by economists, concerns the appropriate tax burden on households of different levels of well-being. It is about how much tax should be paid by a family with $200,000 of income, versus a family with $50,000 of income, versus a family with $10,000 of income.

A tax system can be evaluated against another standard of fairness—to what extent families of the *same* level of well-being end up

bearing the same tax burden. Or, to put it another way, what are justifiable grounds for assigning different tax liabilities to two families of
the same income? This issue, called "horizontal equity" by economists,
is dealt with later. First we will deal with the divisive issue of vertical
equity, or the appropriate degree of tax progressivity.

Recall that a tax structure is called progressive if an individual's or
family's total tax liability, as a fraction of income, rises with income.[4]
If, for example, total taxes for a family with an income of $50,000 are
20 percent of income, and taxes for a family with an income of $100,000
are 30 percent of income, and so on, then the tax structure is progressive. Loosely speaking, one tax structure is more progressive than another if its average tax rate rises more rapidly with income.[5] If, on the
other hand, everyone pays the *same* percentage of income in tax, regardless of income, then the tax is called *proportional*. Finally, a tax that
takes a *smaller* percentage of income from those with higher incomes is
called *regressive*. Using this terminology, the question of vertical equity
usually boils down to whether the tax burden ought to be distributed
in a progressive fashion, and if so, how progressive it should be.

Before plunging in, we must make a frank admission—fairness is
not in the end a question of economics. Neither an A+ in Economics
101 nor a Ph.D. in mathematical economics nor a lifetime of study of
the theory of political economy will reveal the one true answer. Fairness in taxation, like fairness of just about anything, is an ethical issue
that involves value judgments.

The elusiveness of the concept of fairness has not stopped people
from simply asserting, with absolute confidence, what is fair and what
is not. In his 1992 presidential campaign, Bill Clinton advocated making an already progressive U.S. income tax system more progressive,
so as to achieve "an America in which the wealthiest, those making
over $200,000 a year, are asked to pay their fair share."[6] Once in office,
he joined with Congress to raise income tax rates on those very people.
Clinton has also asserted that a flat-rate tax is "not the fair thing to
do" because the middle class would bear more of the tax burden than
they do under the current system.[7] Conservative columnist William
Safire, a well-known stickler for precise language, expresses a not dis-
similar view of the meaning of "tax fairness" when he says "most of
us accept as 'fair' this principle: The poor should pay nothing, the mid-
dlers something, and the rich the highest percentage."[8]

House Majority Leader Richard Armey, on the other hand, contends
that a system that imposes a single, flat percentage tax rate on every-

one's labor income (above an exempt amount) would be truly "fair" because "it treats everyone the same."[9] Robert Hall and Alvin Rabushka, inventors of the flat tax, agree, saying "the meanings of *even, just,* and *equal,* in keeping with rules and logic, better fit a flat rate of taxation than any multiple-rate system that·discriminates among different classes of taxpayers."[10]

A few people express more extreme interpretations of the meaning of "tax fairness." A letter to the editors of *The Wall Street Journal* asserted that a fair tax would feature "the same amount charged to each citizen—much as each member pays a fixed dues to a club, irrespective of assets"—essentially a poll tax.[11] Another letter to the editor that same day contends that a "fair" tax "is never possible, any more than anyone can ever commit a fair murder or a fair rape; for taxation is, without an exception, theft."[12]

Our point is that you can *say* anything about what constitutes a fair tax system, but that doesn't make it true. Careful economic analysis can clarify the issues involved, and can identify the trade-offs that are faced when tax fairness questions are at issue. However, economic reasoning cannot be decisive in the choice about replacing one tax system with another.

In spite of this, economists have often proclaimed at congressional hearings and in the press that one tax system is superior to another. To make such a judgment, the economist is implicitly introducing his or her own values into the choice, values that Congress or the majority of Americans may not share. For this reason, in principle any panel of economists offering their opinions on the best tax system should be followed by a panel of philosophers or theologians who offer their views on the ethics of tax progressivity. In practice, of course, we do not convene such a panel every time an adjustment in the pattern of tax liabilities is considered, and we rely on the political system to make these kind of choices.

Economists have helped to frame the debate by articulating some general principles of tax fairness. Although none of these principles provides a definitive, compelling answer to the question of exactly how we should distribute the burden of taxes, they do offer a helpful conceptual basis for thinking clearly about tax fairness.

We recognize that our tax system is not shaped solely by a clash of principles. More often it is forged through a clash of interests, with the relative political power of groups determining the net fiscal advantage they receive from the government. It is no coincidence that the top individual tax rate fell from 70 percent to 28 percent during the Reagan Administration; this radical change undoubtedly reflected the transfer of political power as much as it reflected a rethinking of first principles. Ideas do matter, though, and it is valuable to discuss what principles, if any, underlie policy decisions.

The Benefit Principle Versus the Ability-to-Pay Principle

Economists have proposed two principles for determining the fair distribution of tax burden among different types of people. The first is the *benefit principle,* which states that each individual ought to pay taxes commensurate to the benefits he or she receives from the government. The second is the *ability-to-pay principle,* which states that the amount each taxpayer pays ought to be related to his or her level of economic well-being.

When we buy ordinary goods and services in the free market, we generally consider it fair to "get what we pay for." The benefit principle of taxation would apply this same reasoning to the financing of government goods and services. In some cases, this is easy. For example, postage is charged on U.S. mail, and local governments charge households for their use of water and sewage facilities. These so-called user charges can be an effective policy when the government is providing what is essentially a private good; the charge not only prices the good based on what citizens "get," but also induces them to use only the amount for which they are willing to pay.

For many important government services, such as national defense or the justice system, it is more difficult to determine exactly how much each citizen benefits. In these cases, implementing the benefit principle would require charging taxes that are related to a rough estimate of the benefits each person receives.

This is the first place where the benefit principle runs into trouble. You certainly can't just ask people what government activities like national defense are worth to them. Imagine how you would respond if you received a survey from the IRS in the mail, asking you to estimate how much the Department of Defense is worth to you. If you even suspected that your tax bill would depend on your answer, you would have a strong temptation to lowball your answer. (It's not as if the government could threaten to not defend those who claimed to not value the Armed Forces.) Those who answered honestly would be caught holding the bill. If the government could credibly promise not to assess taxes based on your survey response, claiming to use the information only to get a sense of the average benefit by income class, then people might respond more honestly. But even with no incentive to lie, many households would undoubtedly find it difficult to provide a sensible answer to a question such as "What are the federal government's activities worth to you?"

So the benefit principle fails on practical grounds as a specific guide to how the tax burden should be distributed. As a general guide, though, it suggests that the tax burden should be higher for households with higher income and wealth, because these people have more to lose from the anarchy that would prevail if the government withdrew from providing defense, a justice system, police and so on. But the benefit principle doesn't tell us how much higher that tax bill should be.

Another objection to the benefit principle is that it permits the government no flexibility in using the tax system to affect the distribution of income. Imagine for a moment that somehow each household's true benefit from government could be determined, and that their tax liability was set at exactly that value so that, on net, everyone comes out "even." There would be no way to go easy on low-income people by assigning them low, or no, taxes; everyone would have to pay their full bill for national defense, police protection, roads, and so on. Nor would there be any scope to supplement the incomes of the very poor by providing benefits such as food stamps, because the value of the food stamps would be exactly offset by a corresponding tax liability. Children who grew up in disadvantaged families could not be provided education free of charge. Social Security could not guarantee that virtually all participants receive at least some minimal survival level of retirement support, as it does now; retirees would only get exactly what they had paid for during their lifetimes, even if it meant many would be impoverished. Thus, a strict application of the benefit principle has radical implications for both how the government raises money and how it spends it.

Most people, though certainly not all, would reject this restriction on what is the appropriate role of government. They would allow that there are cases when redistribution is justified, perhaps only to the extent of providing a minimal level of help for all citizens, making sure they can get a basic education, and so forth. They would allow that, in determining the distribution of the tax burden, the well-being of the potential taxpayers should be considered. But exactly how should taxes be related to the level of well-being? Proponents of the ability-to-pay principle have attempted to answer this question.

According to the ability-to-pay principle, tax burdens should be related not to what a family receives from government, but rather to its ability to bear the tax burden or, in other words, to tolerate a sacrifice. Reasoning from the plausible idea that paying a dollar is a lesser sacrifice for a well-to-do family than for a poor family, an equal sacrifice requires higher tax payments from a well-to-do family. After all, $100 more in taxes may induce an affluent family to cut back on magazine subscriptions, but it may induce a poor family to have less to eat. It makes sense that it would take a whole lot of foregone magazine subscriptions before the sacrifice of the rich family is as great as the one undergone by the poor family.

Although this is a sensible, and even compelling, proposition, it is also an unprovable one. There is no way to compare across individuals the sacrifice caused by having less money, just as it is impossible to compare the pain caused to two people by a pinprick or the joy in one's heart from the birth of a child.

Asserting that a poor family experiences more sacrifice than a rich family from the loss of a dollar, without knowing how much more, is not sufficient to point to a particular relationship between income and tax burden. A proportionate tax, whereby everyone pays the same percentage of income, would take more dollars from a rich family than from a poor family. Indeed, even a regressive tax, with everyone paying 25 percent on the first $20,000 of income, and 10 percent on all additional income, would take more dollars from the rich than from the poor. Whether one of these two schedules, or some other, assigns an appropriate amount of sacrifice across families is impossible to say.

Furthermore, why should everyone make an equal sacrifice? Why not demand greater sacrifice from the affluent than from the poor? Accepting this premise implies that there are two separate layers of indeterminacy in implementing the ability-to-pay principle—how to measure the amount of sacrifice associated with taking one dollar away from someone, and how the level of sacrifice should be related to the level of well-being. Neither of these questions is the sort that can be answered analytically.

We conclude that the ability-to-pay principle is nothing more than an intuitively appealing defense of linking tax liability to some measure of well-being, rather than to an estimate of the benefits from government activities. However, on the compelling questions of the day—such as whether millionaires ought to pay 70 percent, 50 percent, or 30 percent of their income in tax, or whether poor families should pay anything at all—the ability-to-pay principle is silent.

Progressivity and Economic Incentives

In recent years, economists have for the most part given up on seeking operational guidance from first principles of fair taxation. Instead they have concentrated on understanding the economic consequences, or costs, of different levels of tax progressivity. The costs arise because of the disincentive effects of taxation. When all taxes are raised by a poll tax, so that tax liability is the same amount for rich and poor alike, the tax system places no penalty whatsoever on all the efforts people undertake to better themselves—working hard, getting an education, starting a new business, and so on. In contrast, a proportional income tax system levied at a constant 20 percent rate levies a 20 percent penalty on the reward from all such efforts. Tax systems that are progressive place an even higher penalty on getting ahead.

Measuring these costs allows us to pose the critical trade-off that must be faced in resolving the vertical equity question—how to balance the potential social benefits of a more equal distribution of after-tax income against the economic damage imposed by highly progressive taxes. As Henry Simons of the University of Chicago stated so elegantly in his influential 1938 book *Personal Income Taxation*, "Both progress and justice are costly luxuries—costly, above all, in terms of each other."[13] How that trade-off is resolved depends in part on the value society places on a more equal distribution of income, but it also depends on more mundane matters that are the bread and butter of economists—the economic cost of progressive tax systems. These controversies are discussed in the next chapter.

Just How Unequal Is the Distribution of Incomes?

If everyone in our society were equally well off, there would be little reason to worry about tax progressivity. However, in the United States, there is clearly an enormous gap between the best-off and worst-off, as well as a big difference between the best-off and the middle class. Moreover, the degree of inequality has been growing significantly in recent years. This is probably no surprise to anyone who has followed stories in the popular press about the rising fortunes of corporate executives, lawyers, investment bankers, entertainers, and athletes as well as the declining fortunes of those Americans with less valued skills. This large and growing inequality is a major reason why the issue of progressivity raises so much concern and impassioned debate.

Figure 3.1 presents an illustration of the degree of U.S. income inequality and its growth in recent years, calculated by the CBO. In 1990, 51 percent of all income in the United States went to the quintile (or 20 percent) of the population with the highest incomes, compared to 47 percent in 1977. Almost all of this increase was concentrated at the very top; the incomes of the richest 1 percent of households rose from 9 percent to 13 percent of the total. The top 1 percent is a very exclusive group; a family of four needed an income of more than $400,000 (in 1996 dollars) to qualify in 1990, and the average income of all families in this category was over $600,000.[14] The bottom panel of Figure 3.1 shows that average real (inflation-adjusted) incomes declined for people in the bottom two-fifths of the income distribution in 1990 compared to people in that group in 1977. Incomes grew sluggishly in the middle, and surged at the top; average real income among the richest 1 percent rose by a staggering 74 percent.

Wealth is distributed in an even more unequal fashion, and it too appears to have become more concentrated in recent years. A study by Arthur Kennickell of the Board of Governors of the Federal Reserve System and Louise Woodburn of the IRS found that, in 1989, 37.1 percent of net worth in the United States was held by the richest 1 percent of households, up from 31.5 percent in 1983.[15]

There is little doubt that when we view the distribution of incomes in a single-year snapshot, and compare that snapshot with earlier years, as we do in Figure 3.1, things are very unequal and are becoming more so. But it is also true that the people in each income quintile in 1990 are not necessarily the same people who were there in 1977. These single-year snapshots fail to capture income *mobility*—people moving among the different income classes. Some of the single-year snapshot inequality represents temporary fluctuations, such as a family realizing a large capital gain in one year, or a young person who is still in school but will one day earn a high income. If we could look at *lifetime* incomes, the distribution would not appear quite as unequal as it does in Figure 3.1. Nonetheless, the best evidence available on this subject suggests that there is a great degree of inequality even in lifetime incomes, and that this too has been growing. For example, a study by Isabel Sawhill and Mark Condon of the Urban Institute followed the

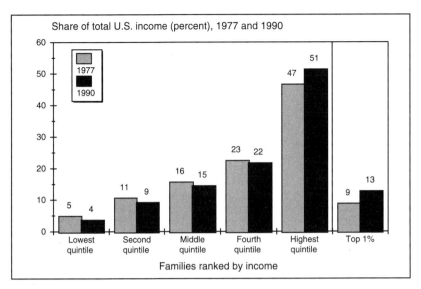

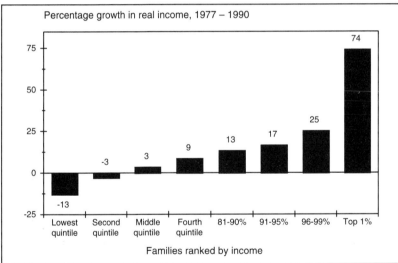

Figure 3.1
Growing income inequality in the United States for the period 1977–1990
Source: Congressional Budget Office analysis, presented in U.S. House of Representatives Committee on Ways and Means (1993).

same group of people over ten years (1977 to 1986), and found that about half of all people who were in the lowest or highest income quintile in the beginning of that period were still in that same category by the end. They also found that income mobility had not increased in that period relative to 1967–1976, indicating that if "snapshot" income inequality was increasing over this period, then so too was lifetime income inequality.[16] Economists Peter Gottschalk of Boston College and Robert Moffitt of Johns Hopkins University calculate that nine-year averages of labor income were considerably more unequal in the 1980s than in the 1970s.[17]

Another important area of controversy is the question of exactly why inequality has been increasing. The figures shown in Figure 3.1 are for *before*-tax income, so taxes cannot be directly responsible for the trend toward greater inequality. However, some have argued that reductions in tax rates may be *indirectly* responsible for some of the surge in incomes at the very top of the income distribution, because lower marginal rates created an incentive for the well-to-do to work harder and to invest more, and reduced their incentive to hide income from the IRS. But many other factors could account for this surge, such as increased demand for the services of a small number of highly skilled lawyers, doctors, investment bankers, and entertainers, which bids up their compensation; some of this increased demand is probably due to the growing ease of marketing these skills globally, rather than being restricted to the U.S. market. The role of taxes in the recent surge of income inequality has become a key issue in the current debate over the economic effects of taxation, one that will be discussed in greater detail in the next chapter.

What are the implications of this growing income inequality for the appropriate degree of progressivity in our tax system? None, if you don't believe in the "ability-to-pay" principle. But if you do accept the ability-to-pay principle, more income inequality may suggest a need for greater tax progressivity. If the rich got richer because of good fortune and market forces that were beyond their control, while the incomes of the poor and middle class stagnated for similar reasons, then you could make a case that some of the increased inequality ought to be offset by a more progressive tax system, and certainly should not be exacerbated by *reducing* the progressivity of the income tax.[18] According to this argument, the problem is flat *wages*, and the solution is not flat *taxes*. Just this case is often made by certain Democratic politicians. On the other hand, if the rich got richer because lower tax rates unleashed a torrent of entrepreneurial effort, as some Republicans argue, it may cause you to increase your estimate of the economic cost of progressive tax rates. In that case, you might desire a less progressive tax system.

What Americans Think Is Fair

Clearly, any first principles of fairness that we can come up with will leave plenty of room for disagreement over the appropriate distribution of the tax burden. Since we live in a democracy, why not forget about first principles, and just ask people what they think is fair? Numerous polls and academic studies have done just that. As Chapter 1 showed, public opinion surveys generally suggest strong support for progressivity in taxation. But the results sometimes seem inconsistent or are difficult to interpret, and can differ greatly depending on how the question is framed.

In 1993, when Congress was considering President Clinton's proposed tax increases on upper-income people, several polls asked whether the "rich" or those with "upper incomes" should pay more in taxes than they did at the time. These polls consistently found overwhelming support for this proposition. For instance, in an April 1993 Gallup poll, 75 percent of respondents said "upper-income" people paid less than their "fair share" in taxes.[19] Similarly, a February 1993 *Time Magazine*/CNN poll found 79 percent support for increasing the personal income tax for families making more than $200,000 a year.[20] The popularity of taxing the rich may not be surprising, when you consider that less than 1 percent of Americans consider themselves to be "rich," and only 7 percent consider themselves to be "upper-income."[21]

Because the federal tax system was already quite progressive at this time, on the surface these polls suggest public support for a strong degree of progressivity. However, it is not clear whether Americans actually believe that the existing tax system is progressive. For example, a June 1986 Roper poll asked the public to estimate how much personal income tax was actually paid by families of four with various income levels. The respondents' median estimate of the tax bill for a hypothetical family making $50,000 was $7,000, a 14 percent average tax rate. But the median estimate of the tax bill for a family with $200,000 in income was only $15,000, a 7.5 percent average tax rate;[22] the actual average income tax rates at the time were about 12 percent for families making $50,000 and 21 percent for those making $200,000.[23] In a 1989 survey, respondents believed on average that 45 percent of millionaires paid no income tax at all. IRS statistics showed the actual figure was less than 2 percent.[24] Thus, the professed desire for *more* progressivity may in part stem from a lack of understanding of how progressive the system really is.

Some recent surveys have focused on flat taxes, in which a single rate replaces the current system of graduated rates. A *Wall Street Journal*/NBC News poll in September 1995 found the public preferred "a graduated income tax" to "a flat tax" by a 57 percent to 38 percent margin, a result nearly identical to their findings in an April 1995 poll.[25] But these results are contradicted by other polls. An April 1995 *Newsweek* survey found that respondents preferred some form of flat tax over "the current tax system" by a 61 percent to 27 percent margin.[26] In a January 1995 survey by Republican pollster Frank Luntz, 51 percent of respondents said they supported a specific flat tax proposal over the current system, while 37 percent opposed it.[27] These conflicting results seem to arise from the wording of the questions—for example, in the questions where the flat tax was preferred, it was compared to the existing system in particular, rather than a graduated income tax in general. In addition, these latter two polls mentioned specific tax rates that were much too low to raise the same revenues as the current system.

A major problem with these polls is that the questions are so simplified that it is difficult to determine what people really think. They provide very little information on the details of what exactly a flat tax is, and how it would differ from the existing system, a topic that will be discussed in Chapters 6 and 7. For example, it is never mentioned that, under many flat tax proposals, all interest, dividends, and capital gains would be excluded from taxation at the personal level. An April 1995 poll done by the *Wall Street Journal* found that people preferred "a tax system that taxes income from investments and wages equally" to one with "higher taxes on wage income but no taxes on investment income" by 57 percent to 32 percent.[28]

A 1991 study by Peggy Hite of Indiana University and Michael Roberts of the University of Alabama provides some of the most detailed information available regarding public opinion on progressivity. They asked a random sample of 593 Americans what they thought the average rate of personal income tax should be at nine different levels of income. The average responses, displayed in the third column of Table

Table 3.1
Personal income tax rates at various income levels desired by survey respondents

Income in 1987 dollars	Income in 1996 dollars	Mean desired average tax rate	Mean desired tax dollars converted into an average tax rate
5,000	6,900	2.4	2.7
10,000	13,800	4.7	4.2
15,000	20,700	8.3	6.6
20,000	27,600	11.7	8.9
25,000	34,500	13.9	10.4
30,000	41,400	16.1	11.8
40,000	55,200	19.1	13.3
50,000	69,000	22.7	15.6
100,000	137,900	29.2	20.1

Note: Survey asked respondents to assign average tax rates and tax dollars to married couples with no children at various income levels.
Source: Hite and Roberts (1991).

3.1, show a strong degree of progressivity, with the average rate increasing uniformly with income. The fourth column is interesting, as well. When the respondents were separately asked to give the appropriate tax liability in dollars, rather than in average tax rates, the mean responses converted into average tax rates were almost uniformly lower, although still quite progressive. It's almost as if the sacrifice of paying taxes became more palpable when the responses were measured in dollars, rather than the more abstract concept of average tax rates, and people therefore shied away from higher taxes. Another possibility is that some people may have trouble distinguishing between *marginal* and *average* tax rates, which could cause upward bias in the average tax rates people said they desired on upper-income people.[29]

When forced to choose among five alternative tax schedules, 34 percent of the respondents chose one that featured a flat rate of 20 percent on all income above $5,000 a year. But two-thirds preferred a more progressive graduated rate structure. Twenty-eight percent chose graduated rates that were about as progressive as the current system, and 38 percent chose rates that were more progressive than the current system. Perhaps not surprisingly, people could not exactly put aside their own self-interest in choosing their preferred tax systems. Lower-income people tended to favor relatively lower rates on low incomes, while higher-income people favored relatively low rates on high incomes.

It has been established that fairness in taxation is an elusive concept about which reasonable people will disagree. It has also been argued that fairness in taxation can't be separated from the issue of how taxation affects economic performance; Chapter 5 will show that neither can it be separated from simplicity, because achieving finer and finer degrees of fairness requires a more complex tax system. It has also been learned that most Americans apparently prefer a progressive tax system. Some would be satisfied with a system that achieves its progressivity by exempting a certain level of income, and then applying a flat rate to all income above that level. Many others seem to prefer an even more progressive system that applies increasingly higher tax rates on successive increments of income. Whether in asserting these preferences people are considering the trade-off with growth or with simplicity is an open and intriguing question.

Tax Incidence—Who Bears the Burden of a Tax?

The next task is to investigate who in fact bears the burden of taxation under the current U.S. income tax system, and see how it compares to Americans' views about the proper distribution of the tax burden. It turns out that this is a much more difficult task than it might seem. It can't be accomplished by adding up how much money people send to the IRS each year and calculating how that differs by income group. This is inappropriate because the person who sends the check to the IRS can often shift at least part of the burden of that tax onto someone else. For example, if the owner of a business can respond to a particular tax levy by raising prices, then even though he or she is the one sending a check to the IRS, the firm's customers are really bearing part of the burden of the tax. To understand where the burden of taxes lies, and whether it is shared fairly, it is necessary to look beyond who writes the checks.

If "paying" taxes means writing checks to the IRS, most wage and salary earners would be surprised to learn that they have no right to complain about income taxes—because they pay no tax at all! Most of the checks to the IRS are written by employers. Of course, all this means is that taxes on wages and salaries are withheld from paychecks by the employer, and forwarded by the employer to the IRS. By April 15 (or the extended deadline), taxpayers must send the IRS the difference between their tax liability and what has already been withheld from their earnings[30]—the amount paid on their behalf by their employers. Because about three-quarters of taxpayers get a refund, most Americans never "pay" any income taxes, if by pay one means to write a check to the IRS. Most Americans are familiar enough with employer withholding to know instinctively that you can bear the burden of taxes without ever writing a check to the government.

Neither is the key to who bears the burden of taxes to be found in where the legal liability to remit taxes resides. If all withholding taxes on wages and salaries became the legal liability of the business employing the labor, and were simply renamed labor *usage* taxes rather than labor income taxes, there would be no change in who really bears the burden of the taxation; only the wording on the pay stubs would change. A weekly stub that now reads $600 wages and $200 federal taxes withheld, resulting in $400 in take-home pay, might read instead $400 in wages, with the employer paying the $200 labor usage tax separately; the bottom line is that the worker takes home $400 either way. Changing the name of the tax won't suddenly make an employer more generous; firms will still try to pay as little as they can to maintain a workforce of the size and quality they desire. Whether the legal liability to pay taxes resides with the buyer of labor services (the firm) or the seller of labor services (the worker), it all works out to the same thing in the end.

There are exceptions to the rule that legal responsibility doesn't matter. For example, it would be relevant in the transition to a new tax regime if the nominal salary were not immediately flexible. If a worker's salary is fixed as part of a long-term collective bargaining agreement, then a change in legal responsibility for income taxes from employee to employer would certainly make the worker better off, at least until the contract could be renegotiated. Similarly, a change in who bears the legal responsibility could matter for someone receiving the minimum wage, because the wage could not be reduced below that level to make up for the change. The employer would either have to put up with a higher cost of employing the worker, or let the worker go.

Nevertheless, these examples remain exceptions to the generally applicable rule. In most cases, and over a reasonable length of time, wages and prices are flexible, so that it doesn't ultimately matter on which side of the transaction the legal responsibility for taxes lies. Although our example featured a tax on labor income, the same conclusion applies to any kind of tax—in the long run, it is irrelevant whether the seller or buyer owes the tax.

So far, it has been explained how *not* to measure the burden of taxes—by calculating who remits taxes or is legally responsible for remitting money to the IRS—but it has yet to be explained how to do it right. Does a tax on labor income make workers worse off by lowering their take-home pay, or does it make employers worse off by increasing the cost of labor? Do taxes on cigarettes burden smokers, the owners of cigarette companies, the people who work for these companies, or tobacco farmers?

The phenomenon that taxes ostensibly levied on a given base may end up being borne by people at a number of places along the production and distribution chain is known as tax *shifting*, and who ends up bearing the burden is known as tax *incidence*. For any given tax, these are very difficult questions to get precise answers about, and there is inevitably disagreement among economists about these issues.

Tax shifting occurs because the price of what is taxed—and perhaps related commodities as well—changes when the tax is imposed. Thus, people bear the burden of a tax not only when they remit taxes, but also when there is a change in the prices of the goods and services they buy and sell.

The essential rule of thumb that determines to what extent a tax is shifted, and therefore who bears the burden of a particular tax, is that the better one's alternatives to what is taxed, the less likely one is to bear a burden. Some examples may help to illustrate this rule of thumb. Will a 5 cents tax per can of Coke® cause the price of Coke to rise, and thus be borne by consumers, or not? The answer is no if most consumers can't tell the difference between Coke and Pepsi®; i.e. if they have good alternatives to the taxed good.[31] If one is as good as the other, the market simply will not tolerate Coke selling for 55 cents a can while Pepsi sells for 50 cents—no one would buy Coke at those prices. In that case, Coke would sell for 50 cents, and Coke's producers would bear the burden of the tax; if their net-of-tax receipts no longer covered their costs, they might have to shut down production entirely. If, on the other hand, neither Pepsi nor any other drink is viewed as a good substitute for Coke, the market price of Coke is likely to rise toward 55 cents, so that the burden of the tax is borne by consumers of Coke.

The alternatives to the taxed good available to the producer are equally important. Consider the incidence of a surprise tax of 10 cents per tomato imposed on unsuspecting farmers as they arrive at the farmers' market. Because the tomatoes will start to rot in 24 hours, the farmers have no alternative but to sell them that day. In that case the likely scenario is that the market price will be not much more than what would have prevailed in the absence of the tax, and the farmers will lose out by receiving a lower net-of-tax price than otherwise. If, however, the tomato tax had been announced months in advance, the farmers would have had the option of growing other crops, or taking their tomatoes to be sold elsewhere. With fewer tomatoes to be sold, the price at market would likely be bid up, so that the tax would to some extent be shifted away from the farmers and borne by those people who shop at the market that imposed the tax, who will be met with more costly tomatoes than otherwise.

In some cases, a tax will cause a change in the price of *untaxed* goods or services that can serve as substitutes; this is called an "implicit" tax. Consider the case of state and local government bonds. Interest on these bonds is excluded from federal taxation, while the returns on federal and corporate bonds are fully taxable. Because of this tax advantage, there is greater demand for state and local bonds. This bids up their price or, in other words, lowers the interest rate they offer. Because of the tax on other investments, holders of state and local bonds bear an implicit tax equal to the difference between the interest rate they receive and the higher rate they would receive on a taxed bond of similar maturity and riskiness. They bear this burden even though they remit no tax at all to the government.

Taxes on labor income can be shifted as well. A tax on wages and salaries will be shifted off of workers to the extent that, because of the tax, wage rates rise. It will be completely shifted if wages rise enough so that after-tax wages are no lower than they would have been absent taxes. How does the rule of thumb about shifting apply to this case? It says that shifting will tend to occur if workers have better alternatives to working than employers have to hiring workers. For workers, the alternative to paid work is leisure or unpaid work at home; for employers, the alternative to hiring labor is to economize on workers by moving to more capital-intensive, or automated, modes of production.

As we will see in Chapter 4, most evidence suggests that labor supply is not highly responsive to the after-tax wage, suggesting that on average people do not perceive they have any alternative but to work. Firms are more flexible in their ability to find alternatives to high-priced labor. The relative flexibility of firms compared to workers implies that very little of an income tax on labor would be shifted off of workers by forcing up wage payments, and the tax will largely be borne by the workers themselves.

An income tax is a tax not only on labor income, but also on business income and the return to saving. It is important to be precise about the incidence of these aspects of income taxation.

Corporations Don't Pay Taxes, People Do

The controversial slogan of the National Rifle Association—"guns don't kill, people do"—may seem like a semantic fine point, but at first blush the tax version seems just plain wrong. Corporations certainly do remit a great deal of taxes; federal, state, and local corporate profits taxes amounted to $203 billion in 1994.[32] Many people favor higher taxes on corporations in the hope that this means that someone else would pay, but not them or their constituents.

Nevertheless, there is an important sense in which corporations do not pay tax. The fact that Chrysler's treasurer signs checks made out to the IRS tells us nothing about which Americans pay the price for government activity. It is certainly not the treasurer who bears the burden of corporation income taxes, but who exactly does bear it? Is it Chrysler's stockholders, its employees, or perhaps its customers? It is simply not meaningful to say that Chrysler will be worse off. It is necessary to identify precisely which people end up bearing the burden of the tax in question.

Unfortunately, tracing the ultimate incidence of a tax levied on corporations, such as the corporation income tax, is a very difficult and controversial matter. But it is an important question, especially because many tax reform proposals involve lowering tax payments of individuals and increasing tax payments by businesses, including corporate businesses.[33]

Who bears the burden of the corporate income tax? To answer this question, imagine imposing a corporate tax in an economy that has no such tax. In the short run, it is holders of corporate stock who will suffer as a result of imposing this tax, as share prices will tumble in anticipation of lower after-tax earnings. This is not the end of the story, though, because further investment in corporations will from now on become less attractive than noncorporate investments, such as partnerships, sole proprietorships, farms, and real estate. Corporate investment dries up, while noncorporate investment expands. But more people seeking noncorporate investments will inevitably drive down the return in these sectors, shifting some of the burden of the tax to the owners of other forms of wealth. Once the reallocation of investment is completed, the after-tax, risk-adjusted return on investment will be the same for corporate investments as it is for noncorporate investments.

Because this is a difficult bit of economic reasoning, the following analogy may be helpful. Imagine there are two highways leading from a suburb to the central city. The two highways each have their own advantages, but get commuters to work in about the same amount of time, and almost everyone has settled into the habit of regularly taking one road or the other. Now imagine a toll booth is constructed on one road. At first, the losers will be those who are accustomed to taking that route to work. Over time, though, more and more commuters will switch to the alternate highway, making that way to work more congested and thereby increasing the commuting time. In this way, the burden of the toll booth on one road is shifted to those who had usually taken the other. Once the dust has settled, it will probably be the case that all commuters are about equally burdened by the toll. Similarly, what is a tax only on the income from corporations will be spread to the recipients of all types of capital income, as funds that otherwise would have been invested in corporations flow into the noncorporate sector, making it a less lucrative venue for investment. With some exceptions, the same principle should apply to personal taxes on capital income; we would expect the burden of taxes on dividends, interest, and capital gains to fall on the recipients of all capital income, whether it is taxable or not.

Do Workers Bear Taxes on Capital?

Some economists argue that the shifting story does not end here, and the burden will be shifted from wealth owners to wage earners. Their argument states that taxes on capital income (including, but not restricted to, corporation income taxes) reduce the rate of return to saving, which in turn reduces the amount of saving that people will willingly undertake. Since saving is what finances capital investment, a decline in saving over time means that there is a less capital-intensive, and therefore less productive, economy. By this string of reasoning, it is workers who ultimately bear the burden of taxes on capital income, because their wages are reduced when the economy is less productive.

This argument is highly controversial because it depends on a couple of hotly debated presumptions about how the U.S. economy works. First, it requires that peoples' saving behavior be responsive to changes in the after-tax return they can earn. The experience of the 1980s, when rates of return surged dramatically but the savings rate gradually declined, has cast considerable doubt on that proposition; the next chapter will explore this issue more thoroughly.

Second, the argument requires that domestic investment must decline if U.S. saving declines. The global economy makes this story much less plausible because, in a global economy, domestic investment need not be financed by U.S. residents' savings. If a tax on the capital income of U.S. citizens reduces our saving, foreign savers have proven only too happy to finance our investment.[34] In this case, the link between the future productivity of American workers and the return to our own investments is broken, and taxes on saving will be borne largely by American savers.

The possibility of foreigners investing in the United States makes it less likely that a tax on U.S. residents' savings will eventually be shifted to become a lower reward to U.S. workers. The possibility of U.S. citizens investing abroad, though, makes it more likely that taxing U.S. domestic investment will be shifted onto workers. Foreign investment is an alternative to domestic investment, making it unlikely that investors will accept a lower return to investing in the United States. An attempt to tax U.S.-located investment to some extent drives investment offshore, leaving U.S. workers with less productive work opportunities. The lesson of the global marketplace is that it is more difficult to impose a burden on activities that are mobile across borders. As of 1996, capital is more mobile than labor, implying that taxes on capital in a particular location will tend to be shifted onto those workers who reside in that location. However, there is evidence that capital is still not perfectly mobile across borders for a large country such as the United States, so even in this case capital owners likely bear some of the tax burden.[35]

The nineteenth-century French pamphleteer and leader of the free-trade movement, Frédéric Bastiat, wrote that there is only one difference between a bad economist and a good economist—the latter considers not only the effects of policy that can be seen, but also those effects that cannot be seen.[36] Because individuals can respond to tax by changing their behavior, the true burden of taxes can be shifted in ways unanticipated and unintended by policymakers. Taxes on capital income can, in principle, be shifted to workers. Taxes on the profits from innovation can, in principle, be shifted to those consumers who would have enjoyed the innovative products the tax discouraged from reaching market. The trouble is that obtaining a completely accurate measurement of how much tax shifting occurs in practice is a difficult task. What economists can offer is an answer to the question using reasonable and defensible assumptions about the critical factors, while making very explicit what those assumptions are and, ideally, providing a range of possible consequences based on a set of other reasonable assumptions.

Who Does Pay?

The results of two recent attempts to assess the incidence of all federal taxes, one by the CBO and the other by the Treasury Department, are shown in Table 3.2. Following our dictum of the previous paragraph, we will be explicit about the incidence assumptions that underlie these

Table 3.2
Recent estimates of the distribution of federal taxes

Families ranked by income	CBO[a] Average federal tax rate	Treasury Department[b] Average federal tax rate	Average personal and corporate income tax rate
Overall	23.7	19.7	11.5
Lowest quintile	5.0	3.2	−2.4
Second quintile	14.9	9.4	2.0
Middle quintile	19.5	16.8	7.1
Fourth quintile	22.3	19.9	9.3
Highest quintile	27.9	22.4	15.4
81 to 90 percent	24.9	21.3	10.8
91 to 95 percent	26.3	22.1	12.8
96 to 99 percent	27.7	21.9	15.7
Top 1 percent	33.2	24.5	22.4

Note: Based on fully phased-in version of law enacted in 1993.
[a]Congressional Budget Office (1994).
[b]U.S. Department of Treasury, Office of Tax Analysis (1996a). Uses a broader definition of income. See text for further details.

estimates. The entire burden of individual income taxes is assumed to fall on those families who have the legal liability, with no shifting at all of tax levied on either labor or capital income. As for the corporate income tax, its burden is assigned to families on the basis of their total capital (not just corporate-source) income. Payroll taxes are attributed to families paying those taxes directly or indirectly through their employers, so that the assignment of legal liability between firm and individual is, as it should be, ignored. Excise taxes are distributed according to consumption of the taxed good or service.[37]

The first two columns of numbers show estimates of how the overall federal tax burden is distributed. Both incorporate the fully phased-in versions of the tax law passed in 1993, which has not changed materially since then. According to both estimates, the distribution of federal taxes is quite progressive. In the CBO version, average tax rates range from 5 percent for those in the lowest quintile to 33.2 percent for those in the top 1 percent of income earners. The Treasury version shows average rates rising from 3.2 percent to 24.5 percent; the pattern of the average tax rates is similar, but rates are generally lower due mainly to different definitions of income. The Treasury uses a broad definition that is close to the economic income concept discussed in Chapter 2, while the CBO definition is closer to adjusted gross income.[38]

The last column of Table 3.2 shows the Treasury's estimate of the distribution of personal and corporate income taxes. Rates range from negative 2.4 percent in the bottom quintile to 22.4 percent at the top percentile. The negative rate at the bottom arises from the earned income tax credit, which provides refundable tax credits to low-income working families. Comparing the last two columns makes clear that income taxation accounts for nearly all of the progressivity of overall federal taxes; most other federal taxes are either flat or regressive in their distribution.

While the underlying incidence assumptions are important, other reasonable assumptions would not change the results dramatically. For example, the CBO has done calculations that assume half or all of the burden of the corporate tax falls on labor, rather than on capital owners. In this case, the tax system is still very progressive, but somewhat less so. The difference is not large because corporate taxes are a relatively small portion of overall taxes.[39]

Figure 3.2 compares the progressivity of the personal income tax with evidence on desired progressivity from the Hite-Roberts survey

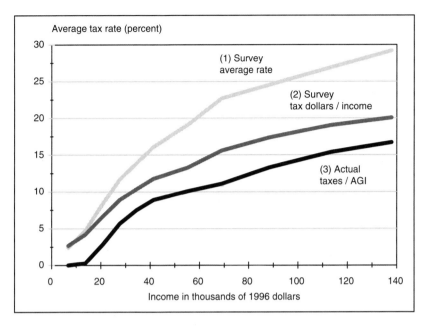

Figure 3.2
Actual progressivity of personal income taxes compared to survey evidence on desired progressivity
Note: Each line represents average rates of federal personal income tax on married couples with no children.
(1) Means of survey respondents' desired average rates.
(2) Means of survey respondents' desired tax dollars, converted to average rates.
(3) Actual average rates for 1991, defined as income tax after credits divided by adjusted
gross income.
Source: Hite and Roberts (1991), and authors' tabulations from the 1991 IRS individual
model files.

results (shown earlier in Table 3.2). Comparing lines 2 and 3 reveal
that the pattern of average rates in the current system is strikingly
similar to the pattern that emerges when the "fair" tax bills assigned
to families at each income level by survey respondents are converted
into average tax rates. The general similarity of these two distributions
suggests one of two things. It may mean that we have managed to get
the sharing of tax burdens about where Americans, on average, want
it to be. Alternatively, it means that when asked their preferences
people tend to mimic the system currently in place. When survey
respondents were asked to assign average tax *rates*, rather than tax
dollars, they chose an even more progressive distribution than the

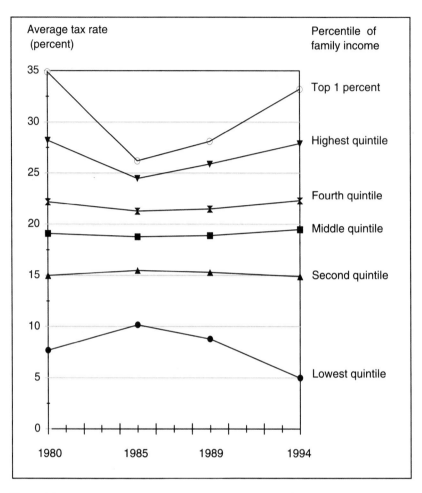

Figure 3.3
Average federal tax rates on families at various income levels for the period 1980–1994
Note: average tax rates for 1994 assume fully phased-in version of law enacted in 1993.
Source: Kasten, Sammartino, and Toder (1994) and CBO (1994).

current system; that it, the slope of line 1 is steeper than the slope of line 3. Some of this, however, might reflect confusion between average and marginal rates on the part of some survey respondents.

Figure 3.3 illustrates how average federal tax rates have changed in recent years for people at different points in the income distribution. Despite all the ballyhoo about taxes between 1980 and 1994, including the "Reagan revolution" in 1981, the landmark Tax Reform Act of 1986, and what was erroneously labeled "the largest tax increase in history" in 1993, there was essentially *no change* in average tax rates for families in the middle 60 percent of the income distribution (quintiles two through four) over that whole period. The only significant changes occurred at the bottom and the extreme top. In 1980, when Jimmy Carter was still the president, the average rate on the top 1 percent of families was 34.9 percent. It fell to just 26.2 percent by 1985 as a result of the Reagan tax cuts. By 1989, it had come back up to 28.1 percent, partially due to the Tax Reform Act of 1986. Enactments in 1990 and 1993 pushed rates on the top 1 percent back near their 1980 levels, to 33.2 percent by 1994. The pattern in the bottom quintile is mainly due to changing real values of the personal exemption and standard deduction, and expansion of the earned income tax credit.[40]

It is often pointed out that even though tax rates on high-income people fell during the 1980s, the share of total taxes they paid actually increased. This is true, and the reason for it is very simple: as Figure 3.1 shows, the share of before-tax income received by the rich increased dramatically during this same time period.

Horizontal Equity—Equal Treatment of Equals

Special Privileges for Everyone!

According to Garrison Keillor, in Lake Wobegon all the children are above average. A similar paradox applies to the U.S. income tax system—everyone gets special privileges. You get a special tax break if you have children, if you are elderly, if you give money to your favorite charity, if you set up an IRA, if you receive fringe benefits from your employer, and the list goes on.

Of course it is no more possible that everyone can get special tax breaks than it is possible that everyone is above average. Remember, we are taxing ourselves. To raise a given amount of revenue, the long list of special tax privileges requires higher tax rates. Allowing large families to take additional dependent exemption allowances lowers their taxes, but inescapably increases taxes on smaller families. The fact that mortgage interest payments are deductible certainly lowers taxes for those itemizing heads of households who have borrowed to buy their homes, but inevitably raises taxes on those who rent housing. A family really only benefits from the whole system of tax breaks if they receive more of them than other similarly situated families—

otherwise, what they save in tax preferences is just offset by the higher-than-otherwise tax rates.

To expose the Wobegonish nature of our income tax system, allow us a flight of fancy in redesigning the tax system a bit. Gone is the current system of first calculating your baseline gross income, and then subtracting off the deductions and credits that are your special privileges. The new system features a radical reduction in all tax rates, but, and there must be a but, in order to pay for the lower rates there are special tax penalties, rather than special tax privileges, for particular characteristics and behaviors. For example, there is a tax penalty for being under 65 years of age, for giving less than 1 percent of your income to a charity, for not setting up an IRA, and for receiving labor compensation in cash rather than in fringe benefits. If this tax redesign were done carefully enough, it could come pretty close to replicating the current pattern of tax liabilities, so that everyone would be right back to where they are now.

We're not suggesting that we go through the hassle of converting our tax system with special privileges for all to one with special penalties for all. However, this exercise does expose the tax system for what it is. In the tax game, we are all in it together, so what is a privilege to some group of people is a penalty to everyone else, because it forces up tax rates.

Is there any justification for imposing special tax penalties—the inevitable consequences of granting privileges—on some families? Or do these penalties imply a failure to achieve what economists call *horizontal equity*, the principle that tax liability ought to be the same for any two families with the same level of well-being—equal treatment of equals?[41] Certainly there are some characteristics on which we could probably all agree it would be inappropriate to base tax liability—such as race or religion. Although your race or religion won't lead to higher taxes today in the United States, many other personal characteristics and choices will. Which, if any, of these are justifiable reasons to penalize someone?

Let's start with spending patterns. Would it be fair that the Hatfields pay more tax than the McCoys just because they like to go to the movies, while the McCoys prefer to watch television? Would it be fair to tax the Astors more than the Vanderbilts because the former prefer to spend their money on yachts, while the latter prefer around-the-world cruises? Such distinctions seem arbitrary and without a place in the tax system. If you agree, then tax penalties based on spending patterns are inappropriate.

This rule surely implies that taxes on selected goods and services are inappropriate, because they will discriminate against families who have a penchant for those goods. Taxes on movies discriminate against movie lovers, taxes on yachts discriminate against yacht lovers, and so on.[42] Note that taxing some goods but not others would not be a major problem for horizontal equity if the taxed goods represented the same share of total income for most people. If, for example, all families spent 20 percent of their income on food, then a 5 percent excise tax on food sales only would be no more horizontally inequitable than a 1 percent income tax; if most, but not all, families spent 20 percent of their income on food, then the food tax would be almost as equitable, but not quite.

Many aspects of the income tax code can be viewed as discriminating against certain people simply because of their tastes. For example, the home mortgage interest deduction penalizes those who prefer to rent. The charitable contributions deduction penalizes those who are not charitable. The deduction for state and local taxes penalizes people who prefer to live in places with low levels of public services. And the dependent exemption effectively penalizes families who would prefer to have a small number of children.

Is there a more positive way to look at those tax features, other than as discriminating? If they encourage behavior that directly benefits other Americans, special tax treatments can serve a legitimate social purpose by in essence subsidizing taxpayers for the benefits they provide to others; in these cases, the horizontal inequity is tolerated in order to achieve a more efficient economic system. The next chapter explores in more detail how to evaluate such arguments.

Tax preferences or penalties may also be justified on the grounds that income is an imperfect measure of a family's level of well-being, and certain adjustments to income are required in order to make it a better measure. According to this argument, these tax features *improve* the horizontal equity of the tax system, for in their absence some families pay too much tax because their taxable income overstates their true well-being, in other words, their true ability to pay. This argument certainly applies to the existing deduction for extraordinary medical expenses. Comparing two families with the same income, one that incurs $10,000 in medical expenses has clearly not fared as well as one that doesn't, and may justifiably be liable for less taxes. What makes this case different than the Hatfields and McCoys is that medical expenses are mainly not a matter of taste—you don't choose to get a serious illness.[43] Allowing a deduction of medical expenses helps out families singled out by circumstances, not by taste, and thus is unlikely to be a source of horizontal inequity. Even in this case, however, there is some discrimination by taste; those who prefer to spend a great deal on the best medical care they can find, instead of economizing, will receive an extra tax benefit.

Each preference or penalty in the tax code needs to be evaluated not only on the basis of its fairness, but also on its economic benefits or costs and on its contribution to complexity. Those latter two issues will be considered in the next two chapters. However, before moving on, it is important to consider some issues that make the principle of horizontal equity a bit less straightforward than it might at first seem.

Misleading Inequity

In some cases of potential horizontal inequity, it is tricky to tell whether circumstances or tastes are involved. Consider the deductibility of casualty losses due to earthquake damages. If earthquakes were truly a random event, not at all predictable by location, then this deduction makes sense as a way to adjust tax liability to reflect the reduced ability-to-pay of earthquake victims; they are victims of circumstance. In fact, earthquakes are much more likely to occur in certain areas, such as California. Living on a fault line is certainly a choice, one that is to some degree compensated by lower-than-otherwise housing prices. In this situation, allowing the deduction rewards to some extent those who are willing to take the risk of an earthquake, which is certainly a matter of taste. The argument gets even murkier when private earthquake insurance is available, because in this case the deduction rewards those who not only choose to live in a risky place but choose not to insure themselves against a catastrophe.

In this example, lower housing prices were partial compensation for earthquake risk, weakening the argument for a tax break. In other cases, the adjustment of prices means that differences in tax liabilities do not necessarily indicate horizontal inequity. For example, the fact that some wealthy investors pay no tax on interest from municipal securities does not indicate horizontal inequity to the extent the market interest rate on these bonds is lower than taxable bonds. Differences in tax payments do not reflect inequity if market prices offset the tax benefits. This offset is more likely to happen if the tax-preferred activity is available widely; when it is restricted to only certain people, the benefit is less likely to be offset by price changes.

Who Are Equals: Families or Individuals?

Another question to consider in our efforts to achieve "equal treatment of equals" is exactly who are equals: individuals or families? This choice inevitably raises some tricky issues.

If all *individuals* of equal levels of well-being are to be treated equally by the tax system, this raises questions about how the income of a family should be attributed to each member of that family. For example, each individual could be taxed on the income he or she earns, period. However, this ignores the pooling of resources between a husband and wife, and does not consider the impact of the tax system on the well-being of children. At the other extreme, we could divide up a family's income among all its members equally, and assess tax on that basis. With a graduated rate structure, for a given family income this would result in a lower tax burden on members of larger families. Because average tax rates rise with income, the members of a six-person family would face a lower tax burden if each member paid tax on his or her "share" of family income than if the rate was imposed on the total of that income.

Our tax system makes no attempt to attribute a level of economic well-being to each individual member of our society, and instead uses the family as the unit of comparison. In practice, it compromises between the two alternative extremes for measuring individual well-being that are mentioned above.

First, consider the issue of children. Under the current system, a family's tax liability declines with each additional child. Each dependent qualifies the family for an additional exemption allowance, which amounts to a deduction from taxable income of $2,500 in the year 1995. The rationale here is that each member of a family with, say, $50,000 of gross income will be worse-off if there are six people in that family than if there are three people. So our tax system treats the larger family more generously.

But there is another issue here; it is not at all clear that parents are made "worse-off" by each additional child that they have. Having children is largely a voluntary choice, and may even be viewed as a matter of personal consumption preference from the point of view of the parents. Some adults prefer to save up and spend their money for a round-the-world trip, while others prefer the joy of children with the attendant costs of food, diapers, Nintendo®, and possibly college. Is it fair to reward adults who prefer to have more children, at the expense of adults who prefer other ways of spending their money?[44]

Undoubtedly some people would object to lumping child-rearing and globe-trotting as two comparable ways to spend money, and would consider the former as a sacred duty rather than a choice. Whether it is a choice or a duty is not an issue that economics can resolve. Moreover, the choice of how many children will be in the family is not voluntary from the children's point of view. So a child in a six-person family may indeed be economically worse-off than a child in a three-person family with the same income.

These are tough issues to resolve, but they are unavoidable in any tax system. Some replacements for the income tax being discussed, such as the retail sales tax and value-added tax, would eliminate any such adjustment based on family size. Others, such as the flat tax, would make these preferences more generous, by making dependent allowances larger.

Common sense suggests that a system that rewards families with children would also reward, or at least not penalize, marriage. Common sense would be wrong for the U.S. tax system. More likely than not, getting married increases a couple's total tax bill.[45]

The marriage tax, as it is usually called, arises because we insist on two requirements for our income tax system—one, that it be progressive and, two, that tax liability be based on total family income and not on how that income is divided between the spouses. Progressivity means that the fraction of income owed in tax increases with income. Combining that requirement with the requirement that what matters is only total family income, and not how it is divided up, leads to the marriage tax. Suppose, for example, that Barbie and Ken each make $30,000, and that the average tax rate on $30,000 annual income is 15 percent; the average tax rate for $60,000 income is 20 percent. They each pay $4,500 as singles; as a married couple they pay $12,000, amounting to a "marriage tax" of $3,000. Note that there would be no marriage tax at all if Barbie earned all the money or for that matter if Ken did.

In this example, the marriage tax happens not because anyone thinks it is good policy, but rather as an unavoidable consequence of progressivity and family-based taxes. Some argue that a marriage tax is appropriate on ability-to-pay grounds, because it reflects savings in the cost-of-living that marriage provides—sharing a kitchen, a telephone, and so on. These savings could, though, be largely achieved by having a roommate, and no one is suggesting that one's tax liability be affected by the number of one's roommates.

If these are not convincing arguments for a marriage penalty, what can be done to alleviate it? One way around the problem is to have separate tax tables for single taxpayers and for married couples, as we do in the United States. Each schedule can be progressive on its own terms, so that the fraction of income owed in tax rises with income for single taxpayers, and also for married taxpayers. If the tax due on the same income is lower for a family compared to a single taxpayer, then the marriage tax can be erased. Let's go back to Barbie and Ken and see how this would work. For single taxpayers, let the average tax rate still be 15 percent for $30,000 income and 20 percent for $60,000 income; this is progressive. For married taxpayers, let the tax rate be 10 percent on $30,000 and 15 percent on $60,000; this is progressive, too (at least when considering only married taxpayers).

This scheme eliminates the marriage tax on Barbie and Ken, because they pay $4,500 each as singles and $9,000 as a married couple. However, the cost of getting rid of the marriage tax is imposing a penalty for being single, and giving a marriage bonus to one-earner couples, because under this system a single taxpayer earning $60,000 pays $12,000 in tax, while a one-earner married couple with exactly the same family income owes only $9,000, a marriage bonus of $3,000.

As long as we desire a progressive tax system based on family income, there is no way out of this dilemma. Any tax schedule will feature either a marriage bonus or a marriage penalty (bonus to being single), or some combination of both depending on the circumstances of the people involved.

In the United States, we have opted for a compromise among the approaches. A two-earner couple typically faces a penalty for getting married, although the penalty is not as large as it would be if all families and individuals were taxed under the same schedule. A single-earner couple faces a marriage bonus, and a single person pays more tax than a single-earner married couple with the same income. We could avoid these problems completely if tax liability were based on individual, rather than family, income, as is the case in several European countries, and was the case in the United States in the early days of the income tax. Under this system, it can be arranged so that marriage has no tax consequences at all. But note that under this system a family's tax liability depends on who earns what; a family in which the total income is divided up fairly equally will owe less than another family with exactly the same total income, but with one primary earner. It also gives rise to incentives to shift income from the higher-earning family member to lower-earning members. Couples can manipulate which spouse receives capital income and incurs deductible expenses; this is difficult for the IRS to monitor.[46] The other way to reduce these horizontal inequities is to make the rate structure less progressive, but this comes at the expense of what many people view as a desirable degree of vertical equity.

Lifetime and Generational Perspectives on Equity

In most cases, both vertical and horizontal equity issues should be addressed in a long-run, rather than an annual, context. If the government announced a special annual tax of $1,000 on half of all taxpayers, to alternate every other year with a special $1,000 grant, everyone would understand that over a two-year horizon the net benefit averages to nothing, even though a one-year analysis would reveal apparently capricious horizontal inequity.

More seriously, when comparing two tax systems for which the timing of tax payments is different, but which add up to the same burden over a longer horizon, one should not be misled by an annual analysis to conclude that there is inequity. Special credits to the elderly don't have significant equity consequences if everyone eventually is elderly. The fact that, over a lifetime, income taxes are paid during one's working years and sales tax payments are spread out more evenly over one's consuming years is not in itself an indication of horizontal inequity, even though in any one year the tax payments of two families with the same income will tend to differ depending on their age. This issue will be important in Chapters 6 and 7, where we discuss replacing the income tax with a consumption tax.

For some tax policy issues, it is important to look beyond even a lifetime perspective, to a generational perspective. As the next chapter will show, this is essential for discussing deficit finance of government expenditures, because borrowing puts off specifying who will bear the burden of taxes, and tends to impose that burden on future generations. As we shall see, it is also a critical issue in the debate over whether to replace the income tax with a consumption tax because, depending on how the transition is handled, that could shift a substantial tax burden onto the elderly, and decrease the tax burden on future generations.

Later, when tax reform options are addressed, the equity of alternative tax systems will be evaluated using the concepts developed here. Before leaving the topic of equity, there is one more aspect that needs to be addressed—inequities that arise from changes in the tax system.

Transitional Equity

Whenever the tax system changes, there are bound to be people who lose out and others who benefit. This is true regardless of whether the change ultimately makes the tax system fairer. The losers lose because they have entered into some long-term commitment that made sense only because of the old tax system. They may have bought houses counting on the mortgage interest deduction, and will lose out if it is abolished. They may have located far from their jobs, counting on cheap gasoline for their commuting, and will lose if gasoline taxes are increased. They may have invested in state and local bonds, counting on the benefit of tax-free interest, and will see the value of these bonds fall if marginal tax rates are reduced, and plummet if the tax exemption is removed entirely.

There will also be those who reap windfall benefits when the tax law changes, people who happen to be in the right place at the right time. For example, people who own stock in high-dividend companies will see their shares rise in value if the tax on dividends is reduced or eliminated. Of course, the political pressure against change always comes from the unlucky losers, not the lucky winners. What should be done about them? Some would say "tough beans" and leave it at that, arguing that there are constantly ups and downs in the economic environment, and everyone has to expect to lose out from time to time. This argument is especially compelling when talk of tax changes has been in the air for a while. In that case, the possibility of windfall losses is probably already reflected in the price of the activity or asset. Talk of a lower tax rate drives down the price of tax-exempt securities, increasing their yield. The bargain price and high interest rate reflect the gamble that tax rates might go down. If that does occur, it wouldn't make sense to fully compensate the holders of the bonds; they took a gamble when they bought the bonds, fully aware of the possibility of a tax reduction, and they've already been partly compensated for this risk through higher interest rates.

In other cases there is simply no way that the tax change could have been anticipated. A family that took out a home mortgage five years ago, counting on the interest deduction, could not have reasonably anticipated that the deduction would be eliminated. If the mortgage deduction were to be eliminated, what can be done to prevent this family from being hurt? The usual fix is to "grandfather" existing mortgages, so that interest on them remains deductible, even as interest on new mortgages is no longer deductible.

This seems reasonable, but grandfathering arrangements and other transition rules can easily become quite complicated. They require two parallel sets of rules, one to apply to decisions taken under the old tax law, and one to apply to decisions taken since; the dividing line requires monitoring to prevent abuse. These arrangements also cost the Treasury revenue, and thus require higher tax rates than otherwise, at least for a while.

Transitional equity is an absolutely critical concern when considering replacing the income tax with a consumption-based tax. Here one important dividing line is age. If people knew from birth that they had to pay a tax equal to 20 percent of their lifetime incomes, it probably wouldn't matter to most of them whether they paid most of it by the time they retired, or whether the tax was spread evenly over their working and retirement years. As long as the payment schedule was known in advance, it shouldn't be a big problem.

However, changing the rules in midlife can be a big problem. Imagine living and paying taxes under an income tax regime all your working life, expecting to pay little or no taxes in retirement, and then waking up on the first day of your retirement to learn that the income tax had been abolished, to be replaced by a 25 percent retail sales tax! No one would blame you for being rather upset. But this is exactly what could happen to millions of elderly people if we were to shift to a consumption tax, depending on how that tax is implemented.

Just as with the mortgage interest deduction, there are fixes. For example, elderly people can be granted an exemption from the sales tax, or at least a lower rate. But, also as with the mortgage deduction, these fixes have problems. The elderly "exemption card" would be valuable indeed. One can imagine making sure your elderly parents buy your next car for you, and give it to you as an anniversary present. Even if such a scheme were preventable, the exemption would require that the sales tax rate on everyone else would have to be much higher, to make up for the lost revenue.

The problem is clear. Even if we could all agree that another tax system is fairer and simpler, getting from here to there might be unfair to many people. If, though, we try to devise rules to compensate losers, the transition can become extremely complicated. Moreover, if only those losers who are politically powerful get compensated, the transition can end up becoming both extremely complicated *and* unfair.

Conclusion

What's fair in taxation will play a crucial role in the coming debate about tax reform, because many reform proposals effect a radical re-shuffling of the tax burden. Some collapse the graduated rate structure to a single rate, substantially lessening the tax system's progressivity. All of the proposals cut back on the special provisions in the tax law that are justified on the grounds that they fine-tune the sharing of the tax burden or reward especially beneficial activities. Whether these changes represent steps toward or away from tax equity will occupy center stage.

These questions cannot be answered in isolation, because fairness is inextricably tied to the topics of the simplicity of the tax system and how it affects economic performance. Fine-tuning tax liability and en-suring progressivity inevitably complicate the tax process, and aban-doning these goals can allow significant simplification. Moreover, the effort to use the tax system to redistribute incomes and single out par-ticular activities for reward may inhibit economic growth.

4   Taxes and Economic Prosperity

The question of how taxes affect the economy has long been at the heart of the American political debate. At one end of the spectrum are politicians who argue that our tax system is severely crippling the economy, and that radical changes could unleash a new era of unbridled growth and prosperity. Ronald Reagan made this a central theme of his presidential campaigns, and rode to landslide victories as he promised and delivered lower marginal income tax rates, with dramatic reductions concentrated at the top.

Jack Kemp and other members of the Republicans' National Commission on Economic Growth and Tax Reform carried this tradition a step further in their 1996 report. They claimed that replacing our progressive income tax altogether with a flat-rate consumption tax could *double* the long-term rate of economic growth from about 2.5 percent to 5 percent.[1] Steve Forbes made a similar assertion about his proposal for a "flat tax" during the 1996 Republican presidential primaries.[2] That our economic growth rate could be doubled is quite a claim; even if it was sustained for only ten years, it would mean an economy 27 percent larger than otherwise would be attained.

At the other end of the spectrum, some Democratic politicians rarely mention the economic costs of taxation, except to say that their opponents are greatly exaggerating them. In between, there are many people of all political persuasions who believe that certain changes to the tax system could be beneficial for the economy, but stop short of the types of claims mentioned above.

Economists' views of the impact of taxation and the potential benefits of reform tend to be considerably more circumspect than those expressed by political advocates, but there's still a broad range of opinion. Stanford economist Robert Hall, a designer of the flat tax, says adopting it would most likely increase incomes by a total of 6 percent over seven years.[3] Some economists would put that figure higher, but hardly any would promise a sustained doubling of the growth rate. Others are less sanguine; for example, William Gale of the Brookings Institution believes the long-run gains would probably be closer to just 1 percent of income.[4] Just as important as the differing estimates, however, is what economists know and agree upon; this often diverges in important ways from the focal issues and claims in the public debate.

Understanding how taxes affect the economy, and how to evaluate claims about those effects, is critically important for anyone who wants to make an informed decision about who should be running our country and what policies they should be pursuing. For one thing, if there are features of our tax code that hinder the economy without good reason, most of us could agree that we should change those features. Often, however, changes to the tax code that could improve economic performance conflict with other cherished goals. In these cases, there is a trade-off or balance to be struck, and the terms of that trade-off depend crucially on how large the economic benefits arising from the tax change would be.

The greatest and most controversial of these trade-offs is one that was alluded to in the last chapter: that between progressivity and economic efficiency. Taxes reduce the incentive to engage in all of the activities people undertake to better themselves—working harder, acquiring education and training, thinking of new products and ways to do business, and so on. The more progressive the tax system, the more these incentives are blunted. However, as shown in the last chapter, progressive taxes also play a big role in determining how economic resources and the burden of paying for government are distributed among people with differing abilities and fortunes. Many view a progressive distribution of the burden as fair. Hence, there is an inescapable trade-off.

In recent years, one of the Republicans' most effective rhetorical weapons has been the parable of the pie, where the pie represents national wealth. Democrats, they claim, are obsessed with how to slice the pie, and with ensuring that their natural constituencies get a good-sized slice. Republicans, in contrast, say they are determined to enact policies that enlarge the size of the pie. A larger pie, they argue, can produce bigger slices for everyone. When framed in this way, the critical question is how much bigger the pie can get. Whether most people are ultimately made better off or worse off by a change in the tax system can depend crucially on the answer to that question.

Many other features of tax reform need not directly conflict with progressivity, but may be in tension with other goals or desires of the public. For instance, reform plans often sacrifice cherished deductions and special preferences in exchange for lower rates. For this and other reasons, any overhaul is likely to have major winners and losers in the transition. Whether such potentially jarring changes are deemed worthwhile also depends critically on the size of the likely economic benefits.

This chapter will explore both the theory and the evidence on the economic impact of taxes. The main topic will be how the design of our tax system affects the level of economic prosperity in the long run. First, however, it is important to examine some issues that are in principle separate from this question, but often get mixed together with the long-run prosperity question. These include the relationship between taxes and the business cycle, the deficit, and the size of government. Once that's out of the way, some historical and international evidence on the relationship between taxes and long-run economic prosperity will be reviewed.

The main task of this chapter will be a systematic examination of specific ways that taxes affect economic behavior, and the evidence on the magnitude of those effects. The focus will be on the three main economic issues that most radical reform proposals would address: the impact of marginal tax rates on work effort; the effect of taxes on the amount of saving and investment; and the economic advantages of a more "neutral" tax system, which would exert less influence on people's choices among different types of investment and consumption. Some other issues frequently raised in the tax reform debate will also be addressed, including: the impact of taxes on risk-taking and entrepreneurship; the question of whether taxes can give us an edge in "international competitiveness"; and promises of "more and better jobs." Two important issues that are less often in the spotlight will also be looked at: how taxes affect investments in education and training; and ways that people can respond to taxes besides changing their real economic behavior, for example, altering the timing of their income or repackaging it so as to avoid taxes. Finally, the chapter concludes by using this information to examine some important disputes often aired in the public debate, including the effect of tax cuts on revenues, and the impact of taxes on the economic behavior of very high-income people.

Separate but Important Issues

Taxes and the Business Cycle

The main focus in this chapter is how taxes affect long-run economic growth and prosperity. As everyone knows, the economy does not proceed steadily along a long-run trend, but instead experiences temporary ups and downs, known as the business cycle. The downs, periods when the economy is sluggish and stuck significantly below its capacity, are known as recessions. Unemployment rates rise above their normal levels, and industrial plant and equipment go underutilized. Recoveries from recessions are periods of unusually rapid growth rates, as we make up lost ground and more fully utilize the capital and labor that are already available. This kind of growth is fundamentally different from the kind of long-run growth that involves an expansion of the economy's capacity or potential—more and better capital and technology, and more and better-skilled labor.

The first thing to note about recessions and recoveries is that they occur for many reasons besides taxes. A recession may be triggered by a drop in consumer or business confidence. If consumers become worried about their jobs and the state of the economy, they may reduce their purchases of cars, homes, and other goods; this in turn reduces the incomes of the workers who produce those things, who in turn buy fewer goods, which produces a downward spiral. If businesses become less optimistic, they may reduce their purchases of investment goods, producing a similar effect. A frightening world event might cause such a drop in confidence—for example, Iraq's 1990 invasion of Kuwait may have contributed to the ensuing 1991 recession by creating worries about world oil supplies.

Most economists believe that, in some situations, the Federal Reserve can affect the business cycle by influencing interest rates. Raising interest rates can slow the economy by making it more expensive for businesses to borrow for investments in plant and equipment, and for consumers to borrow to buy cars, homes, and the like; lower interest rates have the opposite effect. It is likely that the deep recession of 1981–1982 was caused by Fed action to raise interest rates in an effort to curb inflation, and that the recovery had something to do with the Fed's subsequent easing of this policy.

The role of taxes in the business cycle is more controversial among economists. It is true that a tax cut puts more money in people's pockets, and to the extent that people go out and spend some of it, this gives a boost to the economy. However, note that this can only work if government spending is not simultaneously reduced by the same amount, since this would offset the increase in consumer spending; there needs to be an increase in the deficit. More importantly, it can only work if the economy is in a recession, operating below its capacity; if the economy is already at capacity, a big increase in spending can't be met by a big increase in output, so the result will instead be higher prices or higher interest rates.

Recent U.S. history reveals a number of episodes in which tax cuts have been explicitly used in an attempt to spur demand and jump-start a sluggish economy. The Kennedy-Johnson tax cut of 1964 is often cited as an example where a tax cut was intentionally and successfully used for this purpose. In other cases, stimulating demand is not a stated rationale for a tax cut, but it may have that effect anyway. For example, some argue that the recovery from the 1981–1982 recession was spurred in part by increased consumer demand induced by the Reagan tax cut. Finally, income taxes may help dampen recessions even in the absence of legislated changes, by acting as an "automatic stabilizer." Income tax revenues decline automatically in recessions, because incomes are shrinking and people are slipping into lower tax brackets. This may help cushion the blow to consumer demand. For instance, during the 1991–1992 recession, income tax revenues automatically declined and the deficit increased, and some economists believe this helped keep the recession from getting even worse than it did.

In recent years, support for fighting recessions with deficit-increasing tax cuts has waned among economists. Many now argue that a temporary increase in disposable income will mostly be saved rather than spent, and therefore will generate little in the way of an economic stimulus. Besides, by the time the government recognizes a recession and enacts a tax cut, the economy is likely to have begun to rebound on its own, making the cut unnecessary at best, and inflationary at worst. Concern about the negative long-term effects of deficits (discussed below) also diminishes support for such a policy; deficit stimulus might mean short-term gain but long-term pain.

Our point here is not to pass final judgment on the wisdom of using tax cuts as a countercyclical policy, or to join the fray over exactly why recessions occur. Both issues are completely separate from the question of how our tax system should be designed. The real reason for raising these issues is that, in the public debate, some participants tend to attribute everything that happens in the economy to the incentive or "supply-side" effects of taxes—their impact on work effort, innovation, risk-taking, and so forth. For example, those who want to emphasize the incentive effects of the 1981 tax cut will give them credit for all of the rapid economic growth that occurred for a few years after 1982. But, as explained above, much of this growth was undoubtedly due to the fact that we were recovering from a deep recession, and any number of factors could have been responsible for that recovery. For these reasons, when considering evidence regarding taxation's impact on the long-run prosperity of the nation, it is very important to separate that issue from the short-term fluctuations in economic activity due to business cycles.

The Budget Deficit

The budget deficit is a second important issue that, in principle, is separate from the question of how our tax system should be designed. Any tax system could eliminate the budget deficit if its rates are set at the right levels. Moreover, people on all sides of the tax reform issue tend to agree, at least publicly, that the kinds of deficits we have been running persistently since 1981 are a problem.

The deficit does, though, get mixed into the tax reform debate when advocates of radical reform plans argue that tax rates can safely be set much lower than what is conventionally considered "revenue-neutral," because the ensuing economic growth will supposedly increase revenues so much that the increased deficit will eventually go away. This is one more reason why understanding the evidence on the economic impact of taxation is important. But it also means that we need to understand the case against deficits, so we know what is at risk if the extreme optimists are wrong (as we and most other economists believe they are).

The foremost argument is that deficits eat up our national saving, preventing it from going into private investment. When the government runs a budget deficit, it borrows from the public by selling bonds. This causes people to put their savings into government bonds instead of, say, corporate bonds or stocks that would be used to finance productive investments in the private sector. To the extent that budget deficits reduce business investment in machinery, technology, factories, and the like, they reduce the productivity and long-run growth potential of our economy.

A second problem is that running a deficit doesn't reduce the cost of government expenditure; it merely puts off the reckoning of who pays the cost. The massive deficits of recent years mean that one of the biggest government expenditures is interest on the federal debt—it now accounts for about 15 percent of the federal budget.[5] This expense is unavoidable; if we were to stop paying it, it would precipitate financial catastrophe. Our government would lose credibility and would have great difficulty ever borrowing again. Paying this interest requires higher taxes or lower spending on other things, and the more our debt grows, the higher these interest payments become. Repaying the debt itself would require even higher taxes or deeper spending cuts, although this could be avoided by rolling over the debt, which is sustainable as long as the debt doesn't grow too large relative to the size of our economy.

Some economists argue that deficits need not reduce national saving dollar for dollar. First, taxpayers may correctly perceive that deficits imply higher taxes or lower incomes for themselves or their children in the future, and correspondingly increase their own saving and, perhaps, bequests to make up for it. Second, deficits tend to raise interest rates, which could induce people to save a bit more, offsetting some of the government dissaving.[6] But neither of these factors appears to be significant in the United States today; as this chapter will later show, private saving rates have actually gone *down* considerably since the United States started running large budget deficits in the early 1980s. Finally, the nation's level of investment might not be hurt too much by budget deficits if foreigners are attracted by the high rates of return, and direct some of their saving into U.S. investments. This has occurred to some extent in the United States since the 1980s. However, it is of only limited help to us, because foreigners will also end up reaping most of the rewards of that extra investment.

For these reasons, in one way or another, budget deficits are likely to make us and our descendants somewhat worse-off than we could be in the long run.[7] Many analyses of the economic impact of taxation conveniently ignore this fact of life. They predict that a general reduction in taxes will have a beneficial impact on economic activity, because it unleashes demand and reduces the disincentives that taxes create. This may be true to a degree, but it ignores the very real negative consequences that a deficit can have.

How Much Should Government Do?

Another issue that can easily be confounded with tax reform is the question of how big the government should be. Many of the proponents of radical tax reform plans are also strong advocates of sharply reduced federal government spending. But people who disagree on the proper role for government needn't necessarily disagree on what's the best way to finance whatever level of government services we choose.

This is not a book about how big the government should be. There are many arguments regarding why government should or should not undertake certain tasks. Each government function needs to be evaluated on its merits, and this is not the place to do that. For example, whether an additional aircraft carrier should be purchased is in the end a question of whether the benefits it provides by increasing national security exceed its cost; as in many cases, the benefits are difficult to quantify, and the ultimate resolution must come through the political system.

With that said, there are some important connections between the economic impact of taxation and the appropriate size of government. Most importantly, how big the government should be depends in part on how costly to the economy it is to raise taxes. The cost of raising one dollar in taxes is more than one dollar—it also involves some cost in lost economic activity, as well as some cost of collection (a point addressed in the next chapter). So when the government decides to spend a dollar on something, it had better produce benefits worth more than a dollar. If you believe the economic and collection costs of taxes are very large, you may be less willing to accept a high level of government spending.

Second, the distinction between "taxes" and "spending" is sometimes not as clear-cut as it seems. Much of the federal government is a check-writing operation. In particular, many of these checks are written to pay for retirement benefits and health care for the elderly—this now accounts for around one-third of the federal budget.[8] Whether these payments are called "spending," "transfers," "negative taxes," or "entitlements earned through taxes paid earlier in life" is somewhat arbitrary. The justifications for such payments are often no different than those offered in Chapter 3 for tax progressivity—much of it derives from a desire for a "fair" distribution of economic well-being in our country.

For this reason, the debate over tax increases versus spending cuts often boils down to the trade-off between fairness and efficiency. A cutback in Medicare benefits makes elderly Americans worse-off in the same way that a tax increase on upper-income Americans makes that group worse off—so it is a question of whose ox will be gored. Since the beneficiaries of government spending tend to be less well-off than the people who pay the bulk of taxes, the spending cuts on average come at the expense of that segment of society. On the other hand, increasing taxes rather than cutting spending exacerbates the penalty on achieving affluence, blunting the incentive to get ahead.

Even this distinction is not always so clear-cut. Certain ways of limiting government spending can have exactly the same kind of negative economic consequences as high marginal income tax rates. For example, suppose we were to cut spending by "phasing out" 50 cents of Medicare benefits for every dollar of income or saving that an elderly person has. For those people, the result would be similar to a 50 percent marginal tax rate on the rewards to working and saving, and would be a big disincentive to either. There are many examples of this in our current government spending programs; for example, "phase-outs" of welfare and Medicaid benefits, when combined with other tax rates, can produce marginal tax rates near 100 percent for some low-income people.

Finally, some people believe that there is an important connection between spending and taxes because certain approaches to taxation lead to higher levels of government spending than others. In particular, they argue that taxes should be as "visible" as possible, so that people will know exactly how much they are paying for government. Otherwise, they contend, there will be a natural tendency for government to expand beyond what the citizens would prefer if they were better informed. In this sense, visibility might help reduce the economic costs of government. This was a major theme of the Kemp commission report mentioned at the beginning of this chapter. The argument may have some merit, although it depends on the empirical question of whether citizens are actually more likely to get the government they want when taxes are more visible—an unsettled proposition. Some take the argument one step further, arguing that the taxpaying process should be made particularly painful, precisely in order to restrain growth in government. We see little justification for this view, and this book adopts a diametrically opposed perspective. This books seeks to find ways to streamline the tax system, and to make it as efficient and unintrusive as possible. If there are institutional flaws that bias the political system toward overspending, these flaws should be addressed, but not by shackling American taxpayers with a costly and obtrusive tax system.

While it is clear that connections exist between taxation and spending, this book is about how the tax system ought to be designed, given whatever level of government spending is chosen. The economic consequences of tax design will be the main focus of this chapter. The limited scope is chosen not because we believe that the level and composition of government expenditures are exactly right, but because otherwise it is too difficult to reasonably compare the impact of two different tax policies.

How Taxes Affect Long-Run Economic Prosperity: A First Cut at the Evidence

Now that we've put to one side such issues as business cycle management, the deficit, and the appropriate level of government spending, what's left to talk about? The impact of taxes on long-run economic prosperity. In particular, to what extent does our income tax system have a negative impact on our long-run level of economic well-being, and could a better-designed tax system avoid some of these costs? Before getting into the details, we'll take a look at the big picture—the relationship between the level of taxation and economic performance from a historical and international perspective.

Economic Growth, Tax Levels, and Tax Rates in U.S. History

Table 4.1 depicts the historical record on U.S. economic growth since 1950. The first column of data shows real (inflation-adjusted) growth rates for gross domestic product (GDP), a measure of the total output of our economy, and a standard indicator of economic performance. The second column shows growth in GDP per capita, which is a better measure of long-run growth in the well-being of individual Americans, because it adjusts for changes in population growth. However, GDP per capita has the drawback that part of the measured growth in this figure is due to rising labor-force participation rates, particularly among women. As such, it overstates the degree to which Americans have become better off, because some of the growth has come at the expense of other valuable activities, such as leisure, which are not cap-

Table 4.1
U.S. economic growth since 1950

Years	Average Annual Rate of Real Growth (Percent)		
	GDP	GDP per capita	Productivity
1950–73	3.9	2.4	3.1
1973–95	2.5	1.5	1.3
1950–60	3.3	1.6	2.8
1960–70	4.1	2.8	3.3
1970–80	3.1	2.1	1.9
1980–90	2.9	1.9	1.4
1990–95	1.9	0.9	1.2

Note: Productivity measured here as GDP produced in the private business sector, per hour worked in that sector. Figures for 1995 are for the third quarter. Adjusted for inflation using chained price index. Data after 1959 reflect the comprehensive 1996 revisions of the National Income and Product Accounts.
Source: *Economic Report of the President* (1995 and 1996).

tured in GDP. The third column of data depicts growth in "productivity," which is measured here as GDP produced in the private business sector, divided by the total number of hours worked in that sector. This is an even better indicator of changes in living standards, because it is closely connected to growth in hourly wages and compensation. None of these measures, though, account for changes in aspects of well-being unrelated to output, wages, or consumption, such as the quality of the environment; nevertheless, these are the most reliable measures of well-being that are available.

No matter which way you slice it, our economy grew at a much faster rate in the 1950s and 1960s than it has since. In particular, productivity grew at an annual rate of 3.1 percent between 1950 and 1973, but at only 1.3 percent per year from 1973 to 1995. When this diminished growth is combined with the increasing income inequality discussed in Chapter 3, it turns out that the economic well-being of many low- and middle-income people appears to have stagnated for the past two decades. The growth slowdown since 1973 is a phenomenon that has gained a great deal of attention, and it is often blamed for the anger and frustration apparently now felt by much of the voting public.

Another important fact to notice in Table 4.1 is that, despite claims by Republicans that the 1980s represented an "economic miracle," and assertions by Democrats that it was a disaster, neither is really the case. The growth rate of the 1980s as a whole was slightly lower than that of the 1970s, and both were much lower than the "golden era" of the fifties and sixties. So far in the 1990s growth has been even a bit slower, although it is too early for a final assessment of this decade.

Claims that the 1980s were a period of great prosperity depend on picking starting and ending dates so that growth rates are measured from the bottom of a deep recession to the next peak of the business cycle, say from 1982 to 1989. As discussed above, this kind of exercise reveals little about long-term growth trends, because much of that growth merely reflects the natural recovery from a deep recession. Using decades as the dividing point is not perfect either, but it is better because over this period the ends of decades correspond to roughly similar points on the business cycle.

Finally, it is worth noting that doubling the long-run rate of GDP growth from 2.5 percent to 5 percent, as some would-be tax reformers have promised, would put that rate well above even our best historical periods of long-term growth. Such a marked departure from historical experience is unlikely, to say the least.

Critics of high tax rates often give the impression that our taxes were much lower during the "golden age" of economic growth in the fifties and sixties and that many of our current economic problems, including the slowdown of productivity growth since 1973, are caused by the strangling influence of big government and high taxes. By implication, all we need to do to return to the halcyon days of yesteryear is to lift this burden.

One problem with this argument is that, as Chapter 2 details, overall federal taxes were not that different in the fifties and sixties than they are today. In the 1950s, for example, federal taxes averaged 18.4 percent of GDP, compared to 20.5 percent in 1994. The composition of federal taxes has, though, changed greatly since then. For example, Social Security taxes were only 12 percent of federal revenues in 1950, compared to 40 percent today, while corporate income taxes declined from 34 percent of revenues to 12 percent over the same span. Looking only at personal income and Social Security taxes would give the impression of a substantial increase in taxes, but that is misleading because the higher corporate tax payments of the 1950s were inevitably passed on to individuals either in the form of lower wages, lower returns to investment, or higher consumer prices.

Another important change since the 1950s is that personal exemptions and standard deductions were much larger relative to incomes then than they are today. This means that low- and middle-income families probably faced a smaller burden in the old days.[9] So the big difference between federal taxes of the "golden era" and those of today is *not* that they have become much larger; rather, it is that they used to be much more hidden, and that they were probably a bit more progressive and generous to larger families.

It is also true that total taxes, including those of state and local governments, have risen somewhat. They averaged 24.7 percent of GDP in the 1950s and 27.8 percent in the 1960s, compared to 31.5 percent today. But few economists believe that this increase is responsible for much of the slowdown in growth; the culprit is almost certainly not federal income taxes.

So much for the overall level of taxes. But it may be that what is detrimental to a vibrant economy is a particular aspect of the tax system. Some argue that steep marginal tax rates on high-income people are particularly destructive, as they discourage the most highly talented and innovative members of society from pursuing the activities they do best. The emphasis on taxation of high-income households has been dubbed by its detractors as "trickle-down economics," which will be discussed in more detail later. For now, take a look at Figure 4.1, which shows, for certain periods, the top tax rate on individuals and the rate of productivity growth. Rather than telling a trickle-down story, the graph suggests exactly the opposite. The great growth periods were exactly the periods when the top tax rates were the highest.

Don't get us wrong. Our point is certainly not that high marginal tax rates on the rich *cause* faster economic growth. On the contrary, almost all economists would agree that marginal rates in the vicinity of 90 percent are too high to do much good for anyone. Rather, our point is that no simple relationship or single graph can establish how the tax system affects economic prosperity or growth. There are many dimensions to the tax system—rates on individuals, the corporation income tax rate, the tax rate on capital gains, the definition of the tax base, and so on—and all matter. Furthermore, there are many factors unrelated to taxation that probably have a much more profound influence on the economy. There is a raging debate among economists about why

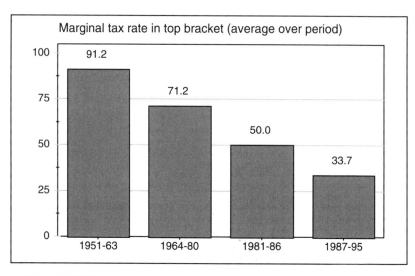

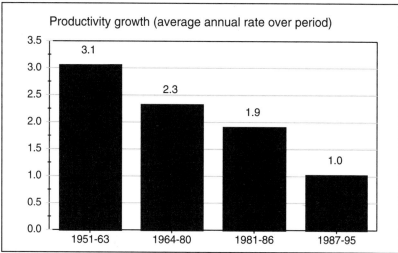

Figure 4.1
Top marginal tax rates and productivity growth in the United States for the period
1951–1995
Source: Top personal income tax rate from U.S. Bureau of the Census *Historical Statistics
of the U.S.* (1975, p. 1095) and IRS *Statistics of Income: Individual Income Tax Returns* (various
years). Productivity is real GDP produced in the private business sector per hour
worked in that sector, from *Economic Report of the President* (1995 and 1996).

growth (not only in the United States, but throughout the world) slowed down after 1973. For example, the unusually fast growth of the fifties and sixties may have resulted from the adoption of many startling technological advances that had been developed over previous decades, but that had not yet been fully utilized to the benefit of consumers because of the Great Depression and World War II. It is impossible to identify precisely what role a slightly increasing overall tax burden and changing features of the tax system have played in the slowdown since then. A more promising approach is to look at the evidence across countries. Have low-tax countries flourished, while high-tax countries have floundered?

International Evidence on Economic Prosperity and the Level of Taxes

Figure 4.2 plots for 24 industrialized OECD countries the relationship between GDP per capita and the ratio of total tax to income. If high taxes destroy prosperity, one would expect that the points on Figure 4.2 would cluster along a line with a northwest-southeast axis, meaning that countries with higher-than-average tax ratios tend to have lower-than-average levels of GDP per capita. But no such pattern emerges from Figure 4.2. Yes, some of the world's most prosperous countries have relatively low tax ratios, such as the United States, Canada, Switzerland, and Japan. But other countries, particularly in Scandinavia, have done quite well, thank you, with far higher tax ratios. That Denmark could maintain a 1993 GDP per capita of $19,300, eight percent above the OECD average, in the face of a whopping 49.9 percent tax-to-income ratio, is a fact that challenges the hypothesis that high taxes are a sure cause of economic decline.

Our disclaimer about Figure 4.1 also applies to Figure 4.2: no simple diagram could possibly settle such a complicated issue as this one. It could still be true that the Scandinavian nations would be even better off than they are now if only they lowered their tax burdens. It could be that all Figure 4.2 is telling us is that history, nature, culture, and demography have enabled some countries to be more prosperous than others, and those countries so favored have chosen to spend relatively more of their bounty on the services provided by government, and to tax themselves more to provide these services. Alternatively, it could be that because richer countries also tend to have a higher literacy rate and to be more urbanized, they are more apt to take advantage of more

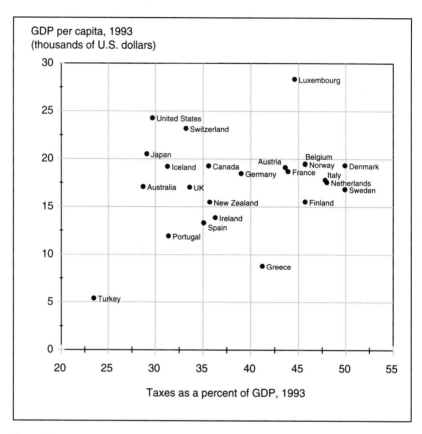

Figure 4.2
Economic prosperity and the level of taxes in OECD countries, 1993
Source: OECD (1995a and 1995b). GDP per capita is converted to 1993 U.S. dollars using
OECD estimates of purchasing-power parity.

efficient ways to raise revenue, such as income taxes. In either of these
cases, comparing the relative levels of prosperity to total tax burdens
would not easily reveal any negative impact of taxation.

A better test would be to see whether there is any relationship between tax ratios and the *growth rate* of economies. Analyzing the rate
of growth frees us from having to explain what caused any country to
have its beginning level of income, and focus on what has caused it to
better itself. Figure 4.3 does just this. For the period 1970 to 1990, it
plots the average tax ratio of the 24 industrialized countries against
their real growth rate.

Yes, there are low-tax countries like Japan that did exceptionally well
over this period, and high-tax countries like Sweden that did relatively

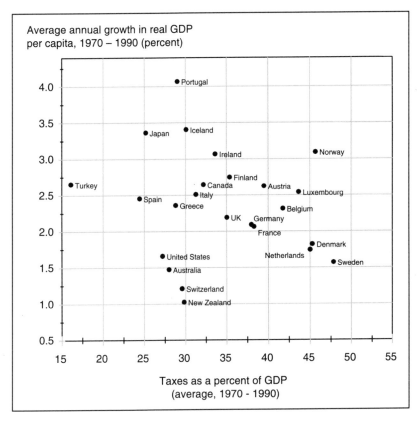

Figure 4.3
Economic growth rates and tax levels in OECD countries for the period 1970–1990
Source: Slemrod (1996), based on data from the *Penn World Tables* (Summers and Heston
1991) and the International Monetary Fund (1995).

poorly. But there are also high-tax countries that did well, and low-tax
countries (like the United States) that performed below average. Again,
no clear relationship emerges. More sophisticated statistical analyses
of the relationship between the level of taxation and economic performance, which attempt to hold constant the impact of other determinants of growth in order to isolate the tax effect, are also generally
inconclusive.[10]

Our point is not that taxes do not affect the economy. On the contrary, in certain situations taxes can have a telling impact. However,
the effect of taxes on economic performance is subtle, and cannot be
established by any one simple graph, not the figures presented here,

or other ones that purport to demonstrate the damaging effects of high taxes. Understanding how taxes affect the economy and which kinds of taxes are worse than others requires looking behind data on overall economic performance, at the kinds of choices taxes affect, and the evidence regarding how exactly taxes influence these choices.

How Taxes Affect Economic Prosperity—The Specifics

It goes without saying that having to pay taxes means having to change your behavior. For every dollar paid to the government, taxpayers have one less dollar to spend or save. Belts must be tightened. This is true just as much for a poll tax (also called a lump-sum tax) as it is for an income tax or a sales tax. But a lump-sum tax is different in one important way from all other taxes—there is nothing you can do to change your tax liability. That characteristic sounds ominous for the family whose income barely exceeds, or even falls short of, the lump-sum tax amount—nothing can be done to reduce this burden. But reversing the emphasis reveals the unique characteristic of the lump-sum tax—nothing you do increases your tax bill. In particular, nothing you do to better your lot increases your taxes—not getting a second job, not buying a new house or car, not even winning the lottery. Under a lump-sum tax, any decision you can think of can be made without a moment's consideration to the tax consequences.

This is quite a contrast to the current situation, where taxes change the terms of just about any decision one faces. A spouse contemplating returning to work must consider that taxes (federal and state income, plus payroll) will possibly take 50 percent of any earnings, while many expenses incurred will not be deductible. A wealthy alumna contemplating a gift of $1,000,000 in stock to her alma mater will undoubtedly be influenced by the fact that, compared to selling the stock, donating it could save her more than $600,000 in taxes. The CEO of Johnson & Johnson may be tempted to open another research lab by the knowledge that 20 percent of the cost may be creditable against tax liability through the research and experimentation tax credit.

The belt tightening that accompanies taxation is an inevitable cost of taxation, but raising taxes does more than force people to tighten their belts. It also changes the cost and reward of most economic decisions, and distorts these choices away from what would otherwise be chosen. What is the cost to the economy when the tax system changes the terms of economic choices?

Economists agree that, in most situations, the baseline for measuring these costs is how the economy would operate in the absence of any taxes other than lump-sum taxes.[11] They believe that firms and individuals, aided by the signals given by market prices, are generally the best judges of what goods and services should be produced, and how resources should be allocated. In the interest of maximizing profits, firms will seek out those investments and opportunities that offer the highest reward, and pursue those opportunities using the most efficient techniques. For their part, individuals will spend, or save, their income the best they can to maximize their well-being according to their own preferences. The result, as Adam Smith observed more than 200 years ago, is that an unfettered free-market economy, whatever its other faults, tends to organize itself (as with an "invisible hand," in Smith's words) so as to make efficient use of the country's physical and human resources. Taxes interfere with that natural efficiency, causing economic choices to be distorted away from taxed activities to relatively untaxed ones, keeping us from making the best use of our resources.

There are exceptions to this presumption when, for reasons such as the difficulty of obtaining necessary information, the presence of activities with spillover effects, or monopoly, markets do not function efficiently on their own—when the invisible hand fails. In such cases we must be careful in assuming that taxes necessarily detract from efficiency; they may, in fact, be corrective. The problem of market failure will figure prominently in our later discussion of a number of tax policy issues that we will address later.

For now, we leave these cases of market failure aside and, in what follows, examine several specific areas of economic behavior where taxes have a distorting effect. Most reform plans aim to alter the distorted incentives created by taxes in these areas, so understanding these issues is crucial for evaluating the potential benefits of reform.

Labor Supply: How Hard People Work

Labor income, in the form of wages, salaries, and benefits, constitutes nearly three-quarters of national income.[12] Therefore, any story about how taxes affect the economy must come to terms with how they affect the incentive to work. If the tax system makes working hard, or working at all, unattractive, then it cannot be contributing to a vibrant economy. A major goal of many tax reformers is to change the tax system so that hard work is rewarded more generously. Before looking at the evidence on this issue, it is important to examine exactly how taxes influence decisions about work.

The initial thing to note is that taxes have two countervailing influences on the decision to work. First of all, taxes reduce the reward for working. Work becomes less attractive because you are able to buy fewer consumption goods and services per hour of your work. The other side of the same coin is that leisure and other nonmarket activities become more attractive, because they are untaxed. So as a result, you are likely to substitute more leisure and nonmarket endeavors for less work and less consumption of goods and services. This impact of taxes is called the *substitution effect,* or sometimes the *incentive effect,* by economists.

The second thing taxes do, however, is make you poorer. As a result, you need to work harder to achieve a given level of consumption. This is known as the *income effect.* Because of the countervailing effects of the substitution and income effects, it is in theory ambiguous whether taxes make people work more or less than they otherwise would.

Note that your decision whether to work a few extra hours or to choose a harder job that pays a little better is affected only by your marginal tax rate, that is, the tax rate on your next few dollars of income. However, what is relevant for the "income effect" is your total tax burden; expressed as a fraction of income, it is your average tax rate that matters.

The relationship between total taxes collected and marginal tax rates is a crucial characteristic of any tax system, and is inextricably linked to how progressive the tax burden is. A lump-sum tax system could, in principle, raise $730 billion per year while imposing a zero tax at the margin for everyone's work decisions. Under a purely proportional tax system, in which tax liability is the same fraction of income for everyone, the marginal tax rate equals the average tax rate. The more progressive the distribution of the tax burden, the higher will be the overall marginal disincentive to work.

Note also that the correct marginal tax rate for measuring the disincentive effect is not necessarily the statutory marginal tax rate. For example, a 20 percent statutory marginal rate levied on labor income excluding fringe benefits is not, in terms of its incentive effect on labor supply, materially different from a 16 percent statutory marginal tax rate levied on labor income including fringe benefits, if fringe benefits constitute about one-fifth of total labor compensation for everyone. What is important is how much real purchasing power an additional hour of work entitles you to. This is an important point to keep in mind when we later discuss the economic effects of broadening the tax base and using the revenue so collected to lower marginal tax rates. That change, in and of itself, does not provide a significantly increased incentive to work.[13]

An example can help illustrate the economic cost of the incentive effect. Consider the case of Roger Brown, who works 40 hours a week on construction sites. Roger is also a talented carpenter, and can earn $20 an hour working at nights and on weekends; he can find ten hours a week of such work. Roger has plenty of hobbies and enjoys spending time with his family, so it goes without saying that he won't work for nothing. In fact, he won't work those extra ten hours unless he can earn at least $15 an hour; in economics jargon, that is the "opportunity cost" of his time, or what his leisure time is worth to him.

In the absence of any taxes, it is clear what Roger decides to do— he moonlights. The $200 he earns for the ten hours of extra work exceeds the $150 he requires to compensate him for the reduced leisure time. Everyone is better off from this decision. Roger's customers are better off, or else they wouldn't have been willing to pay him the $200. Roger is better off. We can even put a dollar measure on how much everyone is better off—$50. This represents the difference between $200, which is the value put on Roger's carpentry by his customers, and $150, which is Roger's own evaluation of the next best use of his time.

Alas, there is taxation, and on an extra $200 per week of income Roger's tax bill turns out to be $60, or 30 percent. He is a dutiful citizen, so does not consider simply not reporting his outside income to the IRS. Given his 30 percent rate of tax, he concludes that his after-tax compensation for carpentry, $14 per hour ($20 minus 30 percent of $20), is not enough to convince him to give up his leisure time. This is an example of the disincentive to work caused by the tax system; it has changed the reward to working, and in this case changed the decision of how much to work.

What is the economic cost of the altered decision? You might jump to an answer of $200, Roger's foregone wages. But that is not correct, because although Roger has decided to forego the $200 in income, by so doing he has ten more hours per week to pursue his other interests, ten more hours he values at $150. The loss to Roger, and to the economy, is the difference between $200 and $150, or $50. Because of the tax system, a transaction that should have been made was not; from a national point of view, we end up having "too much" leisure, and "not enough" work.[14]

Just how high the cost is, per dollar of revenue raised, depends on how responsive labor supply is to changes in the after-tax return to working.[15] If it is not responsive,[16] then the fact that taxes lower the return to working does not translate into significant economic costs because people are not dissuaded from working. The more responsive the decision is, the larger are the economic costs of taxing labor income.

What does the evidence show? The responsiveness of labor supply, both in terms of hours worked and the labor-force participation rate, has been studied extensively, and is a rare example of a question on which there is a broad consensus among economists. Nearly all research concludes that male participation and hours worked respond hardly at all to changes in after-tax wages, and therefore to marginal tax rates. There is evidence that female labor-force participation, and male retirement decisions, are somewhat responsive, but those responses do not contribute enough to total labor supply to alter the conclusion that, overall, labor supply is not greatly affected by taxes.[17]

Table 4.2 illustrates how difficult it is to make a clear link between taxes and labor supply. It shows, by income quintile, how marginal tax rates and total labor supply changed over the 1980s, the latter based on the results of a study by economists Barry Bosworth and Gary Burtless of the Brookings Institution. They estimated the percentage change in hours of work between 1981 and 1989 relative to what would have been predicted by the trend since 1967, and controlled for unemployment rates in an effort to eliminate the effects of the business cycle.

During the 1980s, the marginal tax rate fell sharply for the highest quintile, increased some for the lowest quintile, and stayed roughly the same for everyone else. For men, the change in total hours worked doesn't match up to the tax changes in any obvious way. If the incentive effect was strong, we would have expected the biggest increase in hours to have occurred in the top quintile, but this was not the case. By far the largest increases in hours worked occurred in the lowest quintile, the group whose tax rates increased rather than decreased. Some of this may reflect failure to fully eliminate the impact of the business cycle, which affects poor workers the most; but even the middle-income groups had changes in hours not much different from the top. The pattern of labor supply increase for women in the top four

Table 4.2
Changes in marginal tax rates and hours worked during the 1980s

Income quintile	Marginal Tax Rate on Labor Income[a]		Estimated Percent Change in Hours Worked, 1981–1989[b]	
	1980	1989	Men, aged 25–64	Women, aged 25–64
All quintiles	35.0	34.6	6.0	5.4
Bottom	14.7	19.3	31.0	16.7
Second	26.2	28.0	3.6	−6.9
Middle	28.7	27.3	4.1	6.4
Fourth	32.1	31.1	2.5	10.5
Highest	41.2	33.8	3.2	11.8

[a]Includes personal income tax and Social Security payroll tax.
Source: Kasten, Sammartino, and Toder (1994, Table 9).
[b]Percent change in hours worked between 1981 and 1989, relative to what would have been predicted by the trend since 1967, holding unemployment constant.
Source: Bosworth and Burtless (1992, Table 3).

quintiles does match up slightly better with the tax changes, which is consistent with the other evidence suggesting that on average their labor supply is more responsive to the after-tax return to working.

Other recent studies back up these results. Nada Eissa of the University of California at Berkeley examined changes in hours worked by men with education beyond college, who typically have high incomes. Compared to the recent historical trend, she estimates that these men increased their hours of work by only 2 percent in response to reduced marginal tax rates after 1986. In an earlier study, she found that wives of very high-income husbands increased their hours of work significantly after 1986. But she also notes that the average earnings of married, employed women in the richest tenth of the income distribution was only $11,600 in 1985, so their labor supply decisions cannot have had a major impact on overall national income.[18] Randall Mariger of the Federal Reserve examined data that followed the same group of men between 1985 and 1988, and found no evidence of a strong labor supply response to lower marginal tax rates.[19]

There are many possible explanations for the pattern of labor supply changes depicted in Table 4.2. Tax rates were not the only thing changing during this period. Another important factor, pretax wage rates, were declining for the lower quintiles, and sharply increasing for the top quintile.[20] If incentive effects were strong, this factor would lead us to expect an even bigger increase in hours worked at the top, and this did not occur. A more important factor is that stagnating wages for husbands appear to have pushed many wives from less-than-affluent families into the labor force. But this is the result of lower income, not the result of the attractiveness of higher after-tax wages. The difference is well illustrated by the woman who was part of a focus group pretesting the response to President Clinton's 1996 State of the Union Address, in which he boasted of the seven million jobs created during the three years of his administration. "I know, I have three of them!" was her sarcastic reply.[21]

Before the potential impact of taxes on labor supply is dismissed, a couple of caveats must be mentioned. The first is that economists can measure fairly accurately hours worked, but that is only one part of a broader definition of labor supply that includes work effort, occupational choice, and the acquisition of education and job-specific skills. Taxes may also affect these dimensions of labor supply; unfortunately, we have little understanding of the magnitude involved. Second, it may be that behavioral patterns regarding work are set early on, are hard to break once set, and therefore the effect of taxes on labor supply is felt only gradually as new, impressionable generations reach working age. Assar Lindbeck of the Institute of International Economic Studies in Stockholm has argued that this explanation cannot be dismissed with regard to high-tax Sweden, which has experienced a gradual decline in hours worked over the past two decades.[22] These caveats add uncertainty to the claim that labor supply effects are negligible, but certainly do not provide any decisive evidence against that conclusion.

Robert Triest of the Federal Reserve Bank of Boston has examined the policy implications of these low labor supply responsiveness estimates.[23] He estimates that financing an expansion of the earned income tax credit by increasing the 15 percent and 28 percent tax rates by one point would have an efficiency cost of 16 cents on the dollar; that is, labor supply distortions imply that to deliver a $1 increase in the credit requires that the taxpayers be made worse-off by $1.16. Notably, the cost increases to 52 cents on the dollar when the increased credit is financed by increases in the 28 percent and 35 percent rates. Triest cautions, however, that this latter result arises in part because his model assumes that the responsiveness of labor supply to taxes is higher for people with higher incomes. These figures provide one reasonable quantification of the equity-efficiency trade-off. Based on these estimates, if in your judgment the increased progressivity (more equal "slicing of the pie") is worth 16 cents on the dollar of efficiency cost ("a smaller pie"), then it is appropriate policy.

Saving and Investment

There is a second very important economic choice affected by taxes—
the choice people make about how much of their income to consume
in a given year, versus how much to save up in order to have more to
spend in future years or to bequeath. Income taxes affect the terms of
this choice because, by taxing interest and other returns to capital, they
reduce the rate of return that can be earned on savings. Many would-
be tax reformers support a switch to a consumption tax, which would
effectively eliminate the negative influence of taxes on the incentive to
save. Chapter 6 will explain how consumption taxes accomplish this;
for now, the focus will be on how our current system affects the incentive to save, and how saving behavior is influenced by such incentives.

It's easy to see that a tax of 20 percent on your interest income reduces the reward to saving that income. If the interest rate is 10 percent, you only get an 8 percent return. Another feature of our tax
system can exacerbate this distortion—it fails to adjust the measurement of capital income for inflation. Suppose that in the example
above, inflation was 5 percent. In that case, half of the 10 percent interest you earn is just making up for the decline in the real purchasing
power of your savings. So in this case, the 20 percent tax rate on nominal interest rate turns out to be a 40 percent tax on *real* interest.

Yet another way that our tax system can reduce the reward to saving
is by taxing the returns to investment. Ignoring for a moment international capital flows, savings and investment are two sides of the same
coin. The savings of individuals, often funneled through a financial
intermediary such as a bank, a savings and loan, or an insurance company, eventually are used by businesses to finance real investment in
plants, equipment, inventories, and know-how. Through this process,
individual savings add to the productive capacity of the country and
increase the productivity of the workforce.

Although the connection is not always apparent to the saver, the
return to saving is governed by the return to the productive investment
that the saving finances. If the return to investment is taxed at the
business level, then the amount that can be paid out to those who
financed it, by lending money or buying shares, must fall. As explained in Chapter 2, certain forms of corporate income, such as dividends and some capital gains, are "double-taxed," once under the
corporate tax, and again at the personal level. The extent of this taxation depends not only on the rate of tax applied to net business income,
but also on the depreciation schedules, the generosity of investment

tax credits, and so on. Chapter 6 will explain in more detail how a corporate income tax imposes a burden on the returns to investment. The important point here is that taxation at the business level can reduce the incentive to save even further, by reducing the rate of return that is available to a saver even before personal taxes are levied.

Many of the radical reform options being considered today would, by eliminating all tax on the return to savings and investment, increase the incentive to save, particularly for high-income people who contribute a large portion of our national savings. What effect would such a change have on saving decisions? Just as with labor supply, there are countervailing forces at work. On the one hand, a greater after-tax reward makes you want to save more (via the substitution, or incentive, effect); it makes consuming tomorrow less expensive relative to consuming today, so you may want to plan on some extra future consumption in exchange for less today.

But a higher reward to saving also means you need to save *less* to achieve a given level of future consumption. For example, if you have a fixed goal for your level of retirement income, or a fixed amount you need to save up to pay for your child's college education, a higher reward to saving makes it easier to achieve that goal. So the theoretical direction of the response to taxes is once again ambiguous.[24]

In any event, the encouragement of current spending and discouragement of future spending represents a distortion to consumer decisions, and is certainly a cost of the income tax. Many economists argue that there is a further cost to reduced saving, because individuals are myopic and, on their own, won't adequately provide for their own futures; in that case, to the extent that eliminating the tax on saving encourages people to save more, that is a bigger plus.

The evidence on whether saving responds to its after-tax return does not readily reveal any clear relationship. Figure 4.4, which is derived from a study done by Jane Gravelle of the Congressional Research Service, plots the private saving rate and the real after-tax return to saving.[25] The private saving rate includes saving by individuals and also that done by corporations in the form of retained earnings, but does not include the effects of government "dissaving" through budget deficits. It is expressed as a percentage of disposable income, so it is somewhat larger than other saving rates that are sometimes cited.

If anything, Figure 4.4 suggests a *negative* relationship between saving and the rate of return; the saving rate fell when the incentive to save increased. In the period 1968 to 1980, the average return to saving

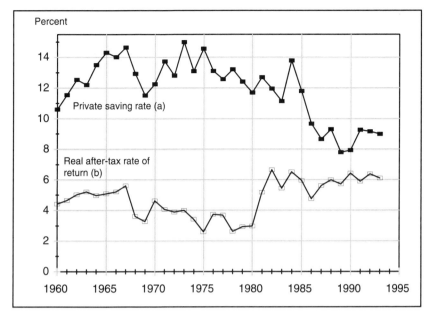

Figure 4.4
Savings rates and the reward for saving in the United States for the period 1960–1993
Note: (a) Net private saving as a percentage of disposable income (GNP less depreciation and taxes), *National Income and Product Accounts.*
(b) Interest rate on Baa corporate bonds, adjusted for expected inflation and the average
marginal tax rate on personal interest income, plus a fixed equity premium.
Source: Gravelle (1994), updated by authors. See endnotes for details.

was 3.5 percent, and the saving rate averaged 13 percent. From 1981 to
1993, the rate of return averaged 5.9 percent, but the saving rate averaged only 10 percent.

There are actually a number of different ways to define the "saving
rate" and the "rate of return," but Gravelle's definitions are quite reasonable ones. Estimating the tax rate on the return to saving is a particularly vexing problem; however, because over this period there was
more variation in the *pretax* return to saving than in the tax rates
on capital income, this is probably not a major difficulty. However
defined, saving rates and the rate of return generally follow similar
patterns.[26]

A more important caution is that over any time period, numerous
factors that influence saving are changing, making it impossible to
draw a clear lesson from a figure like this. There have, though, been
many careful studies that attempt to control, in a statistical sense, for

these other factors. With only one or two exceptions, these studies estimate that any response of the saving rate to the incentive effect of a
higher after-tax rate of return is likely to be fairly small.[27] Given the
patterns shown in Figure 4.4, it would be very difficult to establish
any other conclusion, at least when looking at the last few decades of
U.S. experience.

Neutrality

A third major goal of tax reform is to make our tax system more "neutral" or "uniform," so that it exerts less influence on our economic
choices. As discussed earlier, it is almost always more conducive to
economic prosperity when people make their decisions based on the
economic merits of the alternatives rather than on the tax consequences
of the choices. Reducing the influence of taxes on the incentives to work
and to save are just two important special cases of this principle.

The only tax system that is perfectly "neutral," however, is a lump-
sum tax, because *no* decision you make has any impact on your tax
bill. The kind of neutrality tax reformers have in mind is less ambitious,
but still very important—making sure that tax rates do not differ
across various types of consumption and investment. Our current tax
system is a far cry from this kind of neutrality. A myriad of deductions,
special preferences, compromises in the measurement of capital income, and idiosyncrasies mean that different types of consumption
and investment are taxed at widely different rates. Cleaning up the tax
base, so as to eliminate such distorting features, is a major goal of most
tax reform plans.

Before moving on to a discussion of exactly how our tax system
diverges from this particular brand of neutrality, a couple of qualifica-
tions are in order about its economic advantages. First of all, even a
system that taxes all consumption and investment at a single, uniform
rate will still have at least some distorting influence on economic
choices, because there is always the alternative of an untaxed good,
leisure, to substitute for your consumption or investment. What's more,
even in the absence of lump-sum taxes, uniformity across different
kinds of consumption and investment may not even be the approach
that exerts the least influence on economic decision making. Other
things being equal, it is desirable to place a heavier tax on those goods
for which demand is relatively price-insensitive. Taxing these goods
will change behavior less for any given amount of revenue compared

to taxing price-sensitive goods—it effectively makes the tax system more like a lump-sum tax. This idea has come to be known as the "optimal tax principle" in the economics literature.

While the optimal tax principle may be interesting in theory, it runs into practical problems that make it not particularly useful as a guide to policy. First, identifying which items are more or less responsive to taxation is extremely difficult. Even if economists could measure such things accurately, this approach would conflict with both equity and simplicity. Whenever some goods are taxed at higher rates than others, it penalizes those taxpayers whose tastes happen to favor those goods; this is horizontally inequitable. Moreover, the goods taxed most heavily would probably be necessities, so a disproportionate burden would be placed on the poor. It is also much more costly to operate a tax system that differentially treats goods. And finally, there is little hope that politicians would distinguish among goods based solely on the economic merits; particularly in the face of uncertainty about which goods have relatively price-insensitive demand, the pleadings of special interests would almost certainly carry the day. For these reasons, uniform taxation—either in the form of a broad-based income tax or consumption tax—is still a very good rule of thumb; it is likely to cause much less economic distortion than any other feasible approach, and it allows lower rates of tax because of the broader base it covers.

There is, however, one more qualification that deserves serious consideration. In some special cases, the free market does not lead to efficient outcomes. The most important of these is when an individual's act of consuming or producing a good has an impact on other people, but this fact is not reflected in the incentives faced by the individual. Economists refer to this as an "externality." A classic example of a *negative* externality is pollution; businesses that pollute impose a cost on their neighbors by reducing the quality of air they breathe or the water they drink. But these costs are not reflected in the incentives faced by the owners of these businesses, so too much pollution will be produced. In such a case, taxes can be used to alter incentives and correct the problem.

In our tax system, we tend to subsidize particular activities rather than penalize them. Of course, by requiring higher tax rates, these subsidies cause everything else to be penalized. But such subsidies may be justified if they encourage activities with *positive* externalities. A fairly clear-cut example is research and development, or R&D. Engaging in R&D can be very costly, and when it leads to a good idea, the benefits almost never accrue entirely to the researcher or his or her employer. Although the patent system is designed to ensure that inventors are amply rewarded for their ideas, it is inevitable that people other than the inventor will capitalize on and profit from the idea. What this means is that there are some R&D projects that are not worth doing from a private individual's or firm's perspective, but are worth doing from society's point of view. Our income tax system responds to this externality by granting preferential tax treatment to R&D expenses. Unlike other types of long-lived investment, these expenses can be deducted immediately. Moreover, certain R&D expenditures qualify for a 20 percent tax credit to the extent that they exceed the "normal" level of expenditures for that firm (this provision temporarily expired in 1995). It is hard to tell whether this degree of subsidy is exactly right in this case, but many economists would agree that at least some subsidy is justified.

The externality argument should be a high hurdle for justifying preferential treatment of particular goods or activities. Being "good for the economy" is far short of what is required. Nevertheless, there may be at least a few justifiable exceptions to the rule of neutrality. However, our tax system has departed from the principle of neutrality in a very large number of ways, often for no good economic reason. The Treasury Department has identified over one hundred specific deviations from a uniform, comprehensive income tax base, which in the aggregate cost hundreds of billions of dollars in revenue.[28] Here, we'll note some of the most important of these features, and discuss some of the economic consequences.

First, consider taxation of capital income, or the returns to investment. Different types of investments face vastly different tax treatment under our current system. Because of double taxation at the corporate and personal levels, investments in a traditional C corporation are often taxed more heavily than noncorporate business investments. Both are taxed more heavily than investments in owner-occupied houses, which receive the benefit of a mortgage interest deduction, but incur no tax liability on the services they provide to their occupants. Jane Gravelle has estimated that, in 1989, effective marginal tax rates averaged 43 percent on corporate investments, 22 percent on noncorporate investments, and just 4 percent on investments in owner-occupied housing. The result of such disparities is that much more money has flowed into housing and noncorporate investments than would have occurred otherwise, so that corporations are left with a smaller capital stock, leading to a less productive economy.

Among corporate investments, those that are financed by debt are taxed less heavily than those that are financed by equity (selling shares of stock), which has no good economic rationale. Capital gains are treated more favorably than dividends or interest, so assets whose return comes in the form of appreciation are favored over other types of assets. Depreciation schedules are only rough approximations of true economic depreciation, so they will inevitably cause some distortions. In our system, they cause various types of equipment or structures to be favored over others, and certain industries to receive more generous treatment while others are penalized. An egregious example of this is the depreciation treatment of structures used for extraction of minerals, oil, and gas; as a result, the effective marginal tax rate on these types of investment are estimated at 10 to 12 percent, compared to 43 percent for corporate investments in general.[29] The Tax Reform Act of 1986 reduced many of these kinds of distortions, but many still remain.

There's no better example of the kind of waste that can be caused by these distortions than the commercial real estate boom of the mid-1980s. During this period the tax advantages of real estate were so large that it made good business sense to put up a building even if the expected occupancy rate was very low. The result: a glut of unoccupied office space—nicknamed "see-through" buildings—that was profitable only because of the tax advantages. The tax benefits to real estate caused the invisible hand to fail—what was in the private interest of developers was not in the social interest. The result was a waste of resources, because the bricks, mortar, steel, and time that went into building these unoccupied offices could instead have produced goods and services that people value.

Many features of our tax code also provide special preferences for particular types of consumption spending; most of these arise from deductions, exclusions, and credits in the personal code. Some of the most important preferences are for housing, health care, and charitable contributions, all of which will be addressed in Chapter 6. A few of these exceptions may be justified, but there is broad agreement among economists that eliminating many of these features would have significant benefits. The potential economic gains from making the tax system more uniform are hard to quantify, but they may well be as important as the benefits that could be derived from greater incentives to work and save.

Risk-Taking and Entrepreneurship

Another argument frequently raised in the public debate over taxes is
that our current system is particularly harsh for those small, risky start-
up firms that embody the energies of entrepreneurs who, it is argued,
are an important engine of growth in the U.S. economy. Moreover, it
is claimed that our tax system is biased against risky investments in
general.

First of all, it should be noted that there is little economic rationale
for treating entrepreneurial or risky activities more favorably than
other kinds of activities. Indeed, it wouldn't even be feasible to single
out "entrepreneurial" income for favorable tax treatment, as there is
no meaningful way to define it precisely. But neither is there any good
rationale for penalizing such activities relative to others, and some argue that the current tax code does in fact penalize such activities in a
number of ways.

The most frequent complaint regards capital gains taxes. Risky ventures often receive their return in the form of large capital gains. However, there is also the possibility of a significant capital loss. The U.S.
tax code imposes tax on the gains, but only allows a portion of the
losses to be deducted from income in a given year (although the losses
can be carried over to future years). This tax treatment has a practical
rationale, because if unlimited deductibility of losses were to be allowed, it would open up opportunities for some very sophisticated
and troublesome avoidance schemes. The loss limitation also has the
cost, however, of discouraging risk-taking, because the government
taxes away some of the rewards if the investment is successful, but
doesn't provide symmetrical insurance against a loss.

Capital gains are also blamed for a "lock-in" effect; individuals are
supposedly deterred from selling stocks, because they pay tax only at
the time of sale. The fact that capital gains are taxed only upon realization, and are not taxed at all if held until death, creates such an incentive. Critics contend that investment funds are kept locked up in the
stocks of older, established firms, at the expense of newer entrepreneurial ventures that might offer a higher return. Evidence on whether
there is an important lock-in effect has been very difficult to discern.[30]
Even if there is a strong lock-in effect, moreover, it probably mainly
affects *who* owns particular stocks, rather than which companies receive investment funds.

While these arguments may have some merit, the conventional solution, a cut in capital gains tax rates, has many problems of its own. For

one thing, it is a very blunt instrument for addressing this problem, because innovative entrepreneurial ventures represent only a tiny fraction of the total value of capital gains.[31] There are many other important factors to consider in the taxation of capital gains; these will be addressed in the discussion of options for income tax reform contained in Chapter 8.

Another argument sometimes heard is that the double taxation of corporate equity is particularly harmful to entrepreneurs. Small start-up firms may have trouble obtaining loans because they have little collateral, so they must rely on equity investments, often coming out of their own pockets or those of friends and relatives. To the extent that this is true, corporate entrepreneurial ventures are penalized relative to other investments that have access to more lightly taxed debt.[32]

Finally, progressive income tax rates are also blamed for discouraging entrepreneurship and risk-taking. For one reason, the incentive to engage in such activities depends on a small possibility of a very large return, and progressive rates have their largest impact on just such returns. In addition, the returns to entrepreneurship largely represent the product of hard work, so this is to some extent an argument about how marginal tax rates affect labor supply. The difference is that the work effort of entrepreneurs and other small businesspeople may not be captured by the data on hours worked mentioned above, so there is still some possibility of a strong labor supply response in this sector.

Entrepreneurship is hard to measure and therefore poorly understood, so there is little evidence to contradict the claims that are made about the deleterious effects of the tax system in this area. Such claims should not necessarily be discounted, and the fact that tax reform might help improve incentives in this area, for example by eliminating double taxation, should be viewed as a plus. Yet there is also no hard evidence demonstrating that the potential economic benefits in this area are large. Some have suggested that a burgeoning of entrepreneurial efforts, in response to lower marginal tax rates, was partly responsible for the surge in the incomes of the affluent during the 1980s. This question will be addressed in more detail at the end of this chapter.

International Competitiveness

Another claim sometimes made about tax reform is that it would somehow improve America's "international competitiveness." We put quotation marks around that term because what it really means is unclear.

Are there circumstances under which we should sacrifice the usual standard of evaluating economic policies—expanding national income—to increase something called international competitiveness? We and nearly all other economists think not.

The United States is not in competition with other countries in the same sense that the Chicago Bulls are in competition with the Orlando Magic, in which one side wins and the other side loses. IBM rightly views Toshiba as a competitor in this sense, but the United States should not view Japan in this way. For at least two centuries there has been a broad consensus among economists that the opposite is true—that unfettered commercial relationships benefit all participating countries by allowing them to concentrate their resources on what they do best.[33]

For the most part these battles are fought over international trade and investment policies such as tariffs, local content rules, export subsidies, and preferential government procurement. However, the same issues arise in the international aspects of tax policy. How should we tax foreign investment done by U.S. companies? U.S. investment done by foreign companies? There are some important issues here, which largely have to do with questions of where multinationals locate their operations, as well as concerns about tax administration, avoidance, and evasion. However, arguments that certain approaches will magically give us some sort of sustainable edge in international competitiveness are almost invariably red herrings.

The most common red herring has to do with the value-added tax (VAT). Some American businesspeople and politicians look with envy at a particular feature of European VATs: the tax is levied on imports, while all tax that had been collected on goods for export is rebated to the exporters, rendering exports tax free. At first glance this might seem like an ingenious export promotion scheme, but in fact it is nothing of the sort. All it does is reproduce how a retail sales tax works. States that have sales taxes levy them on goods sold to their residents, regardless of where they were produced, and don't charge sales taxes on goods exported to foreigners. This treatment doesn't give our domestically produced goods any special edge. Suppose we were to implement a 20 percent VAT, and it was tacked on top of the price of everything we buy. Charging a 20 percent VAT on imports would simply mean they are treated equally to domestic goods, just as they are now. The same story holds true for our exports—we wouldn't charge foreigners any VAT on the goods they imported from us, but their home countries would, just as they do for any other goods sold to their residents.

More fundamentally, even if we could figure out some way to give a temporary edge to our domestically produced goods through the tax system, it would soon be dissipated by adjustments in exchange rates. Any apparent advantage to exports would be offset by a combination of strengthening of the U.S. dollar, which makes dollar-priced exports less attractive to foreigners, and of domestic price level increases, which make U.S. markets more attractive to both foreign exporters and U.S. manufacturers. The exchange rate strengthening and/or domestic price increases must eventually occur; if they did not right away, the trade surplus stimulated by the demand for U.S.-produced goods would drive up the value of the dollar, dissipating the temporary advantage obtained. There is simply no magic bullet that would allow us to boost our standard of living at the expense of other countries; our standard of living ultimately depends on our own productivity, resources, and whether we make efficient use of these resources, and this is where we should focus our efforts.

Jobs, Jobs, Jobs

Every politician's favorite promise is "more and better jobs," and advocates of fundamental tax reform are no exception to this rule. Moreover, whenever any kind of tax increase or elimination of a preference is threatened, the affected parties immediately produce a well-publicized study purporting to show how many jobs it will cost. For example, during the debate over the TRA, when eliminating the deductibility of business lunches was being considered, the restaurant industry association warned of thousands of jobs lost in the restaurant business. Such studies will undoubtedly multiply dramatically if we decide to undertake another overhaul of our tax system, as a whole host of sacred preferences would be attacked.

Aside from the natural tendency of interested parties to exaggerate, do such claims about jobs have any economic content? When it comes to the quantity of jobs, these claims can be very misleading. If the economy is functioning normally, the total number of jobs will be determined by the interplay of how much people want to work and labor demand;[34] large-scale unemployment is a feature of recessions, which we have argued is a separate issue from tax design. The idea that tax reform will somehow lead to a larger *number* of jobs in the long run doesn't make sense, unless it induces more people to decide to work more hours than otherwise.

Jobs in certain sectors may indeed be lost as a result of eliminating preferences in the tax code, because the relative demand for those formerly favored items will fall. That doesn't mean there's a permanent reduction in the total quantity of jobs in the economy, however. Rather, there is a shift in demand away from the formerly tax-preferred sectors, and toward the production of other goods and services in the economy. Extra jobs will open up in these sectors as a result. Shifting jobs from one sector to another can be a jarring process, but it happens all the time for reasons unrelated to taxes, and is a key to keeping the economy running efficiently. The transitional costs should not be dismissed, but are likely to be outweighed by the economic benefits that arise if eliminating an unwarranted preference shifts resources into a more productive area; the latter gain persists long after the transitional disruption has past.

While claims about its effect on the quantity of jobs are suspect, there is some economic content to the idea that tax reform could lead to *better* jobs. One way it could do this is if it leads to a more efficient allocation of resources, shifting them from less-productive, tax-preferred sectors to other, more-productive areas. But for the most part, this claim depends on the idea that reduced tax rates on high-income people, combined with greater incentives for saving, will lead to a larger and higher-quality capital stock. This, in turn, would give workers better "tools" to work with, increasing their productivity and raising their wages. This is the essence of how tax changes that are mainly targeted at high-income people are supposed to help the rest of the population. Democrats have often derided this thinking as "trickle-down economics," while Republicans have made it one of their central themes. Although the logic of the argument is sound, the crucial question is the magnitude of the effect; as discussed above, the evidence is uncertain and not extremely promising.

Human Capital—Education and Training

A more direct way to increase worker productivity and generate better jobs is to induce people to acquire more education and skills. Economists refer to the stock of productive skills that people possess as "human capital." Just as investing in physical tools to work with adds to labor productivity, so does investing in skills. Many economists contend that accumulation of human capital, together with research and development, are the most important engines of long-run economic growth for the U.S. economy. Although it is hard to put a dollar value on such things, the aggregate value of human capital is probably at least as large as that of physical capital in our country.[35]

While human capital investment is not often a focus of major tax reform plans, it is certainly a relevant issue. President Clinton raised the stakes on this issue in 1995 by responding to Republican proposals for tax reform with his own modest proposals to spur human capital investment, including a deduction for tuition expenses.

In the same way as adding to the physical capital stock requires foregoing consumption for savings, acquiring human capital also requires such an investment. This investment often takes the form of tuition and other direct outlays—these can be quite substantial, in excess of $20,000 per year at some private universities. The other important cost is income passed up while at school. This cost is also quite substantial; although it is lower than the cost of tuition for some college students, it is many times higher for some MBA and law students.

How does our tax system treat investments in human capital? That depends on the nature of the costs. The investment of time spent at school rather than at work is treated more generously than most investments in physical capital. Although you pay tax on the return to your investment in skills (higher wages), you save any taxes you would have paid on the earnings you pass up while at school. In essence, you get an immediate write-off for your lost wages. In contrast, an investment in long-lived physical capital would typically be depreciated over many years.

The treatment of human capital investment is worse than physical capital when direct costs such as tuition are involved, as it entitles you to no tax deductions whatsoever, yet you pay full tax on the returns. In some cases, there are offsets; for example, you can deduct interest on a home equity loan used for education; interest on some student loans is paid by the government while the student is in school; and scholarships used for tuition are tax-free. On balance, it's unclear whether the treatment is currently better or worse than for physical capital.

Moreover, there are reasons to believe that the tax treatment of human capital ought to be more generous than that accorded to physical capital. Because people can't pledge their future labor earnings as collateral for a loan, private capital markets on their own fail to provide loans even when they are good investments. Government-guaranteed loan programs to some extent deal with this problem.

Most tax reform plans have not specifically dealt with the question of human capital. Plans that reduce marginal tax rates could influence human capital investment indirectly, as they lower the impact of taxes on wages, which are the returns to those investments. But it seems clear that if we were to move to a consumption tax, which allows the cost of all physical investments to be deducted in full immediately, some additional provisions for human capital investments would be needed to maintain neutral tax treatment.

Avoidance and Evasion

Our current tax code provides many opportunities for individuals and firms to reduce their taxes without making any significant changes to important economic decisions, such as how much to work, save, or invest. For example, people with enough accumulated savings can often reduce their tax bills easily by transferring, or relabeling, those assets into IRA accounts; such a transaction requires no actual increase in one's amount of saving. If you know tax rates are going to increase next year, you might try to make sure that any bonuses or royalty checks that are coming your way are paid to you this year. If tax rates go up too much for your tastes, you might simply fail to report some of your income.

We'll classify these types of responses as tax avoidance, when the methods are legal, and tax evasion, when they are not.[36] It turns out that these sorts of responses are very important to understanding how taxes affect the economy. For one reason, they may mitigate the extent to which real economic decisions are affected by taxation; you'd almost always prefer to shuffle your portfolio than to make a real sacrifice such as earning less pay. Second, they can render it very difficult to make sense of the evidence about how taxes are affecting real economic decisions. For example, if the taxable incomes of the rich go down significantly when their tax rates go up, it could mean they're not working as hard, or it could mean that they're reporting less of their income and taking greater advantage of avoidance opportunities. Distinguishing among these kinds of responses is important, because they have very different policy implications. In the example just mentioned, if we care about progressivity, then the appropriate policy response might be to limit opportunities for avoidance and evasion, rather than to abandon a progressive tax structure.

The experience of the 1980s showed that individuals and firms are very willing to take advantage of opportunities for tax avoidance when they present themselves. Probably the best example of this happened in 1986. The tax reform bill of that year was passed by both Houses of Congress in September and signed into law by President Reagan on October 22. According to the law, the tax on long-term gains realized by a top-bracket taxpayer was scheduled to increase from 20 percent to 28 percent as of January 1, 1987. Thus the tax rate was 20 percent *for a limited time only*! Savvy taxpayers took note, and the result was an unprecedented boom in capital gains realizations. Realizations of capital gains increased from $167 billion in 1985 to $322.2 billion in 1986, only to fall back to $137.4 billion in 1987. Even more striking, long-term capital gains of corporate stock in December of 1986, the last month of the tax sale, were seven times their level in the same month of 1985.[37]

A second dramatic example of such a response occurred when the TRA reduced the top marginal tax rate in the personal income tax below that in the corporate income tax for the first time in decades. This, combined with the promise of avoiding double taxation of business income, made it much more attractive to organize a business as an S corporation or a partnership, which are taxed solely under the personal code, instead of as a traditional C corporation, which is taxed under the corporate code. The response was swift and dramatic. The number of S corporations, which had been rising at a 7.7 percent annual pace from 1965–1986, jumped by 17.5 percent a year from 1986 to 1990. The number of C corporations, which had been growing by an average of 3.5 percent per year from 1965 to 1986, dropped by 4.8 percent per year between 1986 and 1990; the biggest decline was among small C corporations, the ones that would be able to switch to S status because of their limitation to 35 shareholders.[38]

There were countless other examples of such responses to the tax changes of the 1980s.[39] All in all, the evidence suggests that there is a hierarchy of behavioral responses to taxation. At the top of the hierarchy—the most clearly responsive to tax incentives—is the timing of certain economic transactions. The pattern of capital gains realizations before and after the 1986 tax reform is the best example, but there are many others, including foreign direct investment into the United

States, which was $16.3 billion in the fourth quarter of 1986, more than double the rate of adjacent quarters, as investors raced to beat the expiration of tax rules favoring mergers and acquisitions. In the second tier of the hierarchy are financial and accounting responses, best exemplified by the shift from C to S corporations after 1986, and the large post-1986 shift away from newly nondeductible personal loans into still-deductible mortgage debt. On the bottom of the hierarchy, where the least response is evident, are the real economic decisions of individuals and firms.

Disputed Issues at the Heart of the Public Debate

Now that we've examined the evidence on how taxes affect economic behavior, we are in a better position to examine some of the claims that play a big role in the public debate over taxes. The first of these is that tax cuts will increase economic growth so much that revenues will not fall much, and may actually increase. A second is that the post-1986 surge in incomes that occurred at the very top of the income distribution reflected a dramatic response to the incentive effects of taxes.

How Do Tax Cuts Affect Revenues?

The proposition that across-the-board tax cuts would lose no revenue is now associated with the economist Arthur Laffer, who claimed in the 1970s that high tax rates might be harming the economy enough that tax cuts would provide more, rather than less, revenue. The free lunch promised by Laffer proved irresistible to politicians, and was one of the ideological underpinnings of the tax cuts in the Economic Recovery Tax Act of 1981. The massive increase in the budget deficit that followed that tax cut weakened support for such views, but they still persist to some degree today. For example, on the campaign trail in 1996, one of Steve Forbes' mantras was that tax cuts in the United States have always increased revenues. Daniel Mitchell of the Heritage Foundation made similar claims recently on the pages of *The Wall Street Journal*.[40]

With a decade of hindsight, it is clear that Laffer's proposition did not apply to the tax rate cuts of 1981. This should not be surprising given all of the evidence we discussed above, such as the apparently small responsiveness of labor supply to taxes. The reduction in tax

rates did not cause the economy to expand enough to recoup the revenues; revenues turned out to be significantly lower than what they
would have been had there been no tax cut. All but the most ardent
supply-siders now concede this point.

Chapter 2 showed that individual income tax revenues did fall relative to GDP after 1981. From 1981 to 1984, they dropped from 9.6 percent of GDP down to 8 percent, despite continued inflation-induced
"bracket creep" that pushed taxpayers into higher tax rates. President
Bush's Treasury Department estimated that, by 1990, the rate reductions of the 1981 act alone were costing the federal government $164
billion per year, assuming no departure from the normal trend of economic growth.[41] The only way such facts could be reconciled with
claims that the 1981 cut caused revenues to *increase* would be if it caused
the economy to grow significantly faster than it otherwise would have.
However, as Table 4.1 shows, the economic growth rate of the 1980s as a
whole was actually slightly below that of the 1970s. Some point to the
growth rate experience in the years immediately after 1982, but this
confuses recovery from deep recession with long-run growth.

Claims about the impact of tax cuts on revenues are worth considering not just because of the bold claims made by some politicians, but
because there is a legitimate question here: exactly how do revenues
respond to changes in tax rates? Advocates of tax cuts often complain
that analyses of their proposals fail to take into account *any* possibility
of induced economic growth. They argue that the revenue-estimating
process of the government should be made "dynamic" (assuming that
economic growth will be affected), rather than "static" (assuming that
growth is unaffected). These critics do have a point, as most economists would concede that tax changes can impact economic performance. But, as we saw above, the evidence on the responsiveness of
economic behavior to taxes is often very uncertain, and there is plenty
of disagreement about its magnitude. So incorporating such dynamic
estimating techniques is problematic.[42] This issue will be considered
later when specific proposals for reform are discussed.

While almost no economists argue that a general cut in tax rates for
all people would raise revenues, some maintain that because high-
income people are exceptionally responsive to taxation, tax cuts targeted to the rich might increase revenues, or at least cost very little.
They often point to the tremendous surge in incomes at the top of the
income distribution during the 1980s as evidence of a strong economic
response to lower marginal tax rates. None of the evidence considered

above explicitly rules out this possibility, so we will turn to this issue next.

How Do Very High-Income People Respond to Tax Cuts?

Table 3.1 presented some evidence of dramatic growth in the incomes at the very top of the income distribution between 1977 and 1990. A study performed by Daniel Feenberg of the National Bureau of Economic Research and James Poterba of the Massachusetts Institute of Technology found that a particularly large jump in incomes of the affluent occurred right around the Tax Reform Act of 1986, which reduced the top marginal tax rate from 50 percent to 28 percent. Between 1984 and 1990, the total adjusted gross income of the highest-income 1 percent of taxpayers rose by 68 percent in real terms, and their share of total adjusted gross income increased from 9.9 percent to 13.4.[43] Data that follows the same taxpayers over time reveals the same pattern— those high-income households for which the 1986 tax reform provided the biggest reductions in marginal tax rates experienced the biggest increases in reported income.[44]

Did the reduced marginal tax rates of the 1980s *cause* the large increase in reported incomes of the affluent, or is it just a coincidence? After all, income inequality, led by an explosion in the incomes at the top of the income distribution, has been steadily increasing since about 1970. There are many explanations for this longer-term trend toward greater inequality. For example, it appears that the demand for the services of a select few highly skilled "superstars" in various fields has been increasing over time. Sherwin Rosen of the University of Chicago discussed this phenomenon in a 1981 article; a new book by Robert Frank of Cornell University and Philip Cook of Duke University, called *The Winner-Take-All Society*, documents many examples of it in the U.S. economy in recent years.[45]

Undoubtedly, there would have been some increase in the share of income earned by the top 1 percent even without any tax changes. But the sharpness of the increase right around 1986 suggests that the tax cut was a major factor in the increase. However, a closer look at the anatomy of the high-income behavioral response suggests that much of it had nothing to do with any dimension of increased labor supply. A study by Gerald Auten of the U.S. Treasury Department and Robert Carroll of Ernst & Young concluded that less than 30 percent of this increase in adjusted gross income was accounted for by wages and salaries. A big chunk was accounted for by the shift in legal organization of firms from C corporations to S corporations, which was described earlier. Such a shift does not reflect the creation of new income or an increase in total tax revenues—although income reported by individuals went up, there was a mirror image decline in corporate taxable income. Another part of the explanation is that the 1986 tax reform sharply reduced the advantages of using partnerships as tax shelters. To the extent these tax losses stopped showing up after 1987 on the tax returns of high-income taxpayers, it looks like their incomes rose, but any such increase reflects only the tightening up of the rules governing tax shelters.

A similar debate arose over the impact of the increase in the top marginal rate enacted in 1993. Bill Clinton was elected in 1992 on a platform that included tax increases on the affluent, and he delivered on that promise starting in tax year 1993, when the top tax rate increased from 31 percent to 39.6 percent. Proponents of this argued that it was appropriate that high-income taxpayers pay their "fair share" of the necessary increase in tax burden. Opponents cautioned that the revenue projections were overstated because they ignored the inevitable behavioral response of high-income taxpayers.

Once the initial evidence regarding tax year 1993 was compiled, Daniel Feenberg and Martin Feldstein of Harvard University examined tabulations of tax return data for 1992 and 1993 and concluded that, compared to previous trend growth and what would have been predicted by the income growth of other taxpayers, the reported taxable incomes of very high-income families fell by 7.8 percent in 1993. This implied that the Treasury collected only half of the revenue they had hoped, and claimed, they would collect from the rate increase.[46] Feenberg and Feldstein argued that this large behavioral response indicated that the ratio of the cost of distorted behavior to revenue raised was very high, and much higher than alternative ways to raise revenue. The policy implication—high taxes on the rich are a bad idea.

There's more to this story, though. Bill Clinton was elected in early November of 1992, leaving plenty of time for high-income taxpayers to move taxable income forward into 1992, when it would be taxed at no higher than 31 percent. In December the financial press was full of stories advising their readers to do just that, and full of stories about prominent citizens who already had. Walt Disney executives Michael Eisner and Frank Wells cashed in stock options worth $257 million. Several baseball players, including David Cone, Mark McGuire, and

Ruben Sierra, made sure their new long-term contracts had front-loaded the bonus payments into 1992, so as to reduce the eventual total tax take. The New York State Bureau of the Budget's annual survey of the year-end bonuses paid to Wall Street high flyers revealed that about two-thirds was paid in December of 1992 and one-third in January of 1993; the usual split was the reverse—one-third in December and two-thirds in January.[47] The Commerce Department has estimated that, all in all, about $20 billion of income in total was shifted forward from 1993 into 1992.[48]

For all these reasons, the lower-than-trend 1993 incomes could reflect nothing more than the fact that taxable income was shifted forward from 1993 to 1992 to escape the expected higher taxes. In fact, compared to data from 1991, which would not be contaminated by the shifting, the 1993 incomes of affluent taxpayers do not look particularly low.[49] It is clear that the evidence from years surrounding announced or anticipated tax changes reveals a mixture of timing responses and the more permanent responses to tax changes, and it is very difficult to sort out one from the other.

Conclusion

There's no question that our tax system imposes costs on the economy, but exactly how large they are no one knows for sure.[50] While a certain amount of this cost cannot be eliminated, tax reform could succeed in reducing these costs. Some tax changes that are "good for the economy" are so because they eliminate unnecessary and misguided features about which there is wide consensus among economists; most of these are violations of neutral tax treatment of economic activities. In other cases the economic gains are achieved by exploiting the inherent trade-off with progressivity, by loosening the link between tax liability and economic success. Depending on one's views about equity, it may be reasonable to reject any economic gains that come only at the cost of penalizing the poor and middle class. For this reason it is important to distinguish these cases carefully. This will be a major theme of Chapters 6 through 8, where we discuss options for tax reform. Before moving on, however, there are two other aspects of a good tax system to consider—simplicity and enforceability.

5   Simplicity and Enforce-ability

To this point, two fundamental criteria for judging a tax system have been explored—fairness and the promotion of economic prosperity. The two other desirable features of a good tax system are that it be simple and easy to enforce. Would-be tax reformers now emphasize more than ever their belief that the current income tax does a poor job on both counts. This chapter will first examine just how complex our income tax is, and then consider what it is that makes it so complex and how to simplify it. Then, we look at the problem of evasion and enforcement in the current income tax, and discuss what features of a tax system make it easy or difficult to enforce. In many cases, but not always, simplicity and enforceability go together. However, achieving these goals often involves sacrificing other cherished objectives, so once again difficult choices must be faced.

How Complicated Is Our Tax System?

Every spring between 1987 and 1993, *Money* magazine invented a tax situation of moderate, but not exceptional, complexity and asked 50 tax professionals to calculate tax liability. In 1993 they got back 41 different answers from the 41 professionals who submitted returns; the answers ranged from $31,846 to $74,450. The actual tax liability was $35,643, although some legitimate differences in interpreting the law could change that total a bit. The preparers' fees for this exercise varied widely as well, ranging from $375 to $3,600.[1]

Another springtime ritual of *Money* was to call the toll-free numbers manned by the IRS and ask the same set of questions to several taxpayer service representatives. In 1992, 86 percent of the questions were answered correctly, far short of a perfect score, but a large improvement over the 55 percent correct figure reported in 1988.[2]

The tax system has become so complicated that, in some situations, neither tax professionals nor the IRS itself can be sure of what tax liability really is. The extent of this uncertainty is just one measure of the tax system's complexity. Another is the sheer length of the tax code. West Publishing Company's 1995 edition of the *Internal Revenue Code* includes 9,722 sections covering 2,540 pages, while the accompanying *Federal Tax Regulations 1995* spans 8,102 pages.[3] The total number of words in these two documents has been estimated at over 5.5 million.[4]

Although these figures are eye-catching, they are not of direct concern to most taxpayers. What does it matter whether the tax code has five, fifty, or five hundred million words, as long as your own tax affairs are straightforward? In fact, having a detailed set of rules could make things simpler, to the extent it clears up gray areas in the tax law. Moreover, many of these rules have been adopted to stop the increasingly complicated tax-avoidance strategies that taxpayers and their advisors are continually inventing. Clearly, more than anecdotes and page numbers are needed to get a good picture of just how complex our tax system is.

The Costs of Compliance

The most informative measure of tax complexity is the resource cost of collecting taxes. This cost certainly includes the budget of the IRS, which in 1995 spent $7.6 billion enforcing all varieties of federal taxation, or about .6 percent of the revenue it collected.[5] However, the IRS budget, the administrative cost of raising taxes, is only the tip of the iceberg of the total cost of collection. It is dwarfed by the costs imposed directly on the taxpayers themselves, known as *compliance costs*. Some of this cost is out-of-pocket, but most of it is the time spent by taxpayers on their tax affairs. Compliance costs also include the expense incurred by third parties to the tax collection process, such as employers withholding tax for their employees. Both the monetary outlay and the time spent are resource costs, because both could be freed up and applied to valued pursuits if it weren't for the tax system.

The most recent study of the compliance cost of the U.S. income tax system by Marsha Blumenthal of the University of St. Thomas and Joel Slemrod concluded that, in 1989, individuals spent about three billion hours, or an average of about 27 hours per year per taxpayer, dealing with both federal and state personal income taxes.[6] This represented an increase from the 22-hour average found in a similar study for 1982, despite the intervening Tax Reform Act of 1986, which was intended to simplify tax matters.[7] About 60 percent of the time was due to re-cordkeeping, while less than 20 percent was spent on preparing the return itself. The remainder was spent in activities such as researching the tax law, meeting with an advisor, or arranging financial affairs to minimize taxes. The survey revealed that the burden of compliance is highly concentrated; more than half the total hours were incurred by just 16 percent of taxpayers. Self-employed taxpayers were particularly hard-hit, spending an average of 60 hours per year on tax matters. People with capital gains, dividends, rental income, and itemized de-ductions also tended to have higher-than-average compliance burdens.

In addition to the cost of taxpayers' own time, there are also direct monetary outlays for professional guidance and supplies. About half of all taxpayers purchase assistance from an accountant or other pro-fessional tax advisor; those who do spend an average of about $158 annually.[8] Other monetary expenses, such as for tax guides and com-puter software, average around $14 per taxpayer annually.[9]

What does this all add up to? If time spent complying with personal income taxes is valued at a reasonable average of $15 per hour, and hours are adjusted to eliminate time spent on state taxes, the total cost of that time comes to about $42 billion for 1995.[10] Professional assis-tance and other monetary expenses add another $8 billion, for a total personal income tax compliance cost of $50 billion.[11]

There are many fewer corporate income tax returns than there are personal returns (4.6 million versus 115 million in 1994),[12] but the amount of time and money spent per corporate return is much greater. The average Fortune 500 company spends over $2 million per year on tax matters; many of the largest spend over $10 million. However, the cost-to-revenue ratio for large firms, 2.6 percent, is apparently lower than for either individuals or smaller businesses. Survey results sug-gest the biggest sources of complexity for large corporations are depre-ciation rules, the alternative minimum tax, the lack of uniformity among states and between the federal income tax rules and those used by the states, and the rules governing income earned abroad. The latter are particularly complex, accounting for 40 percent of the total cost of compliance, although foreign operations account for less than a quar-ter of assets, sales, or employment for these large corporations.[13]

Even after all this expense, neither the company nor the IRS is com-pletely sure what the correct tax liability really is. Audits, appeals, and lawsuits often drag on for years, so it is not at all uncommon for a big corporation to have its tax liability still unsettled ten years after the return was filed.

Small- and medium-size businesses also incur significant compliance costs. Studies consistently find that the smaller the firm, the larger the cost of complying with the tax system per dollar of tax payment or per dollar of sales, assets, or any other measure of the size of the firm.[14] The cost of compliance for some small businesses, particularly sole proprietorships, is already counted in our $50 billion estimate for the personal code; but for many small businesses, it is not.[15]

There is, alas, no reliable estimate of the aggregate cost of business tax compliance. An oft-cited study done for the IRS by the consulting firm Arthur D. Little, Inc., estimated that businesses and their paid advisors spent a total of 3.6 billion hours dealing with income taxation in 1985,[16] but there are serious methodological flaws with the study that suggest this is a gross overestimate.[17] Moreover, any survey-based estimate for business is bound to be only a rough guess, because of the difficulty of separating the accounting and bookkeeping activities that were done solely for tax purposes from those that would have been done anyway for general business purposes. This is a particular problem for small businesses that do not have a separate tax department.

The lack of compelling data for businesses makes it impossible to establish a solid estimate for the aggregate compliance cost for the whole tax system. Our best guess is that business compliance adds about $20 billion per year to the total cost. There are also other hard-to-quantify costs, such as the anxiety suffered by taxpayers. On the other hand, there are mitigating factors not mentioned above. For instance, some of the recordkeeping required for the personal income tax would be required anyway for purposes such as applications for mortgages, college financial aid, and government transfer programs. Taking all of these factors into account, a reasonable estimate of the total annual cost of enforcing and complying with the federal corporate and personal income taxes would be $75 billion, or about 10 cents per dollar raised.

Some other recent studies have produced much larger compliance cost estimates. James L. Payne, in his 1993 book *Costly Returns*, puts the compliance cost of the federal corporate and personal income taxes at $159 billion for 1985, or about 24 percent of revenues raised in that year. Arthur P. Hall of the Tax Foundation projects the same cost at $202 billion for 1995, or 27 percent of revenues. However, both of these studies rely on the flawed Arthur D. Little estimate of the total hours spent by business for tax compliance. Moreover, they use very high estimates of the cost-per-hour for both individuals and businesses, which they arbitrarily base on an average of the IRS budget per employee-hour and the total revenues of a large accounting firm per employee-hour.[18] In Hall's case, the imputed cost per taxpayer hour was $39.60. While there is certainly room for disagreement over the appropriate number to use, this figure is an implausibly high average for individuals.

In the popular press, even more exorbitant compliance cost estimates are routinely cited. For instance, House Ways and Means Committee Chairman Bill Archer has been quoted on the front page of *The Wall Street Journal* as saying "the current income tax system costs, by the most conservative projections, $300 billion a year just for compliance."[19] House Democratic leader Richard Gephardt repeated this figure at a press conference presenting his own tax reform proposal.[20] A recent article in *Fortune* magazine put "the total estimated cost of complying with the current tax law annually" at $593 billion.[21] This figure was based on a generous extrapolation from James Payne's assessment of the *total* costs of the tax system, which he put at $363 billion for 1985. This included not only his figure for the costs of complying with federal taxes, but also his high estimate of the damage caused to the economy by tax disincentives, an important but separate issue we discussed in the previous chapter.

There is no question that it costs a great deal to comply with the income tax. A cost of $75 billion is worth taking very seriously. It represents the value of resources that, if it were not for the complexity of our tax system, could be used to produce goods and services that we value, or time that could be spent on other things. But at the same time, it's important to put this cost into its proper perspective.

It's Not So Complicated for Everyone

How complex the tax system is depends on who you are. For the 42 percent of taxpayers who file Forms 1040EZ or 1040A, it can't be too much of a hassle. About 18 percent of taxpayers use Form 1040EZ. Although it is an 8.5 by 11 inch, two-sided page, it just as well could be put on a (rather large) postcard. All it generally involves is writing down one's wage and interest income, subtracting the personal exemption and standard deduction, and then looking up the tax owed (and in some cases the earned income tax credit) in the tax tables. If the taxpayer desires, the IRS will even do the tax liability calculation. Another 24 percent of taxpayers file Form 1040A, which although not quite as simple as the 1040EZ, is still pretty straightforward. Users of this form may have a few other types of income to report, such as dividends or pensions, some IRA contributions to subtract, or perhaps a child-care credit to compute, but otherwise it's not much different from the 1040EZ. Even some of those who must file the more complicated Form 1040 do not necessarily face a daunting task. Most of the complexity in the personal tax code directly affects only the minority of taxpayers with itemized deductions or significant capital or business income. In the 1989 Blumenthal-Slemrod survey, 30 percent of taxpayers reported spending less than five hours on all tax matters over an entire year; 45 percent spent less than ten hours, and 66 percent spent less than twenty.[22] In any attempt to reform the tax system, we must be careful not to destroy the relative simplicity that already exists for many millions of taxpayers.

However, complexity is often a matter of concern even for the millions of taxpayers with fairly simple tax returns. For one thing, many of these people believe that other, more sophisticated, taxpayers take advantage of the complexity to find loopholes that lower their tax liability, leaving the less sophisticated taxpayers like them holding the revenue bag. To these people, one attraction of a flat tax is its promise to ensure that high-income people have no way to avoid paying their share. Furthermore, some of the cost imposed by complexity on business taxpayers is undoubtedly passed through to ordinary citizens, in the form of higher prices and/or lower wages, in just the same way as an explicit tax liability on businesses would be passed through.

Is Our Tax System Too Complex?

Other things being equal, time and money spent complying with taxes are a waste. For example, all of the intelligent people who are making their livings as tax lawyers or accountants, devising very sophisticated methods for avoiding taxes, could be applying their talents to more socially productive pursuits. But at least some compliance costs are an unavoidable consequence of any tax system. It is not obvious whether a cost of collection for our current income tax of about 10 cents on the dollar is outrageously high or remarkably low. There are not comparable, reliable figures from other countries or alternative tax systems against which we can judge 10 cents.[23] Even if there were, a simple comparison of cost per dollar raised could be very misleading. A lower cost could mean that the tax is being raised in an inequitable way. As an extreme example, we could simplify the taxpaying process for many people if we stopped enforcing it, making it voluntary. Nothing is simpler than not having to file a tax return at all. But this would obviously create a lot of problems, including the unfairness of collecting taxes exclusively from people who view taxpaying as a duty, while allowing others off with no obligations. Before we dismiss the U.S. system as unnecessarily complex, and therefore too costly, we must consider what, if anything, this complexity is buying us. If it is buying us nothing, or is buying us something that is not worth the cost, the tax system certainly ought to be simplified.

What Makes a Tax System Complicated?

Knowing that the tax system is complicated is one thing. But understanding exactly what it is that makes our tax system complex is also essential if we are going to make a serious effort to simplify it. A wide variety of culprits are responsible, some more defensible than others. The desire to achieve equity and fairness provides one set of reasons. Attempts to encourage certain activities deemed socially or economically desirable provide another. Sometimes, purely political factors appear to be responsible. Below, we discuss the major features that make a tax system complicated, and consider why they exist in our current tax system.[24]

Measuring Ability-to-Pay

One reason that paying for government is complicated, costly, and time-consuming is that we are not willing to have one price for all. The line for tickets at a movie theater moves fairly quickly where there is one basic admission price; it moves a bit less quickly when there is a separate charge for children below a certain age. It would move more slowly still if each child had to produce identification to prove his or her age; as it stands, most theaters are willing to take the parents', or child's, word for it. Paying for a meal at a restaurant is usually a simple process, but imagine what it would be like if the bill depended not only on what was ordered, but also on the income, number of children, and annual medical expenditures of each member of the party that ordered the food.

Part of the reason our system is complex is that we think simpler methods of dividing up the tax bill are inequitable. Achieving both kinds of equity discussed in Chapter 3—vertical equity and horizontal equity—puts demands on the tax system. First, consider vertical equity—the appropriate sharing of tax burdens across families of different levels of well-being. A poll tax, under which every adult pays the same amount of tax, period, is unacceptable to most everyone on equity grounds.[25] Instead, we require that tax liability be tied to how well-off a family is. But as soon as the government needs to measure income, wealth, or consumption, things start to get complicated fast.

Measuring labor compensation is often straightforward, although it runs into difficulties when fringe benefits are involved or when the compensation can be relabeled as capital income in order to receive more generous tax treatment. Measuring capital income is often much more complicated. At the business level, it creates the need to measure the depreciation of assets, which is impossible to do precisely. Even the standardized, but approximate, depreciation deductions used by our tax code require considerable recordkeeping and calculation. At the personal level, including capital gains in the tax base as they accrue would be prohibitively complex in some cases, and even including them as they are realized raises nettlesome problems. Other requirements of a completely accurate measure of capital income, such as including the rental value of services from a home and adjusting for inflation, are so complicated that we don't even attempt them. Despite all the compromises we make in our tax code, measuring and reporting capital income are still very burdensome for taxpayers.

If we were to use wealth as the tax base, this could be even more difficult to measure properly. For many types of wealth, such as real estate, and especially closely held businesses, the only time their exact value is known is when they are put on the market and sold.

Even consumption can be difficult to measure if we try to do it at the personal level. Imagine the hassle if each household had to keep track of all its consumption expenditures over the course of the year and report the total to the tax authorities. Alternatively, we could measure each household's consumption as income minus saving, which, if done appropriately, could avoid most of the complexities of measuring income, but would require keeping track of all deposits and withdrawals from savings. On the other hand, taxing consumption at the business level, for example through a sales tax or value-added tax (VAT), could greatly simplify the taxpaying process relative to an income tax, an issue that will be examined in more detail in Chapter 7. But this would limit the degree to which we could adjust tax liabilities according to ability-to-pay.

Achieving horizontal equity—the equal treatment of people with equal ability to pay—also exacts a cost of complexity. If we accept some measure of income or consumption as the basic measure of well-being, how much fine-tuning need be done to account for differences among taxpayers? If two families with the same income are not really equally well-off because one has high unavoidable medical expenses and the other doesn't, should that be reflected in tax liabilities? Doing so inevitably complicates the tax system, and thus there is a tax policy choice that must be made—how to trade off fine-tuning tax liability for family circumstances against the complexity required to implement that fine-tuning. Substantial simplification will require that we give up on the notion that the bill we pay to the government must be personalized in great detail, and settle instead on rough justice only.

Taxing Individuals Instead of Taxing at the Business Level

In general, a system that taxes income or consumption at the business level can be much simpler than one that requires each individual or family to keep track of and report its tax liability. As we noted in Chapter 3, the incidence of a tax (who ultimately bears the burden) is not affected by which side of a transaction remits the tax to the IRS. However, both how simple and how enforceable a tax system is do depend on the mechanics of how tax is collected. For example, a consumption tax that required retailers to charge a fixed percentage tax on every sale and remit it to the government (a retail sales tax) would be much simpler than one that required each individual to keep records of his or her consumption. Similarly, in an income tax, it is simpler to have employers, financial institutions, and corporations report and pay tax on various items of income paid to individuals than to have each individual keep track of the income he or she receives. It is generally more efficient for a relatively small number of businesses to keep records of income or consumption than it is for multitudes of employees, shareholders, or consumers. Moreover, in many cases the firms need to keep these records anyway for business purposes, so there is little duplication of effort.

Our income tax system is relatively simple in the areas where it follows this principle, and more complex where it does not. Taxation of wage and salary income is facilitated because employers are required to keep records of and report the wages and salaries of each employee to the IRS. This adds some compliance burden for the employer, but saves even more for the employee. The more income we treat in this fashion, the simpler the taxpaying process can become. In Japan and the United Kingdom,[26] most taxpayers don't even have to file tax returns in most years, because their systems for withholding on wages are more precise than ours, and because taxes are also withheld on other types of income such as interest.

Graduated Tax Rates

A graduated tax rate structure does not, by itself, directly contribute any significant complexity to the taxpaying process. One of the great red herrings during the debate over the 1986 tax act was that collapsing fourteen tax brackets (fifteen for single filers) to three was an important simplification. Once taxable income is computed, calculating tax liability from the tax tables is a trivial operation that is not perceptibly simplified by having fewer brackets.

But a graduated rate structure does add to the complexity of the tax system because it implies that, due to the need to measure ability-to-pay family by family, one must go beyond taxation at the business level to include individuals in the collection process. In conjunction with other changes, having only one tax rate could facilitate a major simplification. If everyone were subject to the same tax rate, then taxes on most types of income could be remitted at the source of the income payment, rather than by the recipient, and little or no reconciliation would be required of the individual. This becomes much more difficult when there are multiple rates; to get tax liabilities exactly right, each employer, bank, and corporation would need to know exactly how much income was going to each individual from all sources. One reason the United Kingdom's system of final withholding is able to get most people's tax liabilities right without having them file returns is because everyone except those with very high incomes is subject to a single rate.

This same principle applies to consumption taxation as well. If there is a single rate with no exemptions, aggregate consumption can be measured and tax remitted entirely at the business level, with no reconciliation required on the part of individuals.

A graduated marginal rate structure can also contribute indirectly to complexity in one other way. High marginal tax rates increase the incentives for individuals to invest energy and money into complicated tax avoidance schemes, as the marginal tax rate is exactly the return to reducing taxable income by a dollar.

A Messy Tax Base

How we deal with fundamental issues of fairness is responsible for some of the complexity of our current tax system, but a lot of the complexity arises from reasons that are not so fundamental. Consider the deductions and other tax preferences that complicate and narrow the tax base. In the personal code, there are numerous adjustments, credits, and itemized deductions for things such as home mortgage interest, state and local tax payments, and the like. At the business level, there are various tax credits, special depreciation rules, and other preferences. Each of these features requires recordkeeping and calculation. Moreover, each deduction or credit involves ambiguities regarding exactly what kinds of activities qualify. For example, how much of a business expense deduction should someone get for a room in one's home that is sometimes used as an office, or for a personal car that is used occasionally for business purposes? Further complexity ensues as regulations are written to clarify the ambiguities, and taxpayers come up with new ways to circumvent them.

As noted above, some of these adjustments to the tax base represent attempts to accurately measure ability-to-pay. Others are justified as policies for encouraging certain kinds of behavior deemed desirable, or are doled out as political favors. Because nearly every economic issue has a tax angle, just about any time someone comes up with a bright idea about how the government should encourage some economic activity, or discourage another, the tax system gets the call. As a result, our tax system is now an awkward mixture of a revenue-raising system plus scores of incentive programs, and is much more complicated than it would be if its only function were to raise revenue in the most equitable and cost-efficient way possible.

As discussed in the previous chapter, although it is generally better to leave economic decisions up to the free market, there are some situations where it may be legitimate to subsidize certain activities, for example when an activity produces social benefits (externalities) that are not captured directly by the person who engages in it. In such cases, it may actually be cheaper and simpler to subsidize them through the tax code than through a separate program. After all, the administrative machinery already exists for the government to collect and, in some cases, remit money to over 100 million individual taxpayers and 4 million corporations. If we as a society decide to subsidize, say, child-care expenditures, from a purely administrative point of view it doesn't make sense to set up a separate system for processing child-care credit applications and remitting checks to eligible people. Since the IRS is already set up to process tax forms and send out checks, it is surely cost-effective to piggyback a child-care credit onto the taxpaying process.[27] Why not just keep one set of accounts—one-stop shopping—between the government and its citizens?

The biggest problem with this argument is that the policies that are piggybacked onto the revenue-raising system are often thereby obscured, with the result that there are important economic policies hidden in the tax system that would never be enacted as stand-alone policies. As an example, consider the political prospects of the following proposal. The federal government has decided to subsidize the activities of state and local governments. It has decided not to limit the kinds of activities it will subsidize—municipal swimming pools and golf courses will be treated the same as primary education and fire departments. The subsidy will not be remitted to the state and local governments, but rather will be remitted directly to the residents. The rate of subsidy, though, will not be the same for all citizens. Less than one-third of households, mostly high-income ones, will receive the subsidy,[28] and furthermore there will be several rates of subsidy: 15, 28, 31, 36, and even 39.6 percent—the higher one's income, the higher the rate of subsidy. And one last thing—the subsidy is lost to the extent that the families' state and local governments decide to finance their expenditures with a sales tax.

This is certainly a very peculiar kind of subsidy program, and one that, presumably, would never be passed by Congress. It is, though, essentially equivalent to the current deduction for state and local income and property taxes. This deduction can be claimed only by the 29 percent of taxpayers who itemize their deductions, who are typically the most affluent of families; the value of the deduction depends on the household's marginal tax rate, which is higher for higher-income households; income tax and property tax, but not sales tax payments, are deductible.[29] Similar parables could be told about the deduction for home mortgage interest, the exclusion of employer-provided health insurance, and a host of other features of the tax code. The point is that these features are enormously popular because they have been enshrined as "tax reductions," but these exact same features probably wouldn't stand a chance as stand-alone policies.

Part of the reason our tax base is a mess has nothing to do with principles; there are strong political and institutional factors that bias the tax system toward greater complexity. Under the current system, being a member of one of the tax-writing congressional committees— either the House Ways and Means Committee or the Senate Finance Committee—is quite a plum. For example, although members of these committees at the time comprised only 10 percent of Congress, in 1985 they received almost a quarter of the Political Action Committee (PAC) money going to Congress.[30] Obviously, one reason their favor is curried is their potential influence over tax policy. If Congress were to bind itself to make no major changes in tax law during the next congressional session, the contributions would start to dry up, these members' lunch and dinner invitations would tail off,[31] and so on.

Once adopted, each element of the tax code, from the home mortgage interest deduction to the depreciation treatment of oil and gas operations, has a strong lobby behind it. But there is usually no well-organized constituency that opposes the complexity that arises from these preferences. Yes, it is true that business groups bemoan complexity and support simplicity, but when push comes to shove, they are quite willing to accept a provision that saves them $100 million in tax even if it means adding a few more staffers and buying some expensive software to do tax and project planning. Yes, taxpayers complain about having to keep records of their charitable contributions in order to deduct them, but they'd be even more unhappy if this deduction were eliminated, and so would the charities themselves.

As a counterbalance to the institutional pressures toward greater complexity, in the past decade several countries have instigated a formal mechanism for introducing compliance costs into tax policy-making. Since 1985, the United Kingdom has required its officials to produce compliance cost assessments (CCAs) for all regulations affecting business, including tax regulations. The Netherlands has required qualitative CCAs for changes in tax legislation since 1985. The New Zealand government has accepted in principle a similar proposal and, in August 1994, the Australian government announced its intention to accompany all future tax legislation with Tax Impact Statements addressing the compliance costs imposed on taxpayers. The United States does not have such procedures, although for the past several years it has published estimated average times of completion for the major tax forms. The IRS has committed itself in its Business Master Plan to reducing the time burden of paperwork from tax compliance by 7 percent and the expense by 3 percent, by fiscal year 2001.

Eliminating all of the "bells and whistles" and starting over with a clean tax base would go a long way toward simplifying the taxpaying process. Chapter 6 will examine the merits of major preferences in our tax code, considering the equity, economic efficiency, as well as simplicity aspects of each one. When all the factors are considered, many of the exceptions to a clean base become much harder to justify. Whether the political system is ready to undertake such a hardheaded analysis remains an open question.

Attempts to Hide Unpopular Policies from the Public

As already discussed, some tax deductions and preferences represent policies that would probably be quite unpopular on their own, but have become very popular, or at least entrenched, as part of the tax code. There are many examples of this general phenomenon throughout our tax system, aside from the definition of the tax base. Each contributes further to the complexity of the taxpaying process.

One classic example is the "phase-outs" of personal exemptions and some itemized deductions for high-income taxpayers that have been introduced in recent years. In almost all cases, these features are exactly equivalent to raising the marginal tax rate a few percentage points in certain income ranges,[32] and so are really just a way of raising tax rates without making it obvious to the public. As a result, many taxpayers must needlessly go through extra calculations that could have been avoided if the true tax rates were directly incorporated into the tax tables.

Opportunities for "Tax Arbitrage"—Transactional Complexity

Whenever the same transaction is taxed differently depending on how it is "packaged," complexity ensues as taxpayers seek to repackage things to their advantage, and the IRS resists. Economists call this "tax arbitrage." For example, taxing the ordinary income of top-bracket taxpayers at 39.6 percent while taxing realized capital gains at 28 percent offers a large reward to converting ordinary income—wages, salaries, interest, and dividends—into capital gains. This can be accomplished in a variety of ways, such as an executive taking a qualified stock option in lieu of extra salary.

The same argument applies to the differential between the corporation tax rate and the individual rate. When the corporate rate is significantly lower than the individual rate, as it was for high-income individuals until 1986, there is an incentive to retain income within corporations as long as possible and to get it to individuals in backdoor, tax-preferred ways. For this reason the border between what is corporate income and what is individual income creates a major source of complexity, as taxpayers seek to recharacterize income to reduce their taxes, and the IRS seeks to limit such behavior.[33]

Finally, many taxpayers are engaging in tax arbitrage in ways they may not even realize. For example, suppose you borrow $2,000 under a home-equity loan, and in the same year make a $2,000 contribution to your IRA account. Together these two transactions produce no net increase in your saving, as they cancel each other out. But the transactions can reduce your taxes, because you get to defer taxes on the $2,000 IRA contribution and its interest until retirement, and can deduct the interest on the home-equity loan all the while. Such features create an incentive to engage in needless and meaningless financial transactions purely for tax reasons, resulting in added costs of compliance and administration.

Attempts to Limit Tax Avoidance and Evasion

Taxpayers can reduce their tax liabilities in a wide variety of ways. As we discussed in the last chapter, the legal ways, such as the use of legitimate itemized deductions or some forms of tax arbitrage, are called "tax avoidance." The illegal ways, such as failing to report income or overstating deductions, are called "tax evasion." Because of the amount of money at stake, people are continuously developing new and ingenious ways of achieving both. Government attempts to curb these activities often make the tax code even more complicated and burdensome. Alternative minimum tax provisions, rules governing corporate foreign-source income, and loss restrictions are examples that often create very large compliance burdens for those who are subject to them, whether or not they contemplated the potential avenues of avoidance. There are countless other examples of very intricate regulations that are geared toward preventing specific tax-reduction strategies.

One way of achieving simplification in this area would be to eliminate or scale back government efforts to curb avoidance and evasion. For example, many economists advocate the elimination of the corporate alternative minimum tax, the objective of which is to put a limit on the tax savings from legitimate tax-reducing activities. But, in some other cases, halting these efforts could have a major cost in terms of additional avoidance, evasion, and tax shelters, making the tax system considerably less fair and less efficient. Another approach that has been suggested would be to remove incentives for government officials to write complicated regulations. Lawyer Schuyler Moore notes "there is a perverse incentive for the draftsmen of Treasury regulations to write the regulations as long and complex as possible. The draftsmen know that they will probably soon be entering private practice, where they can make a lucrative living pontificating on their own regulations."[34] An existing law prohibits former government employees from immediately representing clients on matters regarding the regulations they wrote, but it does not prevent them from profiting by giving advice, making speeches, or writing books. But perhaps the best approach to this problem would be to redesign the tax system so that many of the opportunities for avoidance, arbitrage, and evasion are not there in the first place.

Now that we've examined the issue of complexity in our income tax system, we next address the related issue of evasion and enforcement. Enforcement has become a major issue in the tax reform debate, in part because people are angry at the IRS and its enforcement efforts. The ease with which a tax system can be enforced, without excessive intrusion into people's lives, is a critical characteristic that is worthy of serious consideration. After discussing the issues of evasion and enforcement in our current system, we'll explore the aspects of a tax system that make it relatively easier or harder to enforce, and conclude by discussing the relationship between enforceability and simplicity.

Evasion and Enforcement

Why Enforcement Is Necessary

For many taxpayers, the real problem with the taxpaying process has little to do with filing their returns, and has a lot to do with the fear and hassle of dealing with the IRS. There are few more anxiety-producing words in our language than "audit." Dissatisfaction with the IRS has grown to the point that the centerpiece of some tax reform proposals is to abolish the IRS completely.

As exhilarating an idea as this may sound, living without the IRS is not a real possibility. It is true that, under a radically different tax system, the tax enforcement apparatus could be scaled down, could be focused entirely on businesses, and could even have another name.[35] But, human nature being what it is, it won't work to just announce how to calculate the tax base and what tax rates to apply, and rely on taxpayers' sense of duty to collect over $700 billion of taxes. Some dutiful people will undoubtedly pay what they owe, but many others would not. Over time the ranks of the dutiful will shrink, as they see how they are being taken advantage of by the others.

The tax system cannot rely on voluntary contributions because the benefits of citizenry are not dependent on the payment of taxes. The auto mechanic who on the weekends also does housepainting for cash without reporting it to the IRS still has access to the national parks. The trucker who overstates his expenses on gas will still be protected from attack by our system of national defense. Even if the mechanic, the trucker, and everyone else agree that it's better to have the government collect taxes to provide highways, defense, and everything else the government does, it is still not in any one individual's interest to contribute voluntarily to the government's coffers. Each citizen has a very strong incentive to ride free on the contributions of others, since one's own individual contribution is just a drop in the bucket and doesn't materially affect what one gets back from the government.

For this reason, paying taxes must be made a legal responsibility of citizens. In the United States, failure to pay one's taxes in a timely manner is a civil offense, subject to a variety of penalties. Fraud can expose the citizen to criminal charges and jail sentences, although this is a very rare occurrence. Even in the face of those penalties, substantial evasion persists.

The Case of the Seven Million Vanishing Exemptions

Tax evasion by the wealthy tends to make the headlines. Recall New York hotel queen Leona Helmsley, who was convicted of evading $1.7 million of federal and state taxes,[36] or baseball star Darryl Strawberry, convicted of evading taxes on $500,000 of income from baseball memorabilia shows.[37] But evasion on a smaller scale is also a pervasive phenomenon. A fascinating recent case concerns exemption allowances for dependents. For a long time the IRS had suspected that many taxpayers were claiming exemptions for dependents that either did not exist or did not qualify as dependents under the tax law. One particular IRS employee by the name of John Szilagyi thought that this overstatement was costing the Treasury—and ultimately all other taxpayers—hundreds of millions of dollars each year, and suggested the following change in the tax return: in order to claim an exemption allowance for a dependent over the age of five, you must report the dependent's Social Security number.

When implemented in tax year 1987, the effect of this change was astonishing to everyone, with the possible exception of Mr. Szilagyi himself. Between tax years 1986 and 1987, the number of dependent exemption allowances claimed fell by seven million! This simple change increased tax revenues by about $2.9 billion per year, or approximately $28 per taxpayer. Undoubtedly, a few of the seven million cases represented legitimate dependents whose parents still hadn't gotten around to obtaining their Social Security numbers, and a few others were children who had been improperly claimed by both parents after a divorce. But certainly the great majority represented people who were claiming their dogs as, or simply inventing, dependents.[38]

How Much Tax Evasion Is There?

Probably most people don't have to read such anecdotes about tax evasion to be convinced that it exists. Moreover, reciting anecdotes does not convey any sense about whether tax evasion is a big problem or a little problem. For obvious reasons—would you honestly answer survey questions about tax evasion?—it is difficult to find out just how big a problem tax evasion really is. While it's easy enough to measure how much tax is paid, it is not at all easy to measure what should be paid. Over the years, the Internal Revenue Service has made several efforts to measure what they call the "tax gap," meaning what should be paid but isn't. They come up with their estimates by combining information from a regular program of random, especially intensive audits, known as the Taxpayer Compliance Measurement Program (TCMP),[39] with information from special studies about sources of income, such as tips, that are difficult to uncover even in an intensive audit.

The last thorough tax gap study was for the year 1987. It was estimated that noncompliance with the individual and corporate income taxes cost the Treasury $84.9 billion in that year,[40] or about 15 percent of actual tax liability.[41] A recent IRS extrapolation put the figure at $119 billion for 1992.[42] Extrapolating a bit further would put it in the vicinity of $150 billion for 1995.[43] At an average tax rate on taxable income of around 20 percent, this implies that there is about $750 billion of unreported income and illegitimate deductions. The procedure for estimating the tax gap is an imperfect one, and even the IRS would admit that their measures are only approximations. In addition, some types of evasion that are very difficult to uncover, such as unreported income from illegal activities, are not included in the estimate.[44] But these are the best numbers around.

Figure 5.1 breaks down the aggregate estimate of the tax gap into its components. About one-quarter comes from corporate evasion, and three-quarters comes from personal evasion. The most important form of evasion is underreporting of income by those who file personal tax

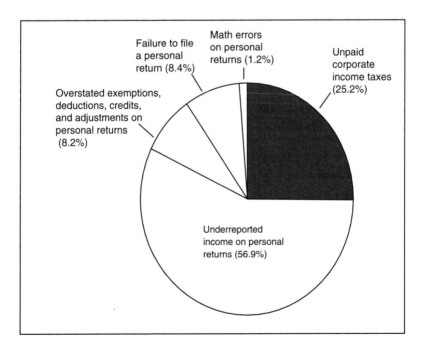

Figure 5.1
Components of the tax gap, 1987
Note: The tax gap is a measure of tax evasion, representing the amount of legal tax liability that is not paid. Estimate excludes illegal-source income and remittance problems.
Source: IRS Research Division (1988).

returns; it accounts for 56.9 percent of the total tax gap. Overstating of exemptions, deductions, adjustments, and credits on personal returns is a significant, but much smaller, problem, accounting for 8.2 percent of the tax gap. People who are required to file a personal return, but do not, cause another 8.4 percent of the gap.

Why Is Tax Evasion a Problem?

For the sake of argument, let's assume there's currently about $150 billion of income tax evasion. Why is this a problem? The answer may appear to be obvious: if evasion vanished, then the deficit could be $150 billion lower than otherwise. Alternatively, we could spend $150 billion more per year to finance health care, job training, child care, infrastructure, and a host of other worthy projects. Or, perhaps the most attractive option of all, federal taxes could be cut by $150 billion; for example, all rates in the personal income tax could be cut by about one-quarter.[45]

But this is not a very satisfactory answer to the question. Reducing the deficit or expanding government programs could be financed in a number of other ways, such as raising tax rates, broadening the income tax base, or adding a new tax or two. A tax reduction could be financed by cuts in overall spending. The real question is whether curbing evasion is superior to alternative methods of achieving our fiscal objectives.

Consider the following hypothetical example. Imagine that all Americans were genetically predisposed to underpay their legal tax liability by 20 percent, sort of the way that most car buyers presume that the actual price of a car is in most cases that much below the sticker price. Thus, a family that initially calculated its true tax liability to be $15,000 would as a matter of course find ways to understate its income so it appeared to owe only $12,000, 20 percent less than $15,000. Similarly, families that legally owe $50,000 fiddle around so that they remit $40,000, and so on. Imagine further that the IRS looked the other way.

In this imaginary world, tax evasion wouldn't matter at all. Government would simply readjust everyone's "sticker price" tax liability upward so that the desired amount of tax would be collected, even after the 20 percent "discount" was taken. Each taxpayer might think that he or she is beating the system, but in fact no one gains compared to a world with no evasion. Evasion is just a shell game that no one wins or loses. In this example, spending money on enforcing the tax laws would be a waste.

Obviously, a lot of things are wrong with this picture as a description of real-life tax evasion, things that turn tax evasion from the benign phenomenon of this imaginary world to one that has real and important implications. First and foremost, not everyone evades tax by the same proportionate amount. There are two sets of reasons why some people may evade a great deal, while others engage in little or no evasion at all. The first are differences in personal characteristics, such as one's intrinsic honesty, one's willingness to gamble, and one's attitudes toward government and the tax system. The second are the opportunities and potential rewards for evasion. As long as people differ in these characteristics or opportunities, evasion can cause serious inequities and inefficiencies.

Evasion creates horizontal inequity because people with equal abilities-to-pay end up paying different amounts. Unlike the imaginary example above, there is no way for tax rates to be adjusted to offset the advantage gained by the evaders, because we don't know which people are evading. Moreover, if opportunities or predilections for evasion were related to one's level of well-being (for instance, if the rich could evade more easily than the poor), then evasion would make it difficult for us to achieve whatever degree of progressivity we deem to be consistent with vertical equity.

A lot of evidence suggests that the world is divided into evaders and nonevaders. According to an IRS-sponsored study in 1979, 42 percent of all returns had some understatement of taxable income.[46] Surveys that have outright asked people about their past tax compliance behavior suggest that between 22 and 28 percent of taxpayers had failed to comply at some point in their lives, and 12 to 20 percent had failed to comply at some point within the past five years.[47] There are obvious reasons why the measured prevalence of compliance would look so much lower in surveys compared to audit-based measures, but what is important here is that a significant fraction of taxpayers comply with the tax law and another significant fraction often do not. This means that, because of tax evasion, some people pay less tax than they ought to, and everyone else pays more.

There is also considerable evidence that evasion depends on opportunities for successful tax evasion, and that these differ widely depending on the circumstances of the taxpayer, including the type of income, occupation, and other factors. The odds that a particular kind of income understatement will be uncovered by the IRS vary from practically zero for a small bit of moonlighting income to very high for wages earned at an established firm that sends the IRS a computer-readable file of all the W–2 forms sent to their employees.

As you would expect, the less the chance of getting caught, the more likely people are to try to get away with tax evasion. This is borne out by the data in Table 5.1, which presents information from the 1987 tax gap study about what percentage of several types of income are actually reported by individuals. It ranges from 99.5 percent for wages and salaries, taxes on which are difficult to evade successfully, down to 41.4 percent for self-employment income. Self-employment includes both formal sole proprietorships and informal work done by sidewalk street vendors, moonlighting craftsmen, unlicensed child-care providers, housepainters, and the like. These are notoriously difficult for the IRS to monitor. Unreported self-employment income from filers alone accounts for a striking 28.7 percent of the overall tax gap. Tip income, which is not shown here, is also very hard for the IRS to find. An earlier study found the reporting rate for tip income to be just 59.8 percent. Other forms of business and capital income in general involve more evasion than wages, salaries, and pension benefits, but less than self-employment income.[48] These facts suggest that significant horizontal inequities persist because of evasion.

The effect of evasion on vertical equity turns out to be less clear. Contrary to what many may suspect, there is some evidence that

Table 5.1
Compliance estimates for selected types of personal income, 1987

Type of personal income	Reported net income as a percentage of true net income from this source (for filers only)	Percentage of total tax gap caused by underreporting of this item by filers
Wages and salaries	99.5	1.7
Pensions and annuities	98.4	0.1
Interest and dividends	94.6	3.8
Capital gains	88.3	7.8
Partnership and S corporation	42.1	3.8
Self-employment income	41.4	28.7

Note: "Total tax gap" refers to all types of evasion for both personal and corporate income taxes, excluding illegal activities and certain remittance problems.
Source: IRS Research Division (1988).

higher-income people actually evade less than those with lower incomes, at least relative to the size of their incomes. Table 5.2 displays the voluntary reporting rates for taxpayers in the 1988 TCMP audit, ranked by income. According to this audit, those with AGIs above $500,000 reported 97.1 percent of their true incomes to the IRS on average, compared to just 78.7 percent for those with AGIs between $5,000 and $10,000. This appears consistent with the old saying among tax professionals, "the poor evade, and the rich avoid," meaning that the rich tend to reduce their taxes through legal "avoidance" measures such as deductions, exclusions, tax arbitrage, and loopholes, while those with lower incomes attempt more outright evasion.

In addition to compromising the equitable sharing of tax burdens, evasion imposes economic costs. Other things being equal, evasion raises tax rates, which will penalize extra work and thrift by honest taxpayers. This is partially offset by lower effective tax rates on the evaders, but not enough to fully make up for the loss. More important, because tax evasion depends on opportunities that are tied to particular activities, it provides an incentive—which is inefficient from a social point of view—to engage in those activities for which it is relatively easy to evade taxes.

Consider the market for housepainting, in which many deals are cash only, in order to facilitate tax evasion. Because the income from housepainting is hard for the IRS to detect, this occupation is more attractive than otherwise. The supply of eager housepainters bids

Table 5.2
Voluntary compliance rates by income, 1988

Adjusted gross income range (dollars)	Voluntary compliance rate (reported income as a percentage of true income)
0–5,000	84.2
5,000–10,000	78.7
10,000–25,000	88.8
25,000–50,000	92.4
50,000–100,000	93.2
100,000–250,000	91.3
250,000–500,000	95.7
Over 500,000	97.1

Source: Christian (1994), based on 1988 TCMP.

down the market price of a housepainting job. Thus, the amount of taxes evaded overstates the benefit of being a tax-evading housepainter. The biggest loser in this game is the honest housepainter, who sees his or her wages bid down by the competition, but who dutifully pays taxes.

Although a supply of eager and cheap housepainters undoubtedly seems like a boon to prospective buyers of that service, in fact it is a symptom of an economic cost of tax evasion—the work of the extra people drawn to housepainting, or any activity that facilitates tax evasion, would have higher value in some alternative occupation. This is just an example of the principle discussed in Chapter 4, that deviations from a uniform tax system, uniformly enforced, have economic costs. While this may seem like an esoteric point, there are so many activities like this that the cost to the economy may in fact be very large. University of Colorado economist James Alm has estimated that our nation is worse off by $100 billion or more because too many resources are diverted into both legal and illegal activities on which it is easy to evade taxes.[49]

From the discussion above, it's clear that widespread evasion endangers the fairness of how we tax ourselves and has a substantial economic cost. The existence of an enforcement agency like the IRS is a necessity for any tax system, and is certainly so for our current one.

How the IRS Enforces the Current Tax System

When most people think of IRS enforcement, they think of the dreaded tax audit. But many are surprised to learn that the IRS now typically audits only about 1 percent of all individual tax returns; in 1994, the figure was 1.1 percent.[50] This fraction has declined dramatically in the last three decades; it was typically about 4 percent during the 1960s.[51] However, in 1995 a special initiative was launched to temporarily increase the number of audits, which should push the audit rate up closer to 2 percent for that year only.[52]

Does this mean that if you file a tax return and omit reporting your wages or capital gains, you have a 1 or 2 percent chance of being caught in the act? Absolutely not, for several reasons.

First of all, the IRS does not just pick out of a hat which returns to audit, so that yours has as good (or bad) a chance as anyone else's. Instead, the probability a return will be examined is determined by a carefully developed secret formula, called the "discriminant index function," or DIF. This formula assigns a score to each return reflecting the estimated likelihood and expected magnitude of noncompliance for that taxpayer, based on reported personal characteristics and the amounts stated on the return for each type of income and deduction. Returns that fit the profile of those that have a significant dollar amount of evasion are the most likely to be examined. For example, in 1992, the fraction of returns audited was about .6 percent for people with incomes between $25,000 and $50,000, but 4.9 percent for those with incomes above $100,000.[53] Among very large corporations, nearly every single one is audited by a team of IRS examiners, which often is given office space within the corporation to facilitate what is essentially a continual audit process.

Second, audits are by no means the only way the IRS checks on the accuracy of tax returns. A very important tool for the IRS is *information reporting*. For example, employers are required to send information reports on wages and salaries for all their employees to the IRS. The IRS computers then match up most of these information reports against tax returns. If there is a discrepancy, a computer-generated notice is automatically sent out to the taxpayer asking him or her to pay up or provide an explanation. Most interest and dividend income and pensions are also subject to information reporting. It is therefore no accident that these types of income, together with wages and salaries, have near 100 percent compliance rates, as reported in Table 5.1. Each year the IRS matches about one billion information reports with taxpayer filing, and sends out about five million notices.[54] The increased use of computer checks based on information reporting has clearly substituted for the decline in face-to-face audits.

A third major enforcement tool of the IRS is withholding of taxes on wage and salary income, a practice it has followed since 1943. All firms above a certain size are required to deduct payroll taxes and personal income taxes from wage and salary income, and then remit them directly to the IRS. About 70 percent of net personal income tax revenues are withheld in this manner.[55] The amount withheld is usually greater than actual tax liability over the course of the year, so the vast majority of individual taxpayers (78 percent in 1992) are eligible for a refund.[56] This creates an added incentive for taxpayers to file their returns in a timely manner. Together, information reporting and withholding are very powerful enforcement mechanisms. Without them, reporting of wages and salaries might not be much different from self-employment income, which, as discussed earlier, has a voluntary reporting rate of around 40 percent.

One additional way the IRS makes sure the proper tax liability gets paid is by helping taxpayers understand and comply with the tax law. There is a substantial segment of the population that would ideally like to comply with the tax laws, but does not because they do not understand what is expected of them, or are frustrated with the process. For this reason, the IRS makes help available over the phone, undertakes education and outreach programs, sets up installment payment plans for people who have been noncompliant in the past, and has even set up an Internet site. Encouraging more voluntary compliance is a central element of the *Compliance 2000* program, a major initiative recently undertaken by the IRS to modernize and improve the enforcement process.

Why More Enforcement May Not Be the Answer

A tax gap of around $150 billion seems awfully large, and this doesn't even include tax evasion on illegal activities. With so much tax cheating going on out there, why not increase enforcement, making the tax system fairer and more efficient, and then use that money to reduce the deficit, cut tax rates, or achieve some other laudable goal? The answer is that although extra enforcement may indeed bring many benefits, we must also consider the costs. Just as stationing a police officer at every corner would certainly reduce street crime, more audits and higher penalties could almost certainly make a big dent in tax evasion. But as a society we choose not to have police everywhere, nor to impose the death penalty for minor infractions. We tolerate some level of crime because we judge that the benefits of eliminating it would not outweigh the costs required; the same is true of the crime of tax evasion.

Would the benefits of extra enforcement by the IRS outweigh the costs? Consider that one analysis of TCMP audit data suggested that for every extra dollar the IRS spends on auditing returns, it could gain between four and seven dollars of additional revenue directly from the audited returns.[57] Such yields could not be achieved immediately, because time would be needed to train new agents, but it is quite plausible that eventually they could be realized. This may even underestimate the potential yield, because it doesn't take into account the deterrent effect of extra enforcement the expanded audit coverage probably would persuade some people that were not audited to become more compliant.

While a four- or seven-to-one ratio of extra revenues to spending is certainly very impressive, it is important to recognize that this is not a comparison of all the costs and benefits of engaging in extra enforcement, and therefore we should not jump to the conclusion that tax enforcement ought to be vastly expanded. There is an "apples-and-oranges" fallacy lurking here. The expenditure on expanded IRS enforcement activities certainly represents a real resource cost to the country—the auditors and computers could be used elsewhere in the economy to produce valuable goods and services. But the increased revenue from greater enforcement does not by itself represent a gain to the economy. Seven dollars handed from a taxpayer to the IRS does not create seven new dollars worth of goods and services. It is merely a transfer from private to public hands, which could be achieved in any number of alternative ways, such as raising tax rates.

That is not to say that there aren't social benefits of increased tax enforcement. These benefits, including a more efficient and equitable tax system, were discussed above. But the benefits are not at all well measured by the extra revenue more enforcement will produce, and are less concrete than dollar revenue.

Critics of increased enforcement point to the social costs associated with enforcement. For every anecdote about flagrant tax evasion, there is another about heavy-handed IRS handling of a taxpayer.[58] Many are concerned about the intrusiveness of the IRS into their lives. Balancing the rights of taxpayers against the desire for an equitably enforced tax system raises critical issues of, among other things, privacy. Many Americans do not want the IRS to get too good at its job, and legitimately object to procedures that would facilitate enforcement of the tax law.

Recently, there has been a movement to reduce the social costs of IRS enforcement, including attempts to enact a "Taxpayer Bill of Rights" that would try to limit the IRS's ability to hassle taxpayers. The IRS has already begun to adopt some of the proposals, in advance of any law changes.[59] For example, more of the burden of verifying disputed figures on a tax return will be placed on IRS agents, instead of the taxpayer. An IRS ombudsman will be given more authority to act on the behalf of taxpayers to resolve disputes. While reductions in the social costs of enforcement are welcome, at some point there is a trade-off between this and the ability of the IRS to do its job.

Taking all the relevant factors into account, it's difficult to come to any hard and fast conclusion about whether the current level of enforcement is about right, or whether it should be increased or decreased. A more fruitful pursuit, which is discussed next, is to consider what elements of a tax system make it harder to enforce than others. These should serve as important guidelines to keep in mind if we really want a tax system that is administered fairly and requires less intrusion into our lives.

What Makes Taxation Difficult to Enforce?

The Absence of Withholding and Information Reporting

Evidence from our existing tax system makes abundantly clear that enforcing the tax code is much easier for both the IRS and the taxpayer with information reporting, and especially with tax withholding at the source of payment. For types of income where these are not used, evasion is much more common. Moreover, the IRS is forced to monitor and investigate more frequently the people who earn these types of income. Changes to the tax code that make it easier to implement information reporting and withholding for more types of income (for example, a single rate) can also make it considerably easier to enforce.

Taxing Individuals Instead of Taxing at the Business Level

Just as it is more complicated to tax income or consumption at the individual instead of the firm level, so too can it be harder to enforce. Taxing at the business level makes information reporting and withholding easier to implement. Moreover, it takes fewer resources to examine, say, 1 percent of businesses than it would to audit 1 percent of individuals, because there are so many fewer businesses than individuals.

Lack of Incentives to Comply

Compliance with taxation is also low when there is little incentive to comply. The threat of audit and penalties for noncompliance provide one kind of incentive, but there are others as well. For example, the fact that most U.S. personal income taxpayers receive a refund gives them a strong incentive to file their forms. Another example is the operation of most VATs throughout the world. In the event of an audit, a business that claims a credit or deduction for an input purchased from another firm must be able to prove that the other firm paid tax on it. So each firm has some incentive to make sure other firms are complying. Whenever incentives of this sort can be worked into the tax system, enforceability is improved.

High Tax Rates

At first blush the most direct cause of tax evasion is high tax rates. To lower evasion, therefore, one could simply lower tax rates. This is not so simple, though, when a fixed amount of revenue must be raised. So the relevant question is whether evasion would be curtailed if marginal tax rates were reduced, holding revenues constant, either by making the system less progressive or broadening the base. In either case the quantitative evidence is not decisive. Even on theoretical grounds, the argument that lower rates reduce evasion is not certain. If penalties for detected evasion are proportional to the understated tax, then lowering the tax rate automatically lowers the penalty, making the effect on evasion indeterminate.[60] Furthermore, for some kinds of evasion, such as nonfiling, the marginal tax rate is immaterial, because the entire tax liability is at stake.

Deductions, Credits, and Exemptions

While deductions, credits, and exemptions are not the major source of evasion in our tax system, they are important. It is unfortunately common for people to overstate deductions for things such as charitable contributions or medical expenses. The fewer of these items that there are, the fewer opportunities there are to overstate them. Moreover, the enforcement authority would be able to devote more of its limited resources to other pursuits, such as verifying whether income has been reported properly.

Trying to Tax Things That Are Easy to Hide

Much of the tax evasion in our country occurs on types of income that are easy to hide. Self-employment income is the most important example. Some types of capital income are also relatively easy to conceal, at least when compared to wages and salaries. One thing that could make the tax system considerably easier to enforce would be to simply give up on trying to tax some of these types of income. For example, a sales tax, VAT, or flat tax would no longer attempt to tax capital income; furthermore, most VAT systems exempt from tax all businesses below a certain size. In some ways, this is similar to the argument that the problem of drug crime could be eliminated by legalizing drugs—in this case, the crime is evading taxes on capital income, which could be eliminated by making this income tax exempt. It will be considered later whether such an approach is fair or efficient overall, but it would at the very least improve horizontal equity between honest and dishonest people who earn capital income. Even solutions of this kind have enforcement problems of their own, though, particularly when they are piecemeal. For example, eliminating all tax on difficult-to-enforce capital gains would greatly increase the incentive to convert ordinary income into capital gains, and put more, rather than less, pressure on enforcement.

Public Perceptions of Complexity and Unfairness

A complex tax system makes it more difficult for taxpayers to comply with the rules. It is also frustrating, and puts people in less of a mood to comply. Moreover, if people feel that other taxpayers are taking advantage of complexity to avoid paying their "fair share," it may make them feel less morally obligated to pay their own taxes honestly. Evidence from surveys provides some support for this notion, although the findings are mixed.[61]

These have been major selling points of the advocates of simpler alternatives to the income tax such as the flat tax, and they no doubt have some merit. Simplifying the tax code could well improve people's attitudes toward compliance. But it's important to remember that we can't rely entirely on public goodwill. It's unclear whether, by itself, moving to a streamlined tax system that is perceived to be fairer would have a dramatic impact on compliance, and it certainly wouldn't eliminate the need for an enforcement authority, as some have implied.

Lack of Documentation and Low Audit Coverage

The more taxpayers are required to document their incomes and deductions, the easier it is to enforce the tax system. The current requirement that a Social Security number be provided for each dependent exemption is one particularly effective example. But most types of deductions, such as those for charitable contributions or employee business expenses, are generally reported without any documentation. If the taxpayer is audited, he or she must provide the documentation, but recall that audits are quite rare. Requiring documentation for more items would make evasion much more difficult. A potentially even more effective approach would be to have the IRS check most or all returns, requiring taxpayers to provide some justification for each item. This may seem far-fetched, but in the Netherlands, the tax authority actually audits every single personal income tax return at least briefly every year.[62]

In contrast to many of the other points discussed above, more documentation and auditing could make the taxpaying process considerably more complicated for both the taxpayer and the IRS, although it would no doubt cut down on evasion. In this case there is a clear trade-off among the multiple objectives of tax policy. In other situations there is substantial flexibility in transferring the costs of enforcement from the government budget to the private sector. For example, requiring more documentation of taxpayers who make some personal use of a business car may facilitate an audit, but it certainly increases the taxpayers' cost of compliance. For a given degree of enforcement effectiveness, whether this is a good idea depends on whether the sum of these costs declines. Shifting the costs off the budget onto the taxpayers does not necessarily constitute an improved process.

Conclusion

Simplicity and enforceability are both important goals for a tax system. In some cases, such as documentation and auditing, efforts to achieve one of these goals are costly in terms of the other. But in many cases, elements of the design of the tax system can foster both goals. For example, settling for rough justice and getting rid of all of the bells and whistles in the tax code would clean up the tax base, making the system simpler and easier to enforce. More dramatic changes such as moving to a single rate or changing to an impersonalized consumption tax base could also help, especially to the extent that they would allow wider use of withholding and less involvement of individuals in the taxpaying process. The simplicity and enforcement benefits of these approaches are a major reason why they are often at the heart of radical tax reform proposals. Of course each of these changes could effect some improvement even if we reject the others.

Now that we have covered all of the major criteria by which to evaluate a tax system—fairness, promotion of economic prosperity, simplicity, and enforceability—we can move on to consider the important features of fundamental reform proposals, and then examine the specific proposals themselves. As we have seen in the past three chapters, there are often conflicts and trade-offs among the various criteria. More progressivity generally is accompanied by greater disincentives to work and otherwise seek economic advancement. More fine-tuning of the tax burden has a cost of complexity. The most radical and most simplifying tax reform options abandon or sharply reduce progressivity, and eliminate all or nearly all personalization of the tax burden. Because each reform proposal strikes a different balance among these criteria, how these trade-offs are made is a major theme of the remainder of this book.

6   Elements of Fundamental Reform

Tax reform proposals fall into two categories—those that accept the current income tax structure as a good starting point, and seek to improve that structure; and those that want to abandon the income tax entirely for something quite different. The next chapter takes a close look at some of these proposals and, using the principles developed in Chapters 3, 4, and 5, evaluates their likely impact and assesses their advantages and disadvantages. This chapter identifies the common elements of many of these plans.

A useful starting point for this exercise is to ponder the buzzword of the day, "flat" taxes. Most, though not all, reform proposals now bill themselves as flat taxes. This is true in spite of the fact that they differ tremendously from each other, and in spite of the fact that some of them are not noticeably flat in any particular dimension.

That flatness has been elevated to the highest compliment to be paid to a tax structure is a bit surprising, if only because in other contexts "flat" is not always a good thing. Just think of beer, musical notes, or tires. *Webster's Unabridged Dictionary* lists 16 major definitions for flat as an adjective, ranging from praiseworthy ones such as "level" and "exact" to much less attractive ones, including "shallow," "dull and stupid," "commercially inactive," and even "having no money." In the context of taxation, the word flat conjures up Webster's definition of "not varying." But even that is open to multiple interpretations.

What exactly is a flat tax? There are three distinct dimensions of flat taxes—a single tax rate, a consumption tax base, and a clean tax base. The single rate is what most people pick up on, but the other two dimensions represent even more radical change in the way we tax ourselves. Some proposals seek flattening in all three dimensions; other plans focus on only one or two aspects of flatness. This chapter will explore each of these aspects of flatness, one at a time.

A Single Rate

The most eye-catching feature of flat taxes is, of course, the flat *rate*. In place of our current system of graduated tax rates that increase with higher incomes, all, or most, taxpayers would be subject to a single rate of tax. While a truly flat-rate tax would apply the single rate to the entire tax base, from the first dollar to the last, flat tax proposals usually exempt a certain amount of the base, be it income or consumption, from taxation. For that reason they are really a form of graduated tax, with an initial bracket to which a zero tax rate applies, plus an open-ended bracket subject to a single tax rate. Under such a system, the average tax rate increases gradually as the tax base increases, and the degree of progressivity can be varied by adjusting the level of tax-exempt income and the tax rate.

To distinguish this aspect of flatness from the others, we will refer to a tax system with this characteristic as a single-rate tax. Abandoning the graduation of tax rates for a single rate can be accomplished independently of any and all of the changes in the tax base, to be discussed below, that are usually associated with flat taxes. A single rate can just as easily be applied to a narrow, preference-ridden base as to a broad, clean base, and it can be applied to all of incomes or just to the portion we consume. Similarly, we can certainly clean up the tax base while maintaining graduated rates, and there are also ways of implementing a consumption tax that allow us to preserve graduated rates.

The first thing to note is that saying we're moving to a flat rate, but not specifying which flat rate, doesn't by itself tell us that much about how the distribution of tax burdens is going to change. Consider the following illustration. Figure 6.1 shows average tax rates for married couples with two children who take the standard deduction, both under the current system and under two single-rate alternatives (the EITC is not taken into account). Line X shows the pattern of average rates under the current system. Under 1996 law, the combination of the standard deduction and four exemptions means that no tax is due on income below $16,900. After that the marginal tax rate is 15 percent until $56,900, 28 percent until $113,600, 31 percent until $164,250, 36 percent until $280,075, and 39.6 percent for any additional income. Under this system, average tax rates rise fairly steadily as income rises, so that the better-off bear a proportionally higher burden than the worse off.

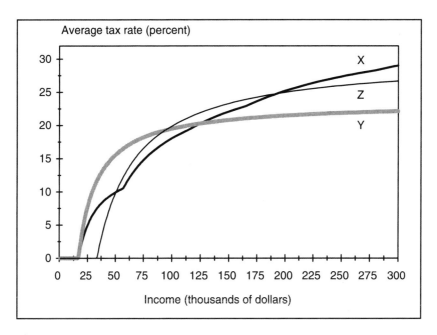

Figure 6.1
Average tax rates for a married couple with two children, under current law and two single-rate alternatives
Note: X = Current federal personal income tax (1996).
Y = Maintain current tax base, replace graduated rates with a single 23.5 percent rate.
Z = Double the standard deduction and personal exemption, and replace graduated rates with a single 30.1 percent rate.
Income is defined here as taxable income plus the standard deduction and personal exemption. Average tax rate is defined as personal income tax before credits as a percentage of income for those who take the standard deduction. Each alternative is estimated to raise the same amount of revenue from all married couples with two children, based on authors' calculations from the 1991 IRS Individual Model File public-use database projected to 1996.

Now suppose we keep the same standard deduction, personal exemption, and tax base (itemized deductions and all) as we have now, but switch to a single rate that raises the same amount of money from four-person families as the current system does.[1] By our calculations, a 23.5 percent rate would be required. Line Y shows what happens to the distribution of tax burdens. Because of the tax-exempt level of income, the average rate doesn't rise to 23.5 percent right away. This flat-rate scheme is still progressive, because people with lower incomes face lower average tax rates. But it is substantially less progressive than the current system. The average rate rises quickly, so that everyone with incomes between $16,900 and $125,000 faces a higher tax liability than they do now, and then flattens, so that everyone above that level gets a tax cut.

Alternatively, suppose we doubled the personal exemption and standard deduction, so that $33,800 of income is exempt from tax for married couples with two children. To raise the same amount of revenue from these families, we would now have to set the single rate at 30.1 percent.[2] Under this approach, depicted by line Z, the single rate produces a tax distribution that is actually *more* progressive than the current one in certain ranges. Everyone below $50,000 now faces a *lower* average rate. Those between $50,000 and $190,000 face a slightly higher burden, and those with incomes above that face a lower burden. What the graph doesn't show is that, at very high incomes, there is a large tax cut. For example, at $1 million of income, the average rate would be 29.1 percent, compared to 36.4 percent under the existing system.

Our point is that it is possible to move to a single rate without throwing progressivity completely out the window. A single rate and a large exemption could in principle raise the same revenue as the current system, and result in a lower burden on low-income people, a somewhat higher burden on a broad swath of the middle, and lower rates on the rich.

The fact that the revenue-neutral single rates are so high in this example highlights the importance of a clean base to the attractiveness of the single rate. If we want to achieve the kind of rates currently being discussed for a flat tax, we have to give up most or all of the cherished itemized deductions and other preferences enshrined in the tax base. Moreover, a clean base enables a single rate to achieve considerably more progressivity than a messy base, because the deductions and preferences benefit high-income people most of all.

Even so, it is practically impossible to get a single rate to replicate the current tax burden on people with very high incomes. As a result, somebody else will have to pay more in taxes, at least in the short run. Some have argued that the flat tax appeals to many people because they think it will make the rich pay *more* in taxes. This is almost certainly not true. As shown in Chapter 3, despite all the loopholes and deductions in the current system, people with very high incomes pay taxes that are a much higher percentage of their incomes than everyone else does. This is true even under a very broad definition of income that includes almost everything that doesn't get included under our current tax code. And recall from Chapter 5 that evasion is by no means entirely an upper-class pursuit. Abandoning graduated rates will lower the tax burdens on very high-income people, even if we get rid of every loophole and every bit of evasion there is. Objections that cutting tax rates on the rich will *increase* the amount of tax they pay need to be taken with a heavy dose of salt. As we discussed in Chapter 4, high-income people have been paying more in taxes in recent years because their incomes have surged, but there are many reasons why this happened other than the tax cuts they received in 1986.

In practice, most of the advocates of a flat tax are also advocates of a flat, *low* tax rate, usually in the high teens or low twenties. If the system is to raise enough revenue, this low a rate requires that the exemption level not be set at too high a level, making it even more likely that tax liability will be shifted away from the highest income classes. As will be discussed later, flat tax proposals that feature a low rate *and* a high exemption level often raise much less revenue than the current system.

So why go to a single rate? Many arguments and much evidence relevant to this question have been discussed so far in the book. Perhaps the most commonly cited reason is to improve economic incentives. High marginal rates discourage work and saving and can cause a whole host of other economic distortions and inefficiencies, which were discussed in Chapter 4. A graduated rate structure means higher marginal rates, and inevitably higher economic costs, so there is a trade-off between progressivity and economic prosperity. However, as shown in Chapter 4, these costs are uncertain, but are almost certainly not as high as they are often made out to be by many political advocates of a flat rate. Other things being equal, lower marginal rates are better for the economy, but economics reveals nothing magical about a single rate. The economic cost of having two low marginal rates, say 15 percent and 25 percent, is not likely to be significantly higher than the cost of a single 20 percent rate.

Some argue that *only* a single-rate tax structure is "neutral" toward distributional issues, and avoids "class warfare." By advocating a single rate, they suggest they are transcending the controversy over "fairness" and are promoting the system that maximizes economic performance. This is a fallacious argument. The only tax system that would truly eliminate all the economic costs of taxation is a lump-sum tax (that is, a poll tax), in which tax *liability*, not the tax *rate*, is the same for everyone, rich or poor. In place of income taxes, we could have a fixed annual charge of $4,000 per adult, whether that adult is Bill

Gates, a homeless person, or yourself.[3] This eliminates any tax penalty tied to work, saving, or investing. Presumably, the reason that the proponents of a single-rate tax prefer it to a lump-sum tax is that they find the latter abjectly unfair (or else they are too timid to admit the opposite.) Thus, the single-rate tax structure already reflects a balancing between equity and efficiency. A two-rate structure reflects another balancing, as does a lump-sum tax. We can argue about how best to make this balancing, but no tax system avoids this inevitable trade-off.

When it comes to simplicity and enforceability, on the other hand, there is indeed something special about a single rate. But, as discussed in Chapter 5, it's not what most people think. Applying the tax rate(s) to your taxable income in order to calculate how much you owe is actually the least complicated part of the whole taxpaying process. Most people can just look it up in a table, in which case it doesn't matter at all whether there are 1, 2, or 20 rates.

Rather, the real advantage is that when there is only one tax rate, it doesn't matter so much whether taxes are remitted at the personal or the business level. Accepting a single rate could allow us to move to a much simpler, business-based system of collecting taxes, such as a value-added tax; although simpler, this would represent a very radical reshuffling of tax burdens. Even if some taxation continues at the personal level in order to further adjust tax burdens for ability-to-pay, as under a flat tax, a single rate still makes it easier to calculate and withhold taxes at the business level, a major simplification and enforcement advantage. This is a key to having tax returns on postcards. Reducing the disparity of tax rates (not the same thing as the number of rates) also reduces the incentives for individuals to shift taxable income from high-rate to low-rate taxable entities, and from high-tax to low-tax periods; this too serves to dampen tax complexity.

While these are all important advantages, it's debatable whether they're worth the distributional consequences of a flat rate. Moreover, making the personal exemption large enough to maintain a strong degree of progressivity, or even adding another rate on top of the main flat rate, doesn't entirely destroy the simplicity advantages. The United Kingdom greatly simplified its income tax system by moving to a single rate for most people and improving its withholding system, but still retained a higher marginal rate at the top. And keeping the same *top* rate across individuals, businesses, and different types of income eliminates most of the opportunities for complex avoidance schemes, even if there are graduated rates below that top rate.

Whether to adopt a single rate is perhaps the most visible aspect of the tax reform debate. The two other main elements—a consumption base and a clean base—are sometimes lost in the shuffle. But in some ways these represent much more dramatic and unprecedented changes in the way we tax ourselves than does altering the rate structure, which we do all the time. As these next two elements are reviewed, keep in mind that each can be achieved independently of what rate structure we choose, and can be achieved independently of each other as well.

A Consumption Base

The second element of many fundamental tax reform plans, a consumption rather than income-based tax, is not commonly associated (by noneconomists) with flatness. But to economists, a consumption tax imposes a uniform, call it flat if you like, tax on current consumption and future consumption. In contrast, an income tax, because it taxes the return to saving, makes consumption in the future more expensive than consumption now.

What Is a Consumption Tax?

For some readers, the word "consumption" may conjure up memories of their introductory college economics class, where they may have first encountered consumption as being something other than an old-fashioned word for tuberculosis. Consumption is just economists' language for what people do when they use up goods and services. A consumption tax simply means that the "tax base" (what is taxed) is consumption, as opposed to income, wealth, or any other indicator of well-being.

There are multiple ways to measure consumption. For a family or the country as a whole, annual income is equal to annual consumption plus saving. This suggests that, for taxation purposes, consumption can either be measured directly or, alternatively, by first measuring income and then subtracting saving. Leaving aside foreign trade and budget deficits (they don't change the basic insight), saving equals investment, and total output equals total income in the economy. So another way of measuring consumption is output minus investment.

Chapter 1 outlined a number of different approaches to taxing consumption, each of which has been proposed as a replacement for our current income tax system. These include a retail sales tax, a VAT, the Hall-Rabushka flat tax, and a personal consumption tax. What they all have in common is that, in the aggregate, the tax base is consumption, measured in one of the ways described above. Each approach differs in how it *appears* to divide that tax base up among consumers, workers, and businesses since different people write the checks. However, as explained in Chapter 3, who writes the checks is irrelevant to who ultimately bears the burden of the tax and to what are its economic effects.

The next chapter will explain in detail how the particular approaches to consumption taxation work, how they are alike, and how they differ from each other. This chapter will address the common features of consumption taxes, and examine how they differ from taxes based on income.

Consumption Taxes and the Incentive to Save

The key distinction between an income tax and a consumption tax is that income taxes have a negative impact on the incentive to save, whereas consumption taxes do not. That the latter is true is a fairly subtle result, but one that is very important to understand. The easiest way to see this is to consider an example. Suppose you get a $100 raise at work, and are trying to decide whether to spend it today or to put in the bank and save it for next year at a 10 percent interest rate. If there were no taxes, you'd have a choice between consuming the $100 today or saving it so you have $110 next year, a 10 percent reward for saving.

First, consider how things change when there's a 20 percent income tax. If you choose to spend your raise immediately, you'll get to consume $80—your take-home pay after the income tax. If you decide instead to save it, your $80 will earn an extra $8 in interest. However, an income tax subjects that interest to taxation as well. After taxes, you only get $6.40 in interest—so your choice is between consuming $80 today or $86.40 next year. The income tax thus reduces your reward for saving from 10 percent to 8 percent.

Now consider what happens when there is a consumption tax of 20 percent. If you spend your $100 raise today, you pay a 20 percent tax immediately, so you get to consume $80 after taxes, just like you would under the income tax. But if instead you save that income, you get to put all $100 in the bank. Because it earns 10 percent interest, you'll have $110 in the bank next year. When you finally do spend that money, you pay a 20 percent tax, leaving you with 80 percent of $110, or $88, to spend. So, under the consumption tax, your choice is between consuming $80 today and consuming $88 in a year. Thus, the reward for saving is still 10 percent, exactly what it would be in the absence of any tax at all.

This is what economists mean when they say that a consumption tax is "neutral" between current and future consumption—the terms of the choice between consumption today and consumption in the future are the same as they would be in the absence of taxes. In our example, you get the 10 percent reward under the consumption tax, just like you would if there were no taxes, while the income tax leaves you with only an 8 percent reward for saving. Our example is admittedly very simplified, but complicating it in any number of ways would not change the basic result. For example, if a larger number of time periods were considered or inflation were introduced, a consumption tax would *still* have no effect on the reward for saving.

At the business level, the difference between an income tax and a consumption tax is that the former only allows deductions for capital goods as they "depreciate" (wear out), while the latter allows the cost of investment goods to be deducted in full immediately, which is known as "expensing." With depreciation deductions, the tax base is total output minus depreciation, or in other words, consumption plus net new investment—both of which add up to net income (where "net" here simply means "subtracting out depreciation"). With expensing, the tax base is total output minus *all* investment, which equals consumption. Modifying our example a bit can show why expensing removes taxation's impact on the incentive to invest in the same way as it eliminates the impact on the return to saving.

Suppose you're the owner of a small business that has just earned a $100 profit. You could pay that $100 to yourself today as say, a dividend. Alternatively, suppose you could spend that money on a machine that will next year produce goods that are worth 10 percent more than the cost of the machine. After producing the goods, it immediately breaks down, becoming useless.

Under either an income or consumption type of business tax, if you pay the profit to yourself today, it will be subject to tax—if the tax rate is 20 percent, you get to pay yourself an $80 dividend after-tax. The difference is in what happens if you buy the machine. Under the income tax, you would still pay a 20 percent tax on your $100 profit today, even if you were to buy the machine; there is no deduction because the machine hasn't worn out yet. So you have $80 left over to spend on such a machine, which will produce $88 in goods for you in the future. Next year, you will have $8 in taxable income—$88 in sales, minus an $80 deduction for depreciation. You would pay .2 × 8 = $1.60 in tax next year, leaving you with $86.40 to pay yourself as a dividend. So the business income tax leaves you with the choice of $80 today or $86.40 next year if you invest—reducing the reward to investing from 10 percent to 8 percent, just as in the personal saving example.

The business consumption tax, on the other hand, has no effect on the reward for investing. If you decide to buy the machine, you get to deduct the full purchase price immediately, so the $100 machine has a net-of-tax cost of $80. Next year, you'll have $110 in sales, but no depreciation deductions. After paying 20 percent taxes on that $110, you will have $88 dollars left to pay yourself in dividends. So under the consumption business tax, your choice is between $80 today and $88 next year—a 10 percent return, just as you would receive in the absence of taxes. Although our example could be made more complicated, for instance by allowing the machine to depreciate over several years, this would not change the basic conclusion that "expensing" makes the rate of return to investment the same as it would be in the absence of taxes.

The Long-Run Equivalence of a Consumption Tax and a Wage Tax

There is another way to eliminate the effect of taxes on the incentive to save and invest—tax wages (or more broadly, labor income) while exempting from tax all interest and other returns to saving. Extending our example to this case is straightforward. Under a 20 percent wage tax, when you earn $100, you receive $80 after tax. Saving it at a 10 percent interest rate would give you $88 next year, and there's no tax on the interest. So just like a consumption tax, the wage tax gives you a choice of consuming $80 today or $88 in a year. Not only is there no impact on the incentive to save—it remains at 10 percent—but the amount you get to consume after-tax is exactly the same in both periods under either the wage tax or the consumption tax.

For these reasons, it is often said that a consumption tax and a wage tax are equivalent. But, in considering the transition to one or the other, there is one very important distinction between them. The adoption of a consumption tax imposes a burden on pre-existing wealth, whereas the adoption of a wage tax does not. Because of this difference, the two would be exactly equivalent only if we were starting society over from scratch. This is a crucial distinction that will be explained in more detail later. But, regardless of the transitional effects, neither a consumption tax nor a wage tax reduces the incentive to save.

Consumption Taxes and the Incentive to Work

One thing that consumption taxes, wage taxes, and income taxes all share is that they reduce the reward to working (the quantity of goods and services that can be purchased per hour of work). The reward to working can be reduced in either of two ways. One is to lower take-home pay, holding fixed the prices of the things you buy. The other is to increase the prices of everything you buy, keeping take-home pay the same. As long as you end up spending all the money you earn, one has just the same effect as the other. A 20 percent tax on wages and salaries is just as bad as a 20 percent sales tax, assuming both are equally comprehensive.[4]

It is sometimes argued that a consumption or wage tax actually reduces the incentive to work *more* than an income tax does. The argument goes like this. Either total consumption or total wages is smaller than the total amount of income. Therefore the tax rates required to raise a given amount of revenue must be higher under a consumption or wage tax than under an income tax with an equally clean base. The problem with this argument is that eliminating the tax on the return to saving *increases* the reward for working, which helps offset the effect of the higher marginal tax rates over a lifetime. In other words, because a consumption or wage tax allows you to earn higher after-tax returns on the portion of your labor income that you save, working becomes more financially attractive.[5]

Is a Consumption Tax More or Less Fair Than an Income Tax?

On a year-by-year basis, a consumption-based tax appears to be much more regressive than an income tax with the same rate structure, because people who have low incomes in any given year on average consume a very high fraction of their incomes, while people with high incomes in a given year save a relatively larger portion of theirs.[6] The apparent conclusion is that shifting to a consumption tax would greatly increase the tax burden on low-income people relative to high-income people.

However, comparing the distribution of tax burdens under an income tax and a consumption tax by looking at a snapshot of income-saving patterns for a single year of data significantly overstates the regressivity of the consumption tax, for a number of reasons. First of all, in any given year there are people with temporarily low income who have maintained a level of spending corresponding to their usual income; conversely, there are people who had an exceptionally good income-earning year who, not expecting their good fortune to continue, keep their spending well below their income, saving up for the years of relatively bad fortune. In both cases, one year's income is not a good measure of how well-off those people really are, and the fact that the consumption-income ratio varies widely across persons, being high for the low-income people and low for the high-income people, is quite misleading.

Second, for most people there is a natural life-cycle pattern of earning and saving. In the early years of working life, family expenses are pressing and income fairly low, so savings are minimal or even negative, as families borrow to finance consumption. In the later working years, incomes have grown to the point where many families begin to save for their retirement and higher education for their children. In retirement, the pattern reverses again, as people live off their accumulated savings. Looking across people of different ages, it would appear that low-income people (young and old) tend to do little or no saving, and high-income people are relatively big savers. That picture would be very misleading because, leaving aside for a moment bequests, inheritances, other intergenerational gifts, and government transfers, over a lifetime one cannot spend more than one earns, and over a lifetime one ends up spending all of what is earned.[7] Thus, from a lifetime perspective it doesn't make much difference whether the tax base is income or consumption—it all adds up the same. Big savers aged 45 to 65, who might appear to be getting off easy under a consumption tax because they consume relatively little of their annual income, will eventually pay more tax when they take their trip around the world, and otherwise live the high life, when they retire. Thus, a single-rate tax on consumption and a single-rate tax on labor income both end up being single-rate levies on lifetime resources. Similarly, over a lifetime, a consumption tax with graduated rates could in principle achieve about the same degree of progressivity as a graduated income tax. One is not inherently more progressive than the other.

Many economists would also argue that, again ignoring bequests and inheritances, consumption taxation is *more* horizontally equitable than a comprehensive income tax on both labor earnings and the return to capital. This is because, when comparing families with equal lifetime incomes, a consumption tax avoids imposing a tax penalty on those who are relatively frugal. Over a lifetime it levies the same present value of taxation regardless of one's saving propensity. In contrast, under an income tax savers are penalized relative to nonsavers.

However, a consumption tax that does not include bequests or inheritances in the tax base will lower the average tax rate over a lifetime on those (generally high-income) families who pass on wealth to their heirs. This turns a flat-rate consumption tax into a somewhat regressive tax on lifetime resources. For this reason some economists who favor a consumption tax do so only if a bequest is treated (that is, taxed) as if it were an act of consumption by the bequeathor.[8]

Fairness and the Transition to a Consumption Tax

As discussed in Chapter 3, whenever the tax system changes, there are bound to be some people who lose in the transition and others who gain. The bigger the tax change, the bigger the likely size of the windfall gains and losses. Replacing the current tax system with any kind of consumption tax is surely a massive change, and there are potentially very large windfall gains and losses in the transition.

The most important distributional issue in the transition to a consumption tax is the treatment of pre-existing wealth. There is about $25 trillion in accumulated wealth held by U.S. households.[9] The transition to a new tax system could mean either a major windfall or a substantial loss for the owners of this wealth, depending on how the change is implemented and in what form the wealth is held.

As mentioned above, there are two ways to remove taxation's impact on the incentive to save—a wage tax and a consumption tax. If we were to replace our income tax with a wage tax, not only could pre-existing wealth now earn interest, dividends, and capital gains tax-free, but that wealth could be withdrawn from saving and spent tax-free as well. As a result, it would provide a windfall to holders of existing wealth, who otherwise would have had to pay tax—explicit or implicit—on the returns to that wealth. It is a windfall because these people gain financially from the new tax rules, even if they don't do any extra new saving at all.

On the other hand, adopting a pure consumption tax could impose a large burden on owners of existing wealth. Suppose we adopted a 20 percent consumption tax, and it caused all prices to rise by 20 percent. The purchasing power of all wages would decline by 20 percent relative to a situation with no taxes, just as it would under a wage tax of the same rate. The difference is that, under a consumption tax, the purchasing power of all existing wealth also falls by 20 percent. For example, suppose you had built up a substantial savings account before the imposition of the new consumption tax. When you withdraw money from the account to spend it, it would be taxed at the full 20 percent rate by a consumption tax, but not taxed at all by a wage tax. For this reason, adopting a consumption tax is equivalent to adopting a wage tax plus levying a one-time tax on existing wealth.

Setting aside for a moment temporary inflexibilities in contracts for wages, bonds, and so forth (we'll address these later), whether the overall level of prices changes or not does not materially affect this story.[10] Even if prices do not rise at all, the purchasing power of both wages and existing wealth should still decline by an average of 20 percent relative to a situation with no taxes. Nominal wages would be forced down because firms would be earning 20 percent less, after taxes, from the output produced by workers. The nominal value of existing capital assets—for example, share prices—which constitute much of "old wealth," would also decline, because the output they produce provides 20 percent less in after-tax revenues.

Whether prices go up or not, it is also necessary to consider what offset is provided by the fact that we would be eliminating our current income tax when we adopted the consumption tax. For wages, the offset would be roughly one-for-one on average; the elimination of income taxes on wages would compensate for the new burden of consumption taxes on wage earners. Different wage earners might gain or lose depending on how the progressivity of the tax burden on wages changes, but this is a separate issue. Fixed nominal wage contracts could also affect the outcome, a point we will address later.

Eliminating income taxes on capital, however, does not offset the one-time tax on existing wealth from instituting a consumption tax nearly as much. It is true that eliminating double taxation of all future dividends and capital gains would provide a counterbalancing gain to corporate shares, as would forgiving the tax on all previously accumulated capital gains.[11] But eliminating the income tax also imposes a loss on owners of capital assets, because firms would no longer be able to take depreciation deductions on previously purchased capital assets to offset taxes on the output they produce. All new investment goods, by contrast, could be purchased tax-free, or deducted from the business tax base immediately, which would offset the taxes owed on the future returns to those new assets. As a result, the demand for existing assets would fall sharply relative to the demand for new assets, reducing the value of existing wealth.

All things considered, the most likely scenario is that owners of existing wealth would take a one-time hit in the switch from the income tax to a consumption tax. This transitional loss would, over the long run, be offset to the extent that wealth owners will in the future receive higher after-tax returns on that wealth.

A key point to recognize here is that the more transition relief that is provided to existing assets in the switch to any consumption tax, the more it becomes like a wage tax. For example, allowing businesses to continue taking depreciation deductions for their past investments would greatly reduce the revenue raised from holders of pre-existing wealth. Wage earners would have to pick up the slack. A similar result occurs in the transition to a personal consumption tax if individuals are allowed to deduct some or all of their existing wealth in the same way as they could deduct new saving; to the extent they can, their tax base is less than their consumption done after the imposition of the tax. So whether the move to a consumption tax provides a windfall or a loss to existing wealth holders depends crucially on the transition provisions that are adopted.

What characterizes the owners of wealth who will be affected most by these transitional gains or losses? They are, on average, very wealthy; the richest 1 percent of the population owns over a third of the nation's private wealth. They are also, on average, elderly; the median net worth of people over age 65 is more than twice as high as it is for the overall population.[12] If Social Security benefits are indexed to compensate for any price change, as they probably would be, then the impact is concentrated on the better off portion of the elderly.

Whether it is "fair" to hit wealth holders, elderly or not, with an unexpected burden is an equity issue on which economic analysis cannot be decisive. The fact that moving to a consumption tax with no transition relief places a burden on the wealthy is probably appealing to many people, especially because the wealthy could benefit greatly in the future from the removal of tax on returns to saving. Those who own lots of old capital are sure to push hard for transition relief nonetheless. The public is likely to be more sympathetic to the plight of retirees. Even here, however, a case can be made that wealthy elderly people deserve at least some extra burden, because they are receiving large subsidies from Medicare and Social Security.[13]

Because many important prices are temporarily inflexible, the transition to a consumption tax can also lead to a variety of other, often capricious, redistributions. Depending on whether the Federal Reserve allows a price change, all sorts of mischief can occur with regard to contracts written in fixed nominal terms, such as bonds, mortgages, and long-term wage contracts. For example, if the adoption of a consumption tax is accompanied by an increase in consumer prices, bondholders suffer the same one-time loss as stock owners, because the real value of their bonds declines. On the other hand, if prices do not rise, the consumption tax will not hurt bondholders, because firms are legally obligated to pay them the full nominal value of their bonds. In this case the owners of businesses who borrowed from those bondholders are hit hard, because they cannot pass through the cost of lost depreciation deductions to the bondholders. Some of these firms might be forced into bankruptcy or layoffs, hurting the employees as well. Similarly, workers with long-term nominal wage contracts will suffer short-term losses to the extent that prices rise.

One other notable issue of transitional fairness concerns government transfer payments that are not automatically indexed for price changes, such as food stamps and welfare. If a consumption tax is accompanied by a price increase, and transfer payments are not increased in value so as to keep real benefits constant, the tax levies an extra burden on the poor.

Economic Reasons for Switching to a Consumption Tax

What would be the long-term economic impact of switching to a consumption tax? The most talked-about potential benefits arise from increasing the incentive to save and invest. A less publicized, but perhaps more important, benefit is that a consumption tax could make it easier to "level the playing field" among different types of investment. Finally, the shifting of tax burdens that occurs in the transition to a new system could have important economic effects.

As demonstrated above, switching to a consumption tax would remove any negative impact of the tax system on the incentive to save and invest. By itself, this is a step in the right direction, because individuals' choices between current and future consumption will more closely reflect the economic merits of the alternatives, rather than the influence of the tax system. There is also a wide consensus that raising national saving and investment from their current levels would be good for the economy as a whole. By providing workers better machines and tools to work with, increased capital accumulation could improve productivity and long-run living standards.

But as shown in Chapter 4, it is unclear whether increasing the incentive to save would actually lead to more saving. The weight of the evidence suggests private saving is probably not very responsive to the after-tax rate of return. The bottom line is that switching to a consumption tax does not guarantee a big boost in saving and investment—our best guess is that at most there would be only a small increase. Because there are more direct ways to increase national saving (for example, lowering the federal deficit), the likely but not assured prospect of a somewhat higher saving rate does not seem to be, by itself, a reason to undertake a wholesale transformation of the tax system.

A second possible benefit of a consumption tax is that it would be easier to achieve "neutrality" or "uniformity" in the tax treatment of various types of investment. As discussed in Chapter 4, under the current income tax different types of investment are effectively taxed at varying rates. For example, corporate business investments are taxed more heavily than noncorporate business investments, which are in turn taxed more heavily than investments in owner-occupied housing. Investments in certain types of capital equipment, or in certain lines of business, are capriciously favored relative to others by depreciation schedules that do not conform to true economic depreciation. Business endeavors that can be packaged into assets that appreciate in value are more attractive than those that pay their returns in the form of dividends or interest, because of the preferential treatment of capital gains. All of these deviations from "neutrality" are economically harmful, because they cause too much money to flow into the favored investments, and not enough into the others.

A consumption tax would eliminate all of these distortions to the choice among different types of investment. It would transform the tax rate on the returns to all investment to a single uniform rate—zero. Of course, in principle an income tax could also be made more neutral, taxing the returns to investment at a uniform, but positive, rate. Thus, to some extent, this is a separate issue from the choice between an income and a consumption tax—it's a matter of having a "clean base," which is discussed below. But this particular aspect of "cleanliness" is much easier to achieve in a consumption tax than in an income tax. Some of the existing distortions arise from compromises that are hard to avoid in an income tax, due to the fact that capital income is very difficult to measure accurately. Some of these compromises were discussed in Chapters 2 and 5. For example, it is impossible to measure depreciation exactly right, so there will inevitably be some distortions caused here. Similarly, it is probably infeasible to include capital gains in taxable income as they accrue, so appreciating assets will be favored. It is theoretically possible to adjust the measurement of capital income for inflation, but in practice it would be complicated and inevitably imperfect. Chapter 8 will look at options for addressing these problems while retaining an income tax. But a consumption tax could end the need to measure any of these things, achieving this dimension of uniformity in a simple way.

The transition to a consumption tax can also have significant economic consequences. From an efficiency point of view, it is not unattractive to place a surprise, one-time tax on holders of existing wealth, as a consumption tax would. Raising revenue from the returns to past investments has no effect on the incentive to work or engage in new investment. Shifting tax burdens onto the elderly—whose working life and saving decisions are finished or nearly finished—also avoids costly disincentives. Since the elderly have a relatively high propensity to consume, moreover, transferring some of the tax burden onto them and away from others could give a boost to national saving. This last effect is likely to be offset, however, by the fact that the wealthy as a whole have a much higher propensity to save than everyone else, and placing an extra burden on them through a consumption tax might reduce their contribution to national saving.[14]

As discussed above, the transition to a consumption tax would impact different firms in very different ways, causing serious, albeit short-term, problems of unemployment and dislocation. As in the case of intergenerational redistribution, whether it is fair to achieve overall economic gains by imposing windfall losses on some members of society is a question of ethics, not just economics. In any event, there is some likelihood that special provisions would be adopted to eliminate some of these transitional economic effects.

A final point to consider is that our current tax system may not actually raise that much revenue from taxing capital income. What is in name an income tax is in fact an awkward hybrid of an income tax and a consumption tax. For example, revenue is collected from taxing nominal interest income, but even more is foregone due to the deduction of nominal interest payments because those deducting the interest tend to be in higher tax brackets than those receiving interest. This problem is made worse by arbitrage opportunities, such as borrowing money to put into IRAs or tax-exempt bonds. Preferential treatment of pension saving and capital gains, plus generous depreciation allowances, all further reduce revenues. There is some evidence that giving up on capital income taxation altogether, which is what a consumption tax would essentially do, ultimately might not cost us that much revenue.[15] This is particularly true in the absence of transition relief, since the tax on old wealth helps make up for any losses.

If capital income taxation isn't generating a great deal of revenue, then eliminating it could get rid of many distortions at little cost. Of course, we could also eliminate many of those distortions by making income taxation more uniform, which would probably increase revenue. Moreover, it suggests that, on average, the tax rate on saving and investment is not that high under the current system, so a major boost in overall saving is even less likely from a consumption tax.

Simplification and Enforcement Aspects of a Consumption Tax

The concept of income is inherently a more complicated one to measure than is consumption. Even with all the compromises we make in our current system, calculating and reporting capital income and deductions is still complex and burdensome. These compromises, in turn, create opportunities to achieve tax savings in complicated and socially unproductive ways, such as devising schemes to rearrange financial and business transactions. In principle, it is simpler to measure consumption accurately than to measure even a compromised version of income, mainly because the need for measuring capital income can be completely avoided. But in practice, it would not be hard to design a consumption tax that is even more difficult to administer and comply with than the current income tax. The simplicity and enforceability of moving to a consumption tax depend crucially on which approach is chosen and how it is operated—these issues will be addressed fully in Chapter 7.

Here too, transitional issues are critically important. Moving cold turkey to a new, pure consumption tax like a VAT or flat tax could immediately make the taxpaying process simpler. But the pleadings of those likely to suffer windfall losses will be difficult to resist, so a switch to a consumption tax is likely to offer various forms of transition relief. Special transitional provisions can be exceedingly complex, because they require the simultaneous operation of parallel tax systems, at least for a while. This is important to keep in mind, because the real choice is then not between the current system and a clean consumption tax, but one encumbered by as-yet-unspecified rules for how to get from here to there, which can be unaesthetic at best, and complicated and loophole-ridden at worst.

There is one other transitional issue that has important implications for evaluating a new system. Depending on how it is implemented, the switch to a consumption tax can lead to enormous incentives to postpone or speed up transactions around the date of switchover. Firms will postpone investment until the expensing rules are in place and, under some plans, individuals will rush to consume as much as possible before the implementation date. This could cost a great deal of revenue, and raises a very delicate problem of minimizing the short-run disruption at the time of transition.

A Clean Tax Base

A third element of proposals for fundamental tax reform is to eliminate many or all of the features that provide special preferences for particular types of consumption or investment. The aim is variously described as "flattening" or "broadening" the tax base, "leveling the playing field," or making the tax system more "neutral." We'll refer to this aspect of flatness as a "clean" tax base. (At least the connotation of clean is less ambiguous than that of flat!)

One important source of messiness in the tax base has to do with compromises or peculiarities regarding the taxation of capital income, such as the failure to index capital income for inflation, and the double taxation of corporate income. These can be important sources of inefficiency, inequity, and complexity. As discussed above, a consumption tax could sweep away many of these problems. Chapter 8 will address specific options for making the taxation of capital income more neutral while retaining an income tax.

A second source of messiness in the tax base involves preferences for particular types of expenditure or activity that are deemed worthy of special treatment. Important examples are housing, health care, charity, taxation and borrowing by state and local governments, and education. Such issues will be the focus of this section. Although we concentrate here on the most important examples, the current personal and corporate income taxes feature scores of other deviations from a clean-based system, from incentives to invest in low-income housing to tax breaks for the production of ethanol. Each needs to be evaluated on its own merits.

Some ambitious proposals for overhauling the tax system, such as the Hall-Rabushka flat tax, would eliminate *all* preferences of this sort. Other proposals eliminate some, but not all, of these features. But no matter what type of tax reform we contemplate, there will almost certainly be a tremendous fight over the most cherished and politically entrenched of these tax goodies. A personalized consumption tax, such as the flat tax, could easily end up retaining many current preferences, or even adding new ones. And even though an impersonalized consumption tax, such as a retail sales tax or VAT, could no longer allow the preferences in their current form, similar ones could be reintroduced by exempting purchases of preferred items.

Throughout this book, a host of reasons why special preferences in the tax base can be a problem have been presented. Every preference is a penalty for someone else, because it requires tax rates to be higher than otherwise. As Chapter 2 explained, more than half of personal income is left out of the tax base; even if we allow for personal exemptions and standard deductions, it's still about one-third. This suggests that all marginal tax rates could be reduced by about one-third if we were able to move to a comprehensive income tax base. Tax deductions are also a regressive way to subsidize activities—people with larger incomes receive bigger subsidies from deductions, because on average they engage more in the deductible activities and have higher marginal tax rates. Those who don't itemize get no benefit at all from the deductions. Except in special cases, tax preferences are inefficient, because they create an incentive to engage "too much" in the lightly taxed activity, and too little in other activities, relative to what the free market would dictate. And, finally, they are a big reason why our tax code is so complicated.

For these reasons, the burden of proof should rest on those who defend deviations from a clean tax base. An exception from this rule must clear one of two hurdles: it must either render the tax system more fair by making the tax base a more accurate measurement of well-being, or it must encourage or discourage an activity with significant externalities—in other words, the activity must create important benefits or costs for others that are not reflected in the incentives faced by the taxpayer. Even if a significant externality is identified, the tax system must be the best alternative for dealing with it. As specific exceptions to a clean base are examined, each of them will be evaluated in light of these high hurdles.

Even if some preferences clear these hurdles, there remains one powerful argument for maintaining a clean base. It is that the political system is incapable of distinguishing legitimate arguments from illegitimate ones, and often succumbs to the political clout of powerful pleaders. Once any preference is allowed, we may begin to slide down the slippery slope to more preferences.

Housing and the Mortgage Interest Deduction

Owner-occupied housing is favored by our tax system in a number of ways. For example, the double taxation of corporate income makes housing investments more attractive by comparison, and capital gains are untaxed on many home sales. But the most politically sacred feature relating to housing is the deduction for home mortgage interest payments. Its sacredness is now being challenged, for it is swept away in some of the more ambitious tax reform proposals. When push comes to shove, however, there would undoubtedly be an all-out fight to retain it.

The home mortgage interest deduction is a very expensive one, costing an estimated $59 billion in revenues in 1996. It requires personal tax rates to be about 9 percent (not 9 percentage *points*) higher than they otherwise could be.[16] So a lot is at stake in this debate. What are the issues?

First of all, let's consider whether there is any good economic reason to favor housing over other types of consumption or investment. To answer yes to this question requires demonstrating that an owner-occupied house provides important benefits to people other than the residents themselves; that the residents take pleasure in ownership is an inadequate argument. While undoubtedly one's neighbors prefer to gaze out their window at a well-kept, rather than a ramshackle, house, and owner-occupiers arguably maintain their houses better than the combination of renters and landlords, these benefits are certainly quite localized and probably fairly small. One sometimes hears vague appeals to the role of home ownership in maintaining a strong democracy, but these arguments are not convincing. Remember, to the extent that the tax system attracts investment into housing, it diverts funds from other business investments, which lowers the productivity of workers and the wage that businesses can profitably pay them. Why isn't broad stock ownership a healthy aspect of democracy? Preferential treatment of housing, in general, is difficult to justify on economic grounds.[17]

In the specific case of the home mortgage interest deduction, however, there is a second possible rationale: it is needed to correctly measure the tax base in a comprehensive income tax. As discussed in Chapter 2, to achieve a comprehensive measure of income, interest payments ought to be deductible, just as interest receipts are taxable. The catch to this argument is that, under a comprehensive income tax, the rental value of owner-occupied housing, net of depreciation and maintenance expenses, should *also* be subject to tax. To be sure, most homeowners don't think of this as income in the same way as their salary or their dividend receipts. But the failure to include this income in the tax base, in conjunction with the deductibility of mortgage interest, adds up to a big preference for residential housing.

Consider a family that is trying to decide whether to buy a $300,000 house, or to instead buy a more modest $200,000 house and invest the extra $100,000 in the stock market. Suppose further that the annual rent for such houses would be 10 percent of their value and that stocks provide an annual pretax return of 10 percent, so that each would be an equally attractive investment in the absence of taxes. Buying the more expensive house will certainly make the family better off; they'll have nicer living quarters, more rooms, a better view, and so on. How much better off they are per year is approximated by the rental value of the extra housing, or $10,000 per year. Investing the $100,000 in stocks, on the other hand, will yield considerably less than $10,000 per year because of the taxes that would be due on the investment return.

The preferential tax treatment could tip the scales in favor of investing in the more expensive house. As a result, in some cases nonhousing investments are passed up in favor of more expensive homes, even though, taxes aside, the return to these investments equals or exceeds the value of the housing services; from a social point of view, this is wasteful. Allowing the deductibility of mortgage interest exacerbates this problem, because it enables one to use tax-deductible debt to finance an investment for which the return, the rental value of the housing, is untaxed. In addition, families and individuals who, for one reason or another, rent housing, end up being penalized; because net rental income of landlords is taxed, rental housing does not get the same preferential tax treatment afforded to owner-occupied housing. This generates an additional source of inefficiency. Not only is there an excessive amount of housing, but some households are induced to own housing when, taxes aside, they would find it more attractive to rent housing.

A second problem is that in our current income tax, there are numerous ways to receive capital income tax-free, such as IRAs, pension plans, municipal bonds, and unrealized capital gains. This makes housing an even more attractive investment for households that do not have the liquid funds to take advantage of these savings vehicles, because they can borrow against their housing, deduct the interest, and put the proceeds into a tax-preferred saving instrument. There are rules that attempt to prevent this, but they are almost impossible to enforce because of the difficulty of establishing the purpose of any particular mortgage balance. This kind of "tax arbitrage" is also wasteful, as it reduces revenues and causes extra complications, without actually creating any new saving or investment.

Unfortunately, in the context of an income tax there is no clean and easy solution to these problems. The mortgage interest deduction would be perfectly appropriate if all capital income were taxed uniformly, and all homeowners were required to estimate the rental value of their housing, subtract depreciation and maintenance expenses, and report the difference as taxable income. Uniform capital income taxation is difficult to achieve, but some improvements could be made; these will be addressed in Chapter 8. Taxing the net rental value of housing would be complicated and imprecise. Moreover, it would undoubtedly be resisted strenuously by the public, so it is probably not a practical option. It is not inconceivable, however, as several European countries actually attempt to do this, albeit in a very rough fashion.[18]

A simpler approach in an income tax would be to eliminate the deduction for home mortgage interest; Canada and Germany are two countries that take this approach.[19] This would certainly make debt-financed housing less attractive, reducing the inefficient bias toward housing investment. But it would do so only for taxpayers who cannot afford housing except by borrowing. For the few who are wealthy enough (or who have wealthy enough relatives) to pay cash, the cost of housing is the foregone, after-tax, return on an alternative investment. This would create an inequitable and still inefficient situation—it would cost mortgage holders the pretax rate of interest to carry housing, but for wealthy individuals who need not borrow the cost would be lower after-tax interest rate.

In an income tax, the treatment of home mortgage interest is a tough question, because the ideal measurement of the tax base dictates such a deduction, along with including as taxable income the rental value of the housing itself. But in a consumption tax, there is no such rationale. Although the USA Tax and some proposed modifications of the Hall-Rabushka flat tax would continue to allow the deduction for mortgage interest, it is completely incongruous in such a consumption tax, because other interest payments are not deductible, and all forms of capital income are untaxed. Deductibility of mortgage interest causes problems of tax arbitrage under the current system, but those problems would be much worse in a consumption tax. Homeowners would find it attractive to be as "mortgaged up" as possible, deducting the mortgage interest and simultaneously earning unlimited amounts of tax-free return from other investments. The only limit to how much you could reduce your taxes would be how much mortgage borrowing you could do. This would be wasteful and unfair, and would exacerbate rather than reduce the bias toward housing investment.

The problem of measuring the rental value of owner-occupied housing can also be easily avoided under a consumption tax. A house's purchase price reflects the value of the future flow of consumption services, so taxing the purchase price effectively "prepays" the tax on that consumption. A consumption tax that treats housing just like other purchases, and does not allow mortgage interest deductions, would be a clean and simple way of eliminating the existing bias toward housing. Deviating from either of these prescriptions, however, could make the bias as bad or worse than it is now.

Home mortgage interest deductions are often defended on the grounds that their elimination would lead to unfair transitional effects. Homeowners are understandably concerned about what eliminating the mortgage interest deduction would do to house prices. Their concerns are only inflamed by studies like the one done for the National Association of Realtors[20] that estimated that eliminating the deduction and moving to a single-rate tax structure would cause residential housing to drop in value by an average of 15 percent. This is a good example of a study commissioned by a party that stands to lose if a deduction is eliminated; for that reason the prediction must be greeted with some skepticism.

There is certainly some truth to the notion that housing prices may fall. By itself, eliminating the home mortgage deduction makes it more expensive to buy a house for anyone who would potentially itemize deductions and who must rely on mortgage finance. This would tend to reduce the demand for housing, which in turn would cause housing prices to drop. The greatest decline in demand would be for high-priced homes; eliminating the tax preference for housing should shift demand from more- to less-expensive homes, and the current deduction is most valuable for people who have high marginal tax rates, who tend to be the buyers of high-priced homes.

If tax reform leads to lower interest rates, the hit to housing prices could be eased. Lower interest rates would make house buying less expensive, which would help support demand and prices. But how pretax interest rates would change is unclear, and depends on whether eliminating the deduction is part of a switch to a consumption tax or a plank of income tax reform. Hall and Rabushka argue that moving to a consumption tax is likely to reduce interest rates. A consumption tax removes tax on lenders' interest income and eliminates the deductibility of borrowers' interest payments; as a result, lenders should be willing to accept a lower pretax interest rate, and borrowers will be less willing to tolerate a high pretax interest rate. This by itself would push interest rates down. However, there are many other factors at work in the switch to a consumption tax that would tend to offset this effect. For example, because a consumption tax removes tax on the normal return to investment, firms would probably increase their demand for loanable funds, which would push interest rates up. In an analysis that takes many of the relevant factors into account, economist Martin Feldstein of Harvard University concludes that interest rates are more likely to go up than down upon adoption of a consumption tax.[21]

Overall, it is hard to forecast the impact on home prices of eliminating mortgage deductions. Dire predictions were made about the Tax Reform Act of 1986, which made the deductibility of mortgage interest less valuable by lowering marginal tax rates, but it has been difficult to discern any negative effects on housing prices from that reform.[22] Canada has no deduction for mortgage interest at all, but has about the same home ownership rate as the United States.[23] Our best guess is that we would see some price declines, but they would be smaller than the sky-is-falling prediction of the National Association of Realtors, and would be concentrated at the high end of the market. The people most affected would often be the same ones who benefit from the lower marginal tax rates in many reform proposals. Transitional losses could be eased further by provisions that preserve some of the deductibility of mortgages initiated before the change in tax law. But such rules can be quite costly and complicated.[24]

Health Care

Health care is a second area where our tax code provides very favorable treatment, and it will undoubtedly be a major source of contention in any reform effort. The most important preference in this area is the exclusion from tax at any level of employer contributions for medical insurance premiums. In 1996, this treatment is estimated to cost $67 billion in revenues, requiring personal tax rates to be 11 percent (not percentage points) higher than otherwise. There is also an itemized deduction for large out-of-pocket medical care expenditures (those that exceed 7.5 percent of adjusted gross income); this costs an estimated $4 billion in revenues.[25]

What rationale is there for subsidizing health care? The main reason appears to be that health care is viewed as a "necessity." To some extent, the exclusion of employer contributions to health insurance is motivated by a sense of fairness; it is a way of redistributing money to people so they can afford to buy health insurance. In some cases, people prefer redistribution for a specific meritorious purpose such as health care over redistribution that can be used for any purpose, good or bad. The itemized deduction for medical expenditures is motivated by horizontal equity concerns; people who experience large, unavoidable, out-of-pocket medical costs are deemed to have a lower "ability-to-pay."

In the case of health insurance, there are other issues involved as well. One is that there are "philanthropic externalities." People who are uninsured often end up getting medical care anyway, either through Medicaid or through uncompensated care from a public or charitable hospital. The costs of caring for them are then passed on to others through higher taxes, or in an arbitrary fashion through higher insurance premiums or lower compensation for doctors. Being uninsured might also make the costs worse than they otherwise would be, because medical care isn't sought until a condition is already very bad.

Here, the gains from making sure everyone has health insurance are similar to those from requiring all drivers to have auto insurance.

Whether or not you agree with these goals, the current tax preference for employer health insurance contributions is a very inequitable and inefficient way to achieve them. To the extent that helping people afford health insurance is the goal, the current approach goes about it backwards. It provides no help to people whose incomes are too low to pay taxes, and it provides very large amounts of help to people who have high marginal tax rates (those with high incomes).

The exclusion is also inefficient because it provides an incentive not only to buy health insurance in the first place (which may be desirable), but also to buy the most expensive health insurance possible (which is not). Consider an employee who faces a 50 percent marginal tax rate, which is not unusual when federal and state income taxes are combined with employer and employee Social Security tax rates. If an employer wants to give that worker $50 more in net-of-tax compensation, it only costs the firm $50 to grant it in the form of a better health insurance policy, but would cost the firm $100 to provide it in the form of a higher wage. This creates a very strong incentive to provide much more generous health benefits than otherwise, which contributes to inefficiently large expenditures on health care. This is a problem *not* because health care is not worthwhile, but because taxpayers are being offered it at a price that is much lower than its true cost to society. This inefficient incentive compounds the well-known problem of "moral hazard," under which insured individuals have no incentive to economize on medical expenses that on the margin are paid for by someone else.

For these reasons, eliminating or capping the exclusion from tax of employer-provided medical benefits is often a feature of proposals for health reform as well as tax reform. Many economists believe that if we want to help people afford health insurance, it would be much more sensible to provide a "voucher" or "credit" of a fixed amount; this would give an equal amount of help to everyone and would eliminate the incentive to buy expensive policies.

The itemized deduction for extraordinary medical expenditures can be justified as an appropriate adjustment for "ability-to-pay." But it too creates an incentive to avoid economizing on health care expenditures, and it adds some complication to the tax system. There would be some advantages to rolling all of the tax system's health care assistance into a single coherent policy, instead of having numerous different provisions that sometimes duplicate each other.

Most of the current proposals for fundamental tax reform would eliminate preferences for health care and insurance expenditures altogether—this is a principal reason why they can apparently feature such a low single rate of tax. The Hall-Rabushka flat tax would actually *penalize* employer-provided health insurance in some cases. The cost of health insurance premiums would be included in the business tax base, and taxed at the single rate; that is, unlike wages and salaries, they would not be deductible from the business tax base. For workers with wages below the large tax-exempt level, it actually becomes cheaper for their employers to provide them cash wages instead of health benefits. These workers do not remit any tax regardless of the form of compensation, but only in the case of cash wages is it deductible to the employer. This penalty could cause problems of its own, because under our current health care system it is often more efficient for businesses to provide insurance to their employees than to have them buy it on their own; in the former case, the risks are pooled over a larger number of people.

Charitable Contributions

Under current law, charitable contributions to qualifying organizations are deductible from taxable income for those who itemize deductions. Let's subject to our two-tiered test this penalty to those not charitably inclined. First, are charitable contributions an indication that the contributing family is less well-off than their income would suggest? As these are voluntary contributions, this doesn't seem to make sense, so we cannot invoke an ability-to-pay justification.

Test number two is whether there is a legitimate externality that requires subsidies in order to encourage charitable giving. This argument is worth taking more seriously. On the one hand, donors give to charities voluntarily, so they must be gaining some satisfaction from their gifts—perhaps they are motivated by the "warm glow" they feel when they help others. On the other hand, charitable activities have benefits that accrue to many members of society who do not themselves contribute, or only contribute a little. For this reason, there is an incentive for people to "free ride" on the contributions of others. In this situation, an extra incentive from the tax code may lead to a higher level of charitable activity that makes everyone better off. Some argue, in addition, that charitable contributions are a more efficient and less intrusive way of financing public goods such as aid to the poor than is government intervention. In an age of government cutbacks, this argument becomes more relevant.

The charitable contributions deduction is not without its costs, however. In 1996, it will reduce income tax revenues by about $24 billion. It adds to complexity and record-keeping requirements. A broad array of things qualify as "charity," so there's no guarantee that the gifts will go to areas that really deserve to be subsidized by the tax system. Contributions can also be very difficult to monitor, so unfortunately there's some inequity arising from cheating. Finally, it's not clear whether the tax deduction really influences the charitable giving that much; it may serve as more of a reward than an inducement. For example, the Tax Reform Act of 1986 significantly reduced the incentive to give by lowering marginal tax rates, but there's not much evidence that contributions declined as a result.[26]

On balance, some form of incentive for charity may be justified. Even so, there is no reason that the rate of subsidy should be tied to the donor's tax rate, and be zero for taxpayers who do not itemize or who have incomes below the filing threshold. If it is an incentive program, rather than an adjustment for ability-to-pay, it ought to be administered as a credit, rather than a deduction, so that we are subsidizing all contributions at an equal rate, and not subsidizing more heavily the contributions of affluent taxpayers. Of course, adopting a single rate would move the subsidy closer to that treatment automatically.[27]

State and Local Government Taxes and Bonds

Two important preferences in our tax code have to do with state and local governments. An itemized deduction for tax payments to state and local governments, not including sales tax, costs the federal government about $44 billion in revenues. The exclusion from federal income tax of interest on state and local government bonds costs an estimated $20 billion.[28]

One potential rationale for the deductibility of state and local taxes is that payment of these taxes reduces a family's ability-to-pay. If all states charged all families the same average tax rate, however, this would be irrelevant; allowing deductibility of state and local taxes would be exactly the same as not allowing it, but having a lower federal tax rate.[29] So the argument is really that people in higher-tax states and municipalities have less ability to pay federal taxes than people in lower-tax places.

The flaw in this argument is that living in a high-tax state is to some extent a voluntary decision, and people in those states presumably benefit from a higher level of public expenditures. Why should someone who chooses to live in a low-tax state, and make do with fewer government services, be penalized for the choice? Of course, the relationship between state and local taxes and the benefits from public services is certainly not one-to-one—they are not benefit taxes. So the ability-to-pay argument has some merit, although it is limited.

Another problem with the deduction is that it provides an inefficient subsidy to state and local spending. The cost to (itemizing) taxpayers of a dollar of state spending is less than a dollar, because part of the cost is shifted to taxpayers in other states. On the margin, this may encourage state governments to undertake projects that would not meet taxpayer approval in the absence of the tax incentive, and that use up resources that would be more appropriately used for other purposes.

Such a subsidy for state and local expenditures might be desirable if those expenditures provide benefits that spread beyond the state's or municipality's borders. This is certainly not true for many expenditures such as garbage collection or municipal swimming pools. It could arguably apply to primary education on the grounds that it builds an "educated citizenry," which benefits all Americans. This argument has some intuitive appeal, but is hard to prove. Even granting that argument, it applies only to a subset of what state and local governments do, and does not justify the general deductibility of state and local taxes. Nor does it justify giving a larger subsidy to more affluent communities, where the residents have higher tax rates.

On balance, if tax reform results in the elimination of deductions for state and local taxes, it would not be a major loss. While it has some merit as an adjustment for ability-to-pay, and perhaps as an encouragement of certain worthy public expenditures, it also involves significant inefficiency, unfairness, and complexity.[30]

Some of these same arguments apply to the exclusion of interest on state and local bonds. In this case, there is no ability-to-pay rationale, because the decision to buy the bonds is entirely voluntary. The main effect of the interest exclusion is to subsidize expenditures in the states and municipalities that issue them, because it enables them to borrow money at a lower interest rate. High-income investors are willing to accept the lower interest rates because they pay no tax on the interest; the increased demand by investors drives the yields on these bonds down near the after-tax rate on similar but taxable bonds.

Not all of the benefits of the interest exclusion go to state and local governments, however. If all potential buyers of these bonds had the same tax rate, say 20 percent, the interest rates on the bonds would end up being about 20 percent lower than on other bonds, so the purchasers would gain little or no benefit; their *implicit* tax would equal the *explicit* tax on other securities. But in a system of graduated rates, in order to sell all the bonds that state and local governments want to issue, the rate of interest must be high enough to attract not just those taxpayers with the highest tax rate—currently 39.6 percent—but also many investors with lower tax rates. This means that taxpayers in the 39.6 percent bracket must surely benefit. In practice, many high-bracket investors benefit greatly from state and local bonds.

Given that the case for subsidizing state and local expenditures is shaky, the interest exclusion seems hard to justify. Because a substantial portion of the subsidy represents a windfall to very high-income people, it is even harder to justify. An alternative to both the exclusion of bond interest and the deductibility of tax payments that would avoid these problems is for the federal government to provide direct subsidies to these governments. This has always been resisted by states and municipalities, largely due to fear that once the subsidy becomes a straightforward appropriation, it could easily go onto the budget chopping block. This is a good example of how the tax system can sustain subsidy programs that, out in the open, would not survive.

Education

Expenditure on education is one item that is not generally deductible under our current personal tax code, but that many people think should be. In 1995, President Clinton proposed a deduction of up to $10,000 for expenditures on postsecondary education and training. Some of the issues regarding the tax treatment of education expenses were discussed in Chapter 4. The argument here is somewhat different than it is for the other types of preferences discussed above. Spending on education and training is in part an investment in "human capital" that yields returns in the form of higher wages later in life. But our tax system does not treat it as generously as investments in physical capital. Moreover, people may underinvest in human capital because it is difficult to borrow against expected future earnings. So there may be some justification for something like a tax deduction for tuition expenses.

On the other hand, education expenses are subsidized in a number of ways outside the tax system, through guaranteed student loans, financial aid and scholarships, state spending on public universities, and the like. Furthermore, some spending on education should probably be regarded as consumption, rather than investment. An education deduction would be expensive and add complexity to the tax code. So the case for such a deduction in our current income tax is not so clear-cut. If we move to a consumption tax, however, the treatment of physical capital becomes more generous, and the case for deductibility of investments in human capital becomes stronger as well.

The Standard Deduction and Rough Justice

To this point, many examples of itemized deductions have been discussed. Recall, though, that less than one-third of all taxpayers actually deduct these expenses, and these are predominantly affluent families. This is because all taxpayers are offered the option of bypassing the itemizing process and instead receiving a "standard" deduction, which varies only by marital status. In 1995 it amounted to $6,550 for a married couple filing jointly, and $3,900 for a single taxpayer.

The standard deduction exists because it would not be cost-efficient for the IRS to have to monitor and occasionally audit the deductions claimed by the 80 million or so taxpayers who do not now itemize, not to mention the cost in time and expense of these taxpayers having to keep track of their expenses. However, by having a standard deduction, the tax system loses its ability to finely differentiate among taxpayers with differing "abilities-to-pay." As it stands now, two otherwise identical families, both with $30,000 of income and both taking the standard deduction, owe the same tax even though one family has incurred $5,000 in medical expenses and the other hasn't. Although in principle we design the tax system so that extraordinary medical expenses reduce income subject to tax, in practice we settle for rough justice, by differentiating tax liability only when relatively large sums of money are involved.

If some or all itemized deductions end up being retained, a larger standard deduction could still simplify taxpaying for many people by cutting down on the number of itemizers. This could save substantial administrative and compliance costs. It would mean settling for even more "rough justice," but the trade-off might be worth it. One simplifying change that would cost no revenue would be to couple a reduction or elimination of personal exemption allowances for the adults in a family with a corresponding increase in the standard deduction. Similarly, if some itemized deductions are retained in a "flat tax," the family allowance could be treated as a large standard deduction.

Conclusion

This chapter has addressed the policy issues that arise in contemplating any major tax reform. As with most contentious policy choices, the contemplated changes often require a balancing among the desirable characteristics of a tax system.

The next two chapters will examine specific proposals for overhauling the tax system. All of these proposals involve some combination of the three elements discussed in this chapter—a single rate (or at least low marginal rates), a consumption base, and a clean base. Throughout the rest of the book, keep in mind that each element is to some extent separable from the others, so that a reform could achieve any or all to varying degrees.

This chapter and the next will examine specific proposals for improving the tax system. We begin in this chapter by addressing the consumption tax alternatives—the retail sales tax, the value-added tax (VAT), the "flat tax," and the personal consumption tax. Each of these proposals would represent a truly sweeping change in the way we tax ourselves, and all are attracting much more attention than in previous rounds of soul-searching about reform.

First, this chapter will explain how each of the four basic approaches to consumption taxation works, and why they are all close relatives. Second, to make the discussion more concrete, the chapter will examine what tax rates would have to be levied to make up for the revenue lost from the income tax. With this as background, we can then move on to the crux of the matter: how to evaluate the consumption tax approaches, and how they stack up to the current system. Since each of the four approaches to consumption taxation can achieve the same basic economic goal—removing taxation's negative impact on the reward for saving—a choice among them must depend on other factors. As is so often the case with issues as complex as this one, the devil is in the details. Deciding which approach is best depends crucially on administrative factors—simplicity and enforceability—and the ease with which the tax base can be adjusted for ability-to-pay. This chapter will show that the VAT and flat tax emerge as superior to the other choices for simplification and enforcement reasons. Moreover, if you are concerned at all about the tax burdens placed on low-income people, the flat tax appears to be the choice among consumption taxes. Finally, we offer an examination of how the distributional and economic impacts of the alternatives are likely to compare to the current system, which is crucial to determining whether the flat tax or any other radical reform is worth undertaking.

How the Consumption Tax Plans Work

There are four basic alternatives for replacing our income tax with a consumption tax. Since these four alternatives appear on the surface to be very different, their essential similarity is often completely misunderstood. Moreover, each of these basic alternatives could be adopted with either a clean or a messy base, and with a single rate or with measures to make it more progressive. Specific proposals in the political arena vary greatly on these latter details.

How a Retail Sales Tax Works

The most familiar type of consumption tax is none other than the retail sales tax (RST), now in use by all but five states and many cities, at rates that range in most cases from 4 to 6 percent. Richard Lugar, a senator from Indiana who ran for the Republican presidential nomination in 1996, has proposed eliminating personal and corporate income taxes and replacing them with a federal retail sales tax. According to his plan, the tax would be administered by the states, so that the IRS could be abolished in the process.

In its ideal form, the retail sales tax is a tax remitted by businesses on all sales to consumers. It should exclude from tax all production inputs, that is, goods and services purchased by businesses to produce their own products. If a business pays sales tax on inputs it purchases from other firms, and then again when it sells to the consumer, its products are being "double taxed." As discussed later, this is one area where, in practice, the retail sales tax often runs into trouble.

A pure, clean-base, single-rate retail sales tax would tax *all* sales of both goods *and* services to consumers. It would be a completely "impersonal" tax in the sense that the rate of tax is not adjusted to account for any characteristic of the consumer, such as income, marital status, number of dependents, or personal tastes. In practice, most states exempt certain items, such as food and medicine, in an attempt to exempt "necessities" and ease the burden on the poor. Many items, particularly certain services, are also exempt in practice because they are difficult to tax. Some states even charge different sales tax rates on different items, or allow certain customers, such as the elderly or the poor, to apply for refunds.[1] Senator Lugar and other advocates of a federal sales tax have suggested their plans would have at least some of these elements. As we will discuss later, this is another area where a national sales tax could cause problems.

If production inputs are successfully excluded from tax, and a perfectly clean base is achieved, the aggregate tax base is the total value of final sales to consumers. Recall from Chapter 3 that, administrative and compliance issues aside, who writes the checks and which side of a transaction bears legal liability for a tax on a given base do not ultimately matter for either the economic ramifications or for who bears the burden of the tax. This point is absolutely critical to keep in mind when investigating some other tax systems that, judging from their mechanics, look to be very different from a retail sales tax but in fact are very close relatives.

How a Value-Added Tax Works

The first close relative to the sales tax is the value-added tax, widely known by its acronym, VAT (pronounced to rhyme with flat). Although rarely used in the United States (except under a different name in Louisiana and Michigan), the VAT has been a staple of European tax systems since the late 1960s, and is now widely used on the national level in almost every industrialized country in the world. Most countries that adopted a VAT used the revenues to replace either retail sales taxes or general business taxes that they had found to be deeply flawed.

In the aggregate, the VAT assesses tax on exactly the same base as the retail sales tax—total final sales from businesses to consumers. The difference is entirely in the mechanics. While the retail sales tax captures this base all at the final stage, when businesses sell to consumers, the VAT accomplishes this in pieces, firm by firm, along the production and distribution chain. For each firm, the tax base for a VAT is very simple—sales revenue minus the cost of purchased inputs, where the definition of purchased inputs does *not* include payments to labor but does include purchases of material inputs and capital goods. So, unlike the income tax, investment in productive machinery, factories, and other capital goods is expensed (deducted immediately) under a VAT, instead of being deducted over several years through depreciation allowances. If investment goods were subject to the VAT as they are sold, but were depreciated rather than being immediately deductible by the firms that purchase them, the tax base would be consumption plus net investment—in other words, it would be a form of income tax instead of a consumption tax.[2]

A simple example can help show why the tax base for a VAT is equal to final sales of goods and services to consumers, just as it is for a retail sales tax. Say you go to a bakery and buy a loaf of bread for $2. Under a retail sales tax, the tax base is simply $2 (assuming, of course, food isn't exempt). To illustrate the VAT, let's greatly simplify the process of making bread into just two steps. First, suppose there is a farmer who grows wheat, grinds it into flour, and sells it to the baker for $1. Then, the baker turns the flour into dough, bakes it into bread, and sells it to you for $2. The value added by the baker is $1—the sale price of the bread minus the cost of the flour. Under the VAT, the tax base is $1 for the farmer and $1 for the baker, adding up to a total of $2, the same tax base as under the retail sales tax. The example could be complicated by adding the cost of other ingredients, an oven, a tractor and seeds for the farmer, a separate flour company, and so on, but the net result would turn out to be identical—the tax base would still be $2.

On the surface, the retail sales tax might look like a tax paid by consumers, and the VAT might look like a tax paid by businesses. But again, the only difference is how the tax base is divided up among various parts of the transaction, which ultimately can't make any difference for who bears the burden of the tax or its economic effects. And don't forget that "business" can't bear the burden—only people can. What's more, if you've ever been to Europe or Canada, you know that a VAT usually doesn't even look different from a retail sales tax on the surface. The VAT (in Canada it's called the "Goods and Services Tax," or GST) generally appears right on top of the sales price whenever you buy something. For instance, if the country has a 10 percent VAT, your cash register receipt will show the before-tax sales price and then tack on the 10 percent VAT, just like a retail sales tax does in the United States.[3] Some advocates of a national retail sales tax have argued that it would somehow be more inherently "visible" than a VAT, but they are mistaken.

There are a couple of different ways that a VAT can be implemented. The first approach, called the "subtraction method," is very rarely used. Under this approach, the VAT is administered like a corporation income tax. Every year (or quarter), a firm's accountants report to the government the total amount of sales, subtract the total cost of purchased inputs, and pay tax on the difference.

Virtually every country that has a VAT actually uses a second approach, known as the "credit-invoice" method. Under this approach, the VAT is administered more like a sales tax; tax is visibly charged on each individual transaction. If there is a 10 percent VAT, every sale a firm makes will have the 10 percent VAT tacked right on top, and every purchase it makes from other firms will also have the 10 percent VAT attached.[4] An "invoice," which records the amount of tax charged, is required for each transaction. Periodically (often monthly), the business remits to the government the amount of VAT it has collected on its sales, less the amount of VAT remitted to other firms on its puchases. In other words, it gets "credit" for the amount of tax it remitted to other firms. Under this approach, the net amount of tax remitted by each firm to the government is identical to what it would be under the subtraction method, but there's more of a paper trail. If a business is audited, it must have invoices to back up the credits it claims—it needs to prove that the VAT has been remitted on its purchases. Thus, firms have an incentive to purchase goods from tax-law-abiding suppliers.

Another mechanical feature of a VAT that is often misunderstood involves the treatment of imports and exports. Most countries "rebate" their VATs on exported goods; in other words, the VAT is removed from the price of goods sold to other countries. Imported goods, on the other hand, are subject to the VAT by the country into which they are imported. Some observers in the United States have envied this aspect of the VAT, viewing it as an ingenious export promotion scheme—but they are simply confused. As explained in detail in Chapter 4, no VAT, nor any other tax system, can so simply give us any kind of "edge" in international competition.

Finally, like the retail sales tax, the VAT is often much messier in practice than it is in theory. For example, many countries levy preferential or zero rates on certain "necessary" or hard-to-tax goods and services and some levy special high rates on luxury goods.[5]

If a VAT is really equivalent to a retail sales tax, except that more businesses are involved in the collection process, why go through all the extra trouble? There must be some reason, since almost every advanced nation that ever had a sales tax has abandoned it in favor of the VAT by now. In a nutshell, the answer is that the retail sales tax suffers from important administrative and enforcement problems that are greatly magnified as the rate gets higher; the VAT gets around these problems in clever ways. Most tax experts believe that a retail sales tax large enough to replace our personal and corporate income taxes would be unadministrable, but that a VAT of that size could be run fairly smoothly. Later in this chapter, when we discuss the simplicity and enforceability aspects of consumption taxes, we will explain why.

How the Hall-Rabushka Flat Tax Works

The term VAT is seldom mentioned in the popular media, and few political candidates ever run explicitly on a VAT platform. Nevertheless, it is important to understand how a VAT works because the "flat tax" that has gained so much attention lately *is* essentially a VAT. Before explaining further, it is necessary to clarify exactly which "flat tax" is being discussed here.

The original flat tax was developed in 1981 by economist Robert E. Hall and political scientist Alvin Rabushka, both of Stanford University. It was laid out in their 1983 book *Low Tax, Simple Tax, Flat Tax* (renamed *The Flat Tax* in its 1995 version), which has come to be known as the flat tax "bible." Hall and Rabushka first attracted attention by claiming that their flat tax returns could fit on a postcard. For most of its short life, the flat tax has had a devoted but small band of supporters. It formed the basis of a few proposals introduced in Congress during the years leading up to the Tax Reform Act of 1986, but the proposals soon fell from serious consideration. When Jerry Brown ran for the 1992 Democratic presidential nomination touting his own "flat tax" proposal, the Hall-Rabushka plan again came into the spotlight, and was compared favorably in the media to Brown's plan. But the flat tax really hit the public consciousness after the Republicans took control of Congress in the 1994 elections. House Majority Leader Richard Armey (R-TX) and Senator Richard Shelby (R-AL) introduced legislation based on the Hall-Rabushka plan in Congress in 1995, and flat tax stories soon proliferated in the popular media. Steve Forbes then made it the centerpiece of his bid for the 1996 Republican presidential nomination. Numerous other politicians have now proposed plans that have at least one element of flatness discussed in Chapter 6—a single rate, a consumption base, or a clean base. But the Hall-Rabushka plan, which involves all three elements of "flatness," was the first, and its innovative design has earned it the right to be called *the* flat tax.

Readers vaguely familiar with the flat tax will probably be surprised that it is lumped together with the retail sales tax and the VAT. The flat tax looks a lot more like the current system than either of the other two, mostly because along with a tax remitted by businesses there is a separate tax on individuals, who must annually file returns, albeit simple ones. Recall that under either a sales tax or a VAT, individuals are completely outside the tax system and need never contemplate their own personal returns.

Although the flat tax looks superficially like our existing income tax, it is fundamentally different. It is really a reconstituted VAT or, in other words, a reconstituted sales tax. Under the flat tax, businesses pay tax on their total sales, minus purchases of material inputs and investment goods (which are deducted immediately), just like a VAT. There is only one main difference; unlike a VAT, the flat tax also allows firms to deduct payments of wages and salaries (but not fringe benefits) to their workers. Wages and salaries are then taxed separately, at the same rate, at the personal level. The flat tax simply takes wages out of the VAT tax base, puts them on the employee's tax return, and labels that return the "individual wage tax." This is where that discussion of "tax incidence" back in Chapter 3 leads to a truly surprising insight. Which side of a transaction gets taxed—in this case, the employer or the employee—ultimately makes no difference, so a version of the Hall-Rabushka flat tax with a single rate and no exemptions would be identical to a VAT or a comprehensive sales tax.

If a flat tax is really just a VAT in disguise, why go through the extra trouble of having individuals fill out returns and pay tax on their wages? The main reason is that it allows some adjustment of individual tax liabilities according to ability-to-pay. The individual wage portion of the flat tax offers a large family allowance, similar to but larger than today's standard deduction and personal exemptions (exact amounts will be discussed in the next section). People with low wage and salary income are exempt from tax, at least at the personal level. As illustrated in the last chapter, the ratio of personal tax to labor income would gradually increase from zero for families with labor income at or below the exemption, up to the uniform flat rate for high-income families. So the flat tax is progressive. This is a much simpler and more efficient method of introducing progressivity than would be possible under a sales tax or VAT, a point addressed in more detail later.

While the Hall-Rabushka flat tax is quite similar to a VAT, there are enormous differences from the existing personal income tax. The only other aspect of the current personal tax code that is retained is the treatment of employer-provided pensions. Pension contributions continue to be deductible by businesses, and benefits paid to retirees continue to be included in the retirees' taxable incomes. That's it. Just two items of income would be reported on one's personal tax return: wages and pension receipts. All other income—interest, dividends, capital gains, rents, royalties, and so on—would be completely exempt from tax at the personal level. All of the familiar deductions and credits are eliminated, including the deduction for mortgage interest payments, charitable contributions, and state and local taxes.

The business portion of the flat tax also differs substantially from the current corporation income tax. All businesses, not just corporations, must pay this tax. So, instead of sole proprietorships and partnerships reporting their income on Form 1040 as they do now, this income would be subject to a separate business tax; this means that business losses could not offset wage and salary income. The business tax base would also be very different than now, especially in three key ways. First, in keeping with the consumption tax concept, capital expenditures would be deducted immediately when made, instead of as they depreciate. All depreciation deductions for past investments would be disallowed, unless special transition rules were introduced. Second, interest payments (and other financial outflows) would no longer be deductible, nor would interest receipts (and financial inflows) be subject to tax. In the absence of transition rules, deductions for interest obligations on old borrowing would also be disallowed. Third, employer contributions to Social Security, health insurance, and other nonpension benefits would no longer be deductible by businesses, nor would tax payments to state and local governments—all would therefore be subject to the flat rate of tax. We would expect the burden of taxing employers' contributions to benefit plans and Social Security to fall on the workers.

The one element that really distinguishes the Hall-Rabushka flat tax from all other plans is the way it defines the tax base, dividing a VAT into a business component and a wage component. Many details could be changed within the context of this base, while retaining its essential character. For example, certain itemized deductions could be allowed under the wage tax; the pros and cons of these types of exceptions were discussed at the end of Chapter 6. Moreover, the Hall-Rabushka tax base could be adopted in conjunction with graduated rates, a possibility that will be addressed later in this chapter.

On the other hand, many reform proposals that have been labeled "flat" involve a fundamentally different tax base. For example, in the 1996 Republican presidential primaries, Phil Gramm and Pat Buchanan proposed "flat taxes" that included interest, capital gains, and other capital income in the personal tax base, and did not change the taxation of business income in the ways described above. These plans are not consumption taxes, but rather income taxes. To keep things straight, in this chapter, whenever we refer to *the* flat tax, we will only be talking about taxes with the Hall-Rabushka consumption tax base.

How a Personal Consumption Tax Works

A fourth approach to consumption taxation goes by a number of different names, such as the savings-exempt tax, the consumed income tax, the progressive consumption tax, or the personal consumption tax. Its mechanics are completely different than the three varieties of consumption taxes already discussed. In this alternative, consumption is measured person by person. No, it doesn't require each household to keep track of everything it buys.[6] Instead it makes use of the fact that consumption equals income minus saving.

Under a personal consumption tax, all income is included in the individual tax base—not just wages and salaries, but also net interest receipts, dividends, and capital gains realizations. What differentiates it from a pure income tax is that there is an unlimited deduction for all net new savings. Think of this as an unlimited, unrestricted Individual Retirement Account (IRA) that allows for the deduction of net additions to savings accounts, investments in stocks, bonds, mutual funds, life insurance, and other assets. Unlike IRAs, there would be no annual limit on deductions, nor would there be any penalties for withdrawals before retirement, although like IRAs, withdrawals from the accounts would be taxable at the taxpayer's marginal rate. To do this right, all new borrowing would have to be subtracted from saving, because borrowing is simply "dissaving." If you were to borrow $10,000 and then put that money into a bank account, your net saving wouldn't have increased at all, so such a transaction shouldn't be allowed to affect your tax liability.

Although sketches and blueprints of personal consumption taxes have been around for a while, a fleshed-out version has recently appeared in the form of the USA Tax, where the USA stands for Unlimited Savings Allowance. In 1995 a bill to replace the current personal and corporate income taxes with the USA Tax was put forward by Senators Sam Nunn of Georgia and Pete Domenici of New Mexico. It features a personal exemption and standard deduction similar in size to today's system, plus a graduated rate structure with three rates of 19, 27, and 40 percent.[7] Deductions for charitable giving and mortgage interest would be retained, and interest on state and local bonds would continue to be excluded from taxable income. A deduction for up to

$2,000 of higher education expenses (for up to four children) is included, as is an earned income tax credit (EITC). The USA Tax would also include an 11 percent business tax akin to a VAT, although a VAT is not a necessary component of a personal consumption tax. Both businesses and individuals would receive tax credits for their Social Security contributions, and in the case of individuals these would be refundable.

Importantly, the USA Tax excludes certain types of borrowing, such as a home mortgage, from the calculation of net saving. Moreover, elaborate transition rules have been written out. These rules allow a certain amount of past savings to be withdrawn without being counted as "dissaving," and also allow businesses to continue taking depreciation deductions on past investments. The treatment of borrowing and the transition rules both create opportunities for complex avoidance schemes, which we will address later.

Appearances Can Be Deceiving: Transitional Similarities and Differences

Some of the approaches discussed above *appear* on the surface more like consumption taxes than others, but as we have demonstrated, such appearances are deceiving. Thinking about the transition to each of these consumption taxes can help clear up such misperceptions and can also highlight some distinctions among the plans that are important.

If we were to replace our income taxes with a retail sales tax or VAT, the most likely scenario is that the price, inclusive of tax, of everything you buy would increase by the full amount of the new taxes. If prices were not allowed to rise in this way, firms would have to reduce the *before-tax* wages of their workers, to reflect the fact that each worker's output was now bringing in smaller sales revenue after taxes. If this could be accomplished, workers' *after-tax* wages would on average not change much; the elimination of income taxes would be offset by a decline in their before-tax wages. The problem is that for many people wages are fixed in the short run by contracts; in these cases, firms would be unable to reduce before-tax wages, so instead many might be forced to lay off workers. To avoid such disruptions, the Federal Reserve, which exerts influence over prices through its control of the money supply, would probably allow tax-inclusive prices to rise by the amount of the new taxes. If this occurs, it's easy to see why the VAT or sales tax is a consumption tax—the price of everything you buy would increase by the amount of a visible tax.

If we were to move to a Hall-Rabushka flat tax, on the other hand, inflexible pretax wages are not a problem. The wage portion of the flat tax could just replace the old personal income tax on your paycheck. For this reason, it is more likely that prices would stay at about the same level. Because the tax would not visibly appear as a rise in the price of everything you buy, and because the business portion of the tax is somewhat hidden, the flat tax may *appear* to be more like a wage tax, which would be a windfall to wealth holders. But this perception is totally wrong. As explained in the last chapter, no matter what happens to the overall price level, what a consumption tax does is reduce the real purchasing power of wages and existing wealth. The business portion of the flat tax is exactly a tax on existing wealth, because it taxes business output while disallowing depreciation deductions on old capital. So the business component makes it a consumption tax, and not a wage tax.

A personal consumption tax would not require an increase in the price level either, because it could be implemented like the current personal income tax, but with an unlimited IRA-type deduction. The USA Tax proposal is a bit more complicated, however, because it also has a VAT, which probably would require some rise in prices. In any event, it is easy to see why such a tax would be a consumption tax, because you would visibly pay taxes on your income minus your saving.

As discussed in Chapter 6, there are some real consequences to whether the price level changes or not, due to temporary inflexibilities in some contracts. For example, if prices did not rise, businesses could not pass the burden of the one-time wealth tax on to bondholders. But the change in the price level has no effect on whether the burden of these taxes falls on consumption, or just wages. Rather, it is the degree of transition relief that determines this. For example, the USA Tax would allow some consumption out of old saving tax free, and would continue to allow depreciation deductions on old capital—pushing it in the direction of a wage tax. If similar provisions were introduced into a flat tax, it would also become more like a wage tax.[8]

At What Rate?

Before evaluating the consumption tax alternatives, it will be helpful to flesh them out by discussing what sort of tax rates and exemption levels would be involved. Promoters of specific plans often advertise rates that would lose money relative to the current system, and in some cases these losses are very large; this can make them, or any tax system, look attractive indeed. This section will focus on the rates that would be required to raise the same amount of revenue as the current system—so-called revenue-neutral rates.

If any one of the four consumption tax proposals was somehow able to tax all personal consumption expenditures in the United States, and had a single rate with no exemptions whatsoever, that rate would have to be about 14.3 percent to replace all the revenues from the federal corporate and personal income taxes (including elimination of the EITC).[9] In practice, however, no consumption tax could achieve a rate this low and still raise enough revenue. Many types of consumption are very difficult to tax and almost certainly would not be included in the tax base. Moreover, there will always be some evasion. Under the current income tax system, several hundred billion dollars of taxable income goes unreported.[10] While it might be possible to reduce evasion under an alternative system, undoubtedly a significant amount will persist. Finally, each proposal would purposefully exempt some income or consumption from the base in an effort to ease the burden on those with low incomes, and some plans also involve graduated rates.

So what kinds of rates would be required? First consider the retail sales tax. How high the tax rate would have to be depends heavily on how extensive the tax base is. Among the states, it is common to exempt medical expenditures (including insurance), food for home consumption, clothing, the imputed rental value of housing, religious and charitable activities, and most services. Goods subject to excise taxes such as motor fuel, liquor, tobacco products, telephone services, and publications are also usually exempted.

If the federal sales tax base were to look like that of the average state, replacing the personal and corporate income taxes would require a rate of about 23.6 percent.[11] Emulating the states with the very broadest sales tax bases could lower the rate to perhaps 16.5 percent.[12] At that level of coverage, the sales tax would fully tax food, which is the most expensive exemption, comprising nearly a quarter of potential sales tax revenue.[13] Both of these figures are gross underestimates for a national sales tax rate, however, because a great deal of state sales tax revenue actually comes from purchases of business inputs, which are supposed to be exempt from a retail sales tax. One recent study[14] estimated that on average only 59 percent of state sales tax revenues actually came from final purchases by resident consumers—almost all of the rest represented taxation of business inputs. Taxing business inputs with a retail sales tax is economically harmful, and becomes much more so as the tax rate gets higher. If business inputs were to be completely eliminated from the base, the national rate would have to be in the high thirties using the tax base of a typical state, or the high twenties if we followed the example of states with the broadest bases. For a revenue-neutral national retail sales tax to feature a rate that even approaches 17 percent, the rate Senator Lugar has proposed, it would have to have a broader base and would have to be administered much more effectively than that of any state in the Union.

In principle, because the VAT base is the same as the retail sales tax base, the same calculations for estimating the revenue-neutral rate should apply. In practice, the VAT does a much better job of avoiding the taxation of business inputs, and involves considerably less evasion. Still, many types of consumption would be very difficult if not impossible to tax under a VAT. The imputed rental value of the existing housing stock, and the value of financial services that are paid for through lower interest rates rather than fees, are just two among many examples. Congressional Budget Office estimates suggest that a comprehensive VAT, which provided no special treatment for purchases of food or housing, could successfully tax about 81 percent of personal consumption expenditures. A base of this size implies that a rate of about 17.6 percent would be required to replace federal revenue from the individual and corporate income tax systems.[15] Preferential treatment of any kind increases the revenue-neutral VAT rate.

A flat tax requires a higher rate than a VAT, because the family allowances reduce the tax base significantly. On the other hand, the separate wage tax means that unlike a VAT, labor compensation in some hard-to-tax sectors such as financial services can easily be taxed, providing some offset. Similarly, the labor income of government employees would be taxed under the flat tax, but not under the VAT. Exactly what the revenue-neutral rate would be for the flat tax depends heavily on the size of the family allowances and exactly how the tax base is defined.[16]

In their book on the flat tax, Hall and Rabushka propose a 19 percent rate on individuals and businesses, and set the exempt level of income for a family of four at $25,500 for 1995.[17] They present a calculation suggesting this plan would raise as much revenue as the current tax system. As they admit, their calculation is "back-of-the-envelope" and assumes no evasion; it also involves a few small errors.[18] Using a methodology based on actual tax returns, the U.S. Treasury Department has calculated more reliable estimates for a number of related, but slightly different, flat tax proposals. They estimate that the Armey-Shelby version, which has a $31,400 exemption for a family of four in 1996, and would eliminate the EITC and estate and gift taxes, would require a rate of 20.8 percent to be revenue-neutral; the same plan could achieve a 17 percent rate if the allowance for a family of four were reduced to $15,000.[19] This suggests that, for each percentage point reduction in the single tax rate, a decrease in the tax-exempt level for a family of four of about $4,300 is required to keep revenue constant.[20] Adding back in some itemized deductions or changing the tax base in other ways could raise the required rate for a flat tax significantly. For instance, allowing deductibility of home mortgage interest and charitable deductions would push the revenue-neutral rate on the July 1995 Armey-Shelby plan from 20.8 percent to about 22.7 percent.[21]

There is no one rate to examine for a graduated personal consumption tax. However, the drafters of the USA Tax put a high priority on raising enough revenue, and the rates mentioned above for that system are certainly in the ballpark of revenue neutrality.

It is possible that if tax reform were to induce greater economic growth, the revenue-neutral rates on any of these plans could eventually be somewhat lower than the ones we have discussed. This is an important question, but one that will be deferred until discussion of the economic impact of specific proposals later in this chapter. Spending cuts could also allow some reduction in rates, although these cuts would have to come on top of all the other cuts that would already be needed to balance the budget. Moreover, the level of spending is really a separate issue from tax reform, and the reduced rates that spending cuts allow could make any tax system, including the existing one, look more attractive.

Simplicity and Enforceability of the Consumption Tax Plans

Now that what rate of tax we're talking about has been established, an evaluation of the consumption tax plans can begin. Some very important administrative questions must be reviewed first—how simple or complicated is each approach, and how easy is it to enforce? The answers to these questions turn out to be crucial for determining which approach to consumption taxation is the best, and are also an important factor in deciding whether any of them would be better than the existing system or a reformed income tax.

Administrative Problems of a Retail Sales Tax Compared to a VAT

On the surface, the retail sales tax seems like a fairly simple and straightforward way to raise money and, to the average citizen, it probably appears to work reasonably well. But, as mentioned before, virtually every developed country that ever had a national retail sales tax has by now replaced it with a VAT. The reason is that there are serious administrative problems with the retail sales tax that most average Americans never hear about. These problems are not too glaring when rates are low, as they are in most states (usually in the 4 to 6 percent range). But at the rates that would be required to replace U.S. personal and corporate taxation, these problems would be very serious indeed.

It is true that our current state retail sales taxes seem to be simpler and relatively less costly to administer than our income tax system. Recent studies suggest that the total cost of enforcing and complying with current state retail sales taxes is on the order of 2.4 percent to 4.8 percent of revenues raised.[22] This is lower than the 10 percent that is estimated for the current income tax system, but is not necessarily a reliable indicator of what the costs would be like for a national retail sales tax. Current administrative costs do not give a flavor of the kinds of problems that could be created at very high rates.

The first problem with the RST is the taxation of business inputs. A retail sales tax is supposed to tax only the final purchases of consumers, and not the purchases of businesses. If businesses pay sales taxes on their inputs, and then again when they sell their outputs, a problem of "cascading" develops. Goods that require more intermediate steps in production and distribution end up being taxed more heavily. This distorts incentives in the economy, leading to inefficient changes in the types of goods that get produced and consumed, and the way businesses are organized. Most states try to avoid this problem by giving businesses a registration number to present when purchasing goods from other firms, exempting them from sales tax liability. But this procedure works very poorly in practice, as evidenced by the very high percentage of RST revenues that apparently come from business purchases. This is not a very noticeable problem at low rates of tax, but would be very serious if rates were approaching 30 percent or more, as they would if a national RST were added on top of the state taxes. At high rates, a mirror-image problem would also emerge—consumers inappropriately making use of business registration numbers to avoid the sales tax. These problems are largely avoided under a VAT, as the whole system is designed to allow businesses to deduct or receive credit for taxes paid to other businesses. Moreover, only businesses that file tax returns are able to take advantage of the VAT credit.

A second and perhaps more fundamental problem with the retail sales tax is that at high tax rates, it becomes extremely difficult to enforce. The reason is that it collects all of the tax liability from what is, for compliance purposes, the weakest link in the production and distribution chain. Consumers have no incentive to make sure retailers are paying their sales tax, and retailers have no incentive to pay aside from the threat of audit. In contrast, under a standard credit-invoice style VAT, firms have an incentive to make sure that any other firm they are buying from has paid its VAT, so they can claim credit for it on their tax returns. Moreover, a retailer that evades a 10 percent RST costs the government tax revenue equal to the full 10 percent of the final value of the good or service. The VAT only puts at risk, at most, the revenue from the portion of the final value of the good or service produced at the given firm, which in the case of a retailer is a fairly small percentage. Under a credit-method VAT, a firm that does not file a return or collect the VAT on its sales can actually end up paying *more* tax, because it does not get a refund of taxes on its purchases. While evasion under current state retail sales taxes may not appear that serious, the problem would be much worse at higher rates. As one leading expert, Alan Tait of the International Monetary Fund, has put it: "at 5 percent, the incentive to evade tax is probably not worth the penalties of prosecution; at 10 percent, evasion is more attractive, and at 15–20 percent, it becomes extremely tempting."[23]

Just as with an income tax, there are also all sorts of difficult issues of interpretation under the sales tax. The difference is that, unless you run a retail sales business, the typical American never hears about these problems. Whenever there are exempt commodities, where the line is drawn is important. Consider the problem if expenditures on food, but not restaurant meals, are exempt. What is the appropriate tax treatment of salad bars in grocery stores or fast food restaurants, where the customer may eat in or take out? These sorts of problems become much more troublesome as the rate rises.

Worst of all, there is no historical precedent to reassure us that these problems are manageable in a retail sales tax. Undoubtedly for the reasons discussed above, in history only five countries have operated retail sales taxes at rates over 10 percent. Three of them, Norway, Sweden, and Iceland, decided to switch to a VAT.[24] Based on a review of worldwide practice, Vito Tanzi, the director of the Fiscal Analysis Division of the International Monetary Fund, concludes that 10 percent is probably the maximum rate feasible for a retail sales tax.[25] We believe that, because of compliance and enforcement problems, replacing the income tax with a retail sales tax would be unwise, especially given that a VAT can achieve the same goals while avoiding most of these problems.

Just How Simple and Easy to Enforce Is a VAT?

The VAT clearly has many administrative advantages over a retail sales tax. Although the VAT involves more businesses in the collection process, it makes it much easier to prevent taxation of business inputs, and it is considerably easier to enforce. Just how simple and easy would it be to enforce a VAT, and how would this compare to the current system?

To be sure, replacing the income tax with a comprehensive, single-rate VAT could provide an enormous amount of simplification. Not only could individual income tax returns be completely eliminated, but business tax returns could be significantly simplified, requiring little more information than is now collected in the normal course of business. Complex depreciation deductions would be eliminated. It would also be easier to enforce than the combined personal and corporate income tax codes.

A few recent studies have estimated the enforcement and compliance costs of adopting a VAT. Consider first the costs to the enforcement agency, whether it be the IRS or some renamed authority. A U.S. Treasury Department estimate from 1984 suggests that a relatively simple version of a VAT would cost the government about $1.5 billion (in 1996 dollars) to administer and enforce when fully operational, assuming a 2.2 percent audit rate.[26] A 1993 study by the General Accounting Office (GAO) suggests the cost with a 7.8 percent audit rate would be close to $2 billion.[27] An important consideration is whether, and at what level, small businesses are exempt from the VAT system. The GAO estimated that exempting all businesses with revenues below $100,000 would cut the cost by about one-third. These administrative cost estimates can be roughly compared to the current IRS budget of about $7 billion, although the IRS oversees more than the income tax system.

As Chapter 5 made clear, for most taxes the largest fraction of the cost of running a tax system is not the administrative budget, but rather the cost expended by the taxpayers themselves. The VAT is no exception. An analysis by the Congressional Budget Office (CBO) suggests that the combined administrative and compliance costs of raising $150 billion from a relatively clean European-style VAT would be between $5 and $8 billion, or between 3.3 and 5.3 percent of revenues collected.[28] They note that these costs would be "largely independent" of the amount of revenue raised, suggesting that the cost-revenue ratio for a $700 billion-plus VAT could be substantially lower, but to an unknown degree. Taken at face value, the CBO estimate certainly suggests a large potential cost saving compared to our estimates of the cost of the current income tax. However, before jumping to the apparent conclusion of large simplification, several points should be noted.

First, a portion of the apparent compliance cost saving of replacing the income tax with a VAT stems from the elimination of individual tax returns. This saving would be largely lost if the states do not abolish their own personal income tax systems. Because most of the information required to calculate income is currently used for both federal and state income tax purposes, eliminating only the federal return requirement would not spare most individuals the need to file returns and keep track of the requisite information.

Second, the cost estimates done by the CBO and others presume that businesses with turnover less than a certain amount will be exempt from VAT liability. In a VAT, exemption means that the firm is completely outside the tax system. It does not charge or remit to the government VAT on its sales, nor is it allowed to take a credit for VAT charged on its purchases from suppliers. Exemptions for retailers cost the government revenue on the final slice of a product's value. But exempting a firm in the middle of the production and distribution chain can actually *increase* revenues, because neither the exempt firm nor the next firm in the chain can take a credit for taxes paid at earlier stages in the chain. So overall, exempting small firms is unlikely to cost the government much revenue. It does involve some economic costs, however, as it can distort firms' decisions regarding size and organizational form, and can tax different types of goods more heavily or lightly depending on how many firms in the good's production and distribution chain are exempt and where in the chain these firms are located.

The fact that the cost estimates presume small businesses are exempt also makes the comparison with the current income tax somewhat unfair. Recall that small business is the most costly sector to tax, as judged by the cost-to-revenue ratio, under an income tax as well as under a VAT. So exempting small business from tax would effect considerable simplification under the income tax, too. To put it another way, part of the calculated compliance and administrative cost savings from adopting a VAT come from dropping hard-to-tax entities out of the tax system, which has nothing inherently to do with a VAT. Moreover, some of the simplification reflects elimination of complicated features that are not essential to the corporate income tax—such as the alternative minimum tax. The possibility of simplifying the existing personal and corporate codes will be addressed in more detail in the next chapter.

Finally, it must be said that the VAT introduces some tricky administrative issues that do not arise under an income tax, such as how to tax financial transactions. The VAT base applies only to real operations—sales revenue minus the cost of inputs—and not to the financial operations of a firm. But for a financial institution, the financial transactions are the real purpose of the business, and the pricing of the services offered is often implicit in the interest charges and payments. Thus, by placing net interest receipts outside of the tax base, one may be seriously mismeasuring the true value-added of a financial firm, or of a nonfinancial firm with financial operations. Procedures must be developed to deal with, for example, installment sales of automobiles, because a firm has the incentive to characterize its receipts as (untaxed) interest, while a consumer would be indifferent as to what his or her payments are labeled.

Although these problems with a VAT are difficult, there are also three decades of experience in other countries, particularly in Europe, on which to draw. In contrast to the retail sales tax, VATs of the size necessary to replace the U.S. income tax are not out of the range of historical experience. The standard rate, applied to most goods and services, is 20 percent or more in several European countries. Although 10.4 percent—the ratio of federal personal and corporate income tax receipts to GDP in the United States—is higher than that collected by value-added taxation in any other OECD country, it is not higher by much. Among the nations with the largest VATs as a percent of GDP are Iceland (9.9 percent), Denmark (9.8 percent), Greece (9.3 percent), and Norway (9.1 percent). Of the largest European countries, France raises 7.4 percent, Germany 6.8 percent, and the United Kingdom 6.6 percent.[29]

The fact that VATs have been around a while, at levels comparable to what the United States would need to replace the income tax, is both the good news and the bad news. It is the good news because we would not be stepping into unknown territory, as would be the case with a retail sales tax. It is the bad news because the experience from other countries is not encouraging about the possibility of actually realizing the simplification potential of a VAT. For the most part the European countries do not levy the kind of broad-base, uniform-rate VAT we have been discussing, or perhaps fantasizing about. Instead the European VATs have multiple rates and numerous exemptions, features that require difficult-to-make distinctions, invite abuse, and call for close monitoring.

The scant quantitative evidence that exists suggests that, warts and all, the European VATs are no less costly to collect than their income taxes. A careful study of the British tax system of 1986–1987 concluded that the ratio of collection cost to revenue raised was only slightly lower for the VAT compared to the personal income tax—4.7 percent for the VAT (1 percent for administration, and 3.7 percent for taxpayer costs) and 4.9 percent for the personal income tax (1.5 percent for administration, 3.4 percent for taxpayer costs).[30] A recent study of the Swedish tax system suggests that its VAT is *more* expensive to operate than its income tax, costing 3.1 percent of revenue to collect compared to 2.7 percent for the income tax, prompting the author of the study to remark that "the VAT is evidently not the simple tax it has been marketed as."[31] Undoubtedly, in both these cases the failure of the VAT to display a collection cost advantage reflects both that actual VATs are more expensive than ideal VATs, and also apparently that European income taxes are less costly to collect than the U.S. income tax. It is also possible that these other studies make somewhat more conservative estimates of compliance costs for both types of tax, compared to those cited for the United States in Chapter 5, although this is very hard to gauge.

Nor do enforcement problems disappear, in spite of the theoretical self-enforcement feature of the invoice-credit method of administering the VAT. Estimates of evasion range from 2–4 percent in the United

Kingdom to 40 percent in Italy.[32] A VAT requires a strong enforcement system to monitor unregistered business, exaggerated refund claims, unrecorded cash purchases, underreported sales, false export claims, and so on.

All in all, there is no doubt that a VAT *potentially* represents a major simplification compared to our current income tax. But the failure of European VATs to be as simple as the drawing board version of a VAT suggests caution when comparing the messy real world to an ideal. More practically, it is a warning that, if the United States were to adopt a VAT, it would be well advised to keep it simple, above all, levying a uniform rate on all firms and all goods and services.

Simplicity and Enforceability of a Flat Tax

As shown above, the Hall-Rabushka flat tax adds an extra step to the VAT, by taking wages and salaries out of the VAT base and requiring individuals to fill out their own returns on which they report that income. This extra step makes a big difference in the ease with which tax burdens can be adjusted according to ability-to-pay. But it also adds some degree of extra compliance costs and enforcement problems. Nonetheless, a clean version of the Hall-Rabushka flat tax would undoubtedly be much simpler to comply with and easier to enforce than the current system.

At the business level, the flat tax involves a subtraction-method VAT (with labor costs deductible), rather than the credit-invoice method used in most other countries. The reason is that by removing the labor portion of value-added from the business tax base, it becomes impossible to have some fixed tax rate charged on every transaction between businesses. The exact rate would depend on the share of capital versus labor used to produce that particular good or service, which varies greatly. There is some possibility that a flat tax could be implemented in a credit-invoice framework, but it would be more difficult and the details have not been worked out.[33]

A subtraction-method VAT lacks some of the enforcement advantages of a credit-invoice VAT, which is why almost all countries use the latter method. Since a fixed tax rate can no longer be charged on each transaction, it becomes harder to monitor whether tax is paid on each transaction. The flat business tax thus becomes more like a corporate income tax for administrative purposes. A subtraction-method VAT also makes exempting small businesses somewhat more difficult, although it is still possible.[34] Neither the Hall-Rabushka flat tax blue-print nor the Armey-Shelby version mention a small business exemption. In its absence, the substantial cost savings of being able to ignore the hardest-to-tax sector are lost. The flat tax would suffer from some of the same problems as a VAT, such as the incentive for businesses to redefine "sales to consumers" as nontaxable interest received from consumers. It would have the advantage, however, of taxing the labor portion of hard-to-tax services separately.

Contrary to what Hall and Rabushka claim, moreover, flat tax business returns would probably not be able to fit on postcards. Doing so would require combining many different items into single entries, making it very difficult for the IRS to verify the results. In any event, the postcard would merely summarize what could be millions of transactions, understating the difficulty of monitoring the tax return. Still, the flat business tax would in principle be considerably simpler and easier to enforce than a corporate income tax, in part because of the replacement of depreciation deductions with expensing and the fact that financial transactions generally have no tax consequences. It would also have the advantage of eliminating many of the complicated special provisions in the current corporate code, although this could be accomplished within the context of the income tax as well.

At the personal level, the flat tax is obviously more complicated than a VAT, because a VAT eliminates personal returns altogether. But it is vastly simpler and easier to enforce than the current income tax system. Since only wage and pension income need be reported, all of the complications associated with reporting personal capital income are eliminated. The Hall-Rabushka claim that personal returns could be made to fit on postcards may indeed be feasible. With a single rate, moreover, withholding could also be much more accurate, making the process that much simpler. Workers whose wages are subject to information reporting and withholding would have very high compliance rates, as under the current system, although the self-employed would continue to pose an administrative and compliance problem; for example, the knotty issue of whether a car is for business or personal purposes looms just as large, even larger. A clean flat tax also eliminates most opportunities for "tax arbitrage," a major source of complex avoidance schemes discussed earlier. In general, a single tax rate is imposed on the tax base, no matter what the taxpayer labels it. There would surely still be some ways to "game the system," but these opportunities would be greatly reduced.[35]

It is difficult to come up with a precise estimate of the compliance and enforcement costs associated with a flat tax, especially because no other country has ever operated such a system. The total cost would surely be lower than our estimate of $75 billion per year for the current system, perhaps half as large.

It's important to recognize that the simplification promises of the flat tax depend on a lot of big "ifs." What starts as a very simple plan could end up becoming a mess as it winds its way through the political process. For instance, allowing lots of itemized deductions would make the personal system more complicated, and retaining home mortgage interest deductions in particular would create arbitrage problems discussed in the previous chapter. Transition rules could make things even more complicated than the current system in the short run. Some flat tax advocates have also proposed eliminating withholding of taxes on wages, which would undoubtedly cause major enforcement problems. And simplifying the federal code would only help taxpayers to the extent that the states followed suit. It's also worth noting that some of the simplification, such as eliminating itemized deductions, could be achieved while retaining the existing income tax structure. Nonetheless, the basic simplicity of the flat tax approach to progressive consumption taxation cannot be denied.

The Personal Consumption Tax: Complexity and Enforcement Problems

Unlike the other kinds of consumption tax discussed so far, the personal consumption tax would complicate tax matters for many individuals. It is true that some of the difficult compromises made by the current income tax—such as including capital gains in taxable income only upon realization—are handled easily by a personal consumption tax; for example, if accrued capital gains are left unrealized, they are both income and saving, so they have no tax consequences. However, the tax affairs of the average taxpayer, for whom the conceptual measurement difficulties of capital income are now of little concern, would be complicated by the addition to the tax base of borrowing and savings account withdrawals. If done correctly, even credit card borrowing would have to be reported.

For those families with extensive capital income flows, calculating taxable income can be simplified to the extent that assets are kept within the IRA-type accounts. However, some features of the new requirement to keep track of net saving will be complex, and aspects of personal financial affairs that currently have no tax implications would under a personal consumption tax. Note that although a personal consumption tax is akin to having an unlimited, unrestricted IRA, in the IRA case participation is a voluntary decision taken to reduce tax liability. Under a personal consumption tax all taxpayers would be required to measure and report their net savings, which is significantly more difficult than reporting limited deposits to an IRA account, and only reporting withdrawals during retirement.

A whole host of new enforcement issues and complex avoidance schemes arise under a personal consumption tax. For example, while taxpayers would have the incentive to report all the deductions for new saving to which they are entitled, they would have an incentive not to report withdrawals or borrowing. The Treasury Department's 1984 study of this issue concluded that compliance with a personal consumption tax would require "a more extensive system of information reporting and monitoring than does an income tax," including "a comprehensive inventory of all existing wealth upon enactment of the tax, registration of private borrowing, and a far-reaching system of exchange controls to facilitate policing of foreign transactions."[36] Martin Ginsburg of Georgetown Law Center recently took a close look at life under the USA Tax and concluded that the plan was fundamentally flawed. He noted numerous ways that high-income taxpayers could manipulate the definition of net saving to avoid taxes, leading to bizarre situations in which "municipal bonds pay interest in even years only, executive compensation and the yield on at least one class of each corporation's stock is paid only in odd years, and the rich with borrowed money buy raw land or works of art they admire but may not keep forever."[37] Some of the problems are caused by the transition rules, deductions, and compromises in the USA Tax in particular, but others are hard to avoid in any personal consumption tax of this type.

In its favor, a personal consumption tax eliminates the need for a complex business tax, as it can stand alone or be accompanied by a VAT, the simplification advantages of which have already been discussed. However, given the overwhelming desire for a simplified and less intrusive tax system, the complications caused by a personal consumption tax outweigh the potential simplification at the business level. It would be a shame to undertake a massive overhaul of our tax system, with all the associated transition costs, and end up with a system that is no less complicated than the current system. This is particularly true given that many of the same goals of the personal consumption tax could be achieved using the Hall-Rabushka consumption tax base.

Distributional Effects of the Consumption Tax Alternatives

Of course, simplicity and enforceability are not the only criteria for choosing a tax system, nor are they necessarily the most important. Most everyone also has a strong and abiding interest in the distributional consequences of tax reform—which plans will make your tax bill larger or smaller, and more generally, how will the burdens end up being shared by people with different abilities to carry the load?

Distributional Consequences of a Retail Sales Tax or VAT

Although a retail sales tax and a VAT have essentially the same economic and distributional effects, the VAT has important administrative advantages. As a result, there seems to be little reason to adopt a retail sales tax. In what follows, therefore, we will mainly refer to the effects of a VAT, although the same basic results should hold for the sales tax as well.

Chapter 6 argued that, over a lifetime, a single-rate VAT would exact from individuals a burden that is approximately proportional to their lifetime incomes, although somewhat regressive to the extent that inheritances and bequests escape tax and to the extent that transfers are not indexed to keep up with any price increase the tax causes. It doesn't take a complex analysis to reach the conclusion that, compared to an income tax with a generous level of tax-free income, graduated rates, and an earned income credit for the working poor, a VAT would increase the burden substantially on low-income households. For example, someone who spends an entire lifetime at the poverty level would remit no income taxes under the current system, because tax-exempt levels are currently set to approximate the poverty line. In fact, if such a person were poor in spite of working, he or she would currently receive a refund, because of the EITC. In stark contrast, a 17 percent VAT would impose a tax burden equal to approximately 17 percent of that person's lifetime income. Similar reasoning suggests the tax burden on high-income households will fall greatly if the graduated income tax is replaced by a flat-rate VAT. Both low- and middle-income people would be likely to pick up the slack through higher tax burdens.

The question then is whether the potential gains—from simplification and potential economic growth effects—justify a redistribution of tax burden of this magnitude. No economic analysis can provide a decisive answer to this question, because it involves evaluating a policy that makes some people better-off and others worse-off. Even with the possibility that the economy could grow and eventually compensate the less well off for some of the increased tax burden, such an evaluation inescapably involves value judgments that must ultimately be resolved by our political system. We suspect, though, that most Americans do not favor such a dramatic shift in the tax burden, and for this reason would not support the VAT as a replacement for the income tax.

Can the VAT be saved, by somehow dampening redistributional consequences? The answer is yes, but at significant cost in terms of simplicity and economic efficiency. One way to soften the regressivity of a switch to a VAT is to abandon tax rate uniformity and instead to impose a zero, or lower than average, tax rate on those commodities that figure more heavily in the expenditures of poorer families, such as food, shelter, and health care. However, the European experience with the VAT shows that multiple-rate VAT systems are significantly more complex and therefore more expensive to administer; preferential taxation of necessities also sharply reduces revenues, requiring an even higher tax rate on other goods. Most important, because a large fraction of expenditure on the preferentially taxed commodities is made by middle- and high-income families, this is a very poorly targeted way to increase the progressivity of the VAT. It also causes significant economic distortions, creating an inefficient incentive to consume more of the goods and services that are untaxed, and less of the ones that are taxed. Since tax rates well above 20 percent would be required for a VAT with exempt commodities, the distortion to incentives would be quite large.

A second alternative is to impose a uniform-rate VAT simultaneously with a large increase in income maintenance programs designed to offset the impact of the VAT on lower-income households, or perhaps a new universal tax credit paid to all individuals and families. This is not an unreasonable option, but such an approach would probably be unpopular, especially considering current public opinion regarding welfare. It would also entail additional administrative costs and enforcement problems. In the case of the credit, it would require that a whole new administrative apparatus be set up in addition to the one needed to run the VAT.

Distributional Consequences of a Flat Tax

None of the alternatives mentioned for the VAT addresses the vertical equity issue as easily as a flat tax, whose genesis was exactly as a scheme to administer a VAT with an efficient method for achieving some progressivity. The tax-exempt level of labor income in the flat tax makes it equivalent to a VAT plus a limited (and nonrefundable) credit for earned income set at the flat rate.

How would a flat tax distribute the burden of taxes relative to the current system? The U.S. Treasury Department's Office of Tax Analysis has estimated the distributional impact of a few specific flat tax proposals. Their projections are done on an annual basis, rather than the theoretically preferable but difficult-to-implement lifetime basis. The estimates depend on explicit assumptions about incidence: that both the old corporate income tax and the new VAT-like business tax would be borne by individuals in proportion to their capital income, that the old individual income tax is borne by those households that remit the tax, and that all taxes on labor compensation are borne by workers.

These assumptions are by no means uncontroversial, but they provide a reasonable baseline approximation of the distributional impact of a change to a flat tax.[38] Moreover, these analyses are clearly better than the examples often seen in the popular media, which usually just look at the individual wage portion of the flat tax. By ignoring the business tax and new taxes on employer contributions for Social Security and fringe benefits, such examples can give a misleading impression of the true impact on tax burdens. In addition, the Treasury analysis adjusts the rates or exemptions in the flat tax proposals so that they will raise the same revenue as the current system, in order to make an appropriate comparison. Finally, the results do not account for the effects of any economic growth that might occur because of the reforms—an issue that will be taken up later.

Table 7.1 illustrates the Treasury's estimates of tax burdens as a percentage of total income[39] under the current personal and corporate income tax system and three recent flat tax proposals. Alternative (1) is

Table 7.1
Treasury estimates of the distributional impact of flat tax proposals: Average tax rates

Family Income		Average Tax Rates			
Percentile rank	1996 income range (thousands of dollars)	(1) Current personal & corporate income taxes	(2) 20.8% flat tax, $31,400 exemption, no EITC	(2) 17% flat tax, $15,000 exemption, no EITC	(3) 22.9% flat tax, $35,750 exemption, keep EITC
Lowest quintile	0–16	−2.4	3.8	4.6	−1.5
Second quintile	16–30	2.0	6.7	8.3	3.1
Middle quintile	30–49	7.1	9.5	10.9	8.5
Fourth quintile	49–79	9.3	11.2	12.3	11.1
81 to 90 percent	79–109	10.8	12.9	13.1	13.2
91 to 95 percent	109–145	12.8	14.2	13.5	14.6
96 to 99 percent	145–349	15.7	14.8	13.2	15.0
Top 1 percent	349+	22.4	13.5	11.3	14.3

Note: Each flat tax plan above is estimated by the Treasury to be revenue-neutral, assuming no induced economic growth. Assumes the burden of labor taxes falls on workers, and the burden of business taxes fall on capital income generally. Exemption levels are for a married couple with two children in 1996. The 17 and 20.8 percent flat tax options assume repeal of estate and gift taxes.
Source: U.S. Department of Treasury, Office of Tax Analysis (1996), and Samuels (1995).

the July 1995 Armey-Shelby plan, which would provide a family of four with an exempt level of $31,400, and would eliminate both the EITC as well as estate and gift taxes, requiring a rate of 20.8 percent. Alternative (2) is the same plan, but with a $15,000 exemption for a family of four and a 17 percent rate. Alternative (3) has a $35,750 exemption, a 22.9 percent rate, and keeps the EITC and estate and gift taxes.[40] Note that in all three cases the exemptions are lower for single individuals and smaller families, as in the current system.

The Treasury analysis suggests that each of the three plans involves a stark shifting of the tax burden away from those with very high incomes, onto everyone else. Under all three flat taxes, average tax rates decline sharply for those in the top 1 percent of the income distribution, drop moderately for those in the next highest 4 percent, and go up for all other income groups. For example, the 20.8 percent flat tax alternative slashes the average rate on the top 1 percent of taxpayers from 22.4 percent to just 13.5 percent. At the same time, families and individuals in the middle fifth of the income distribution, with annual total income between $30,000 and $49,000, would see their average tax

rate rise from 7.1 percent to 9.5 percent. For a family in the midpoint
of this range, that's a tax increase of about $960 per year.

Table 7.2 converts these results to percentage changes in after-tax
income. Again, all groups outside of the top 5 percent would see
their after-tax incomes decline. Under the first two alternatives, the
largest percentage declines occur among the poorest. For example,
people in the bottom fifth of the income distribution, with incomes
below $16,000, would see their after-tax incomes decline by 6.8 percent
under the first flat tax alternative. Much of this is due to the elimination
of the refundable EITC, which in 1996 pays 40 cents for every dollar
earned up to about $8,890 of wages for families with two children,
with a maximum credit of $3,556 (see Chapter 2 for details). Elimina-
tion of the EITC reduces the incomes of eligible families significantly;
the flat tax's family allowance offers no offsetting benefit, as these families are already exempt from paying income tax under the current
system.

The 22.9 percent flat tax of alternative (3) is noticeably more progressive than the other two options, because it retains the EITC and has a

Table 7.2
Treasury estimates of the distributional impact of flat tax proposals: Percent change in
after-tax incomes

Family Income		Percent Change in After-Tax Income		
Percentile rank	1996 income range (thousands of dollars)	(1) 20.8% flat tax, $31,400 exemption, no EITC	(2) 17% flat tax, $15,000 exemption, no EITC	(3) 22.9% flat tax, $35,750 exemption, keep EITC
Lowest quintile	0–16	−6.8	−7.7	−1.0
Second quintile	16–30	−5.4	−7.2	−1.2
Middle quintile	30–49	−2.9	−4.7	−1.8
Fourth quintile	49–79	−2.4	−3.8	−2.2
81 to 90 percent	79–109	−2.7	−2.9	−3.0
91 to 95 percent	109–145	−1.8	−1.0	−2.4
96 to 99 percent	145–349	1.2	3.2	0.9
Top 1 percent	349+	11.7	14.7	10.8

Note: Each flat tax plan above is estimated by the Treasury to be revenue-neutral,
assuming no induced economic growth. Assumes the burden of labor taxes falls on
workers, and the burden of business taxes falls on capital income generally. Exemption
levels are for a married couple with two children in 1996. The 17 and 20.8 percent flat
tax options assume repeal of estate and gift taxes.
Source: U.S. Department of Treasury, Office of Tax Analysis (1996), and Samuels (1995).

larger family allowance. Under this alternative, the decline in after-tax income for most people ranges from 1 to 3 percent. It is certainly possible to design a flat tax where the income loss for most people is modest, as long as the exemption level is kept large and the EITC or some close substitute is retained. Such a plan would, however, require a rate higher than is usually advertised—in this case, about 23 percent.

These distributional estimates ignore any improvements to the economy that might arise from tax reform. Many aspects of the flat tax, as well as other possible reforms, would likely provide some boost to the economy. Some economists' estimates of the likely size of the boost will be discussed in the next section.

Table 7.2 is helpful for thinking about how large the economic effects would have to be for one of these flat tax proposals to make you better-off, if you're not up in the top 5 percent of incomes. The immediate percentage decline in your after-tax income due to the flat tax is a rough approximation of how much the hoped-for boost in economic growth would have to benefit you in order to make you better-off. It's not perfect, because each income category includes many different types of families and individuals who are affected differently. Moreover, such economic benefits would take a while to materialize, moving the goalposts out a bit further. But, on the other hand, the economic growth would also allow tax rates to decline a bit, moving the goalposts a bit closer. Finally, if the extra income simply comes from you working harder for longer hours, it isn't a costless gain. You'll have lost leisure time that could have been spent with your family or doing something else you enjoy.

With these important caveats in mind, consider the following examples. If you have an income between $16,000 and $30,000, flat tax alternative (2) might make you better-off if it improved the economy enough, relative to what would have happened anyway, to raise your income by more than 7.2 percent. When thought of in these terms, the idea that a flat tax could eventually make most people better-off seems less implausible. Keep in mind, though, that many economists doubt that a switch to a flat tax would deliver that much extra income and the gain in income would have to be large enough to offset not only higher taxes, but also any lost leisure. The possibility is a bit more likely for a plan like alternative (3), which is considerably more progressive than the others and, according to the Treasury's calculations, only reduces most peoples' incomes by a couple of percentage points in the short run.

In weighing the impact of a flat tax on different peoples' levels of well-being, we shouldn't forget the benefits of having a much simpler tax. As discussed above, these benefits could be substantial for a flat tax, potentially involving total savings of nearly $40 billion per year. For most of the people who would pay higher taxes under the flat tax, however, the income tax is already fairly simple, so making things a bit simpler wouldn't provide much, if any, direct offset. Most of the direct gains from simplification would go to people with higher incomes, because they're typically the ones with the complicated tax affairs. This doesn't diminish the fact that the simplicity is a valuable gain; other things being equal, all that time and effort devoted to tax affairs is a waste that doesn't do anybody any good. But it also means that the gains from simplicity don't change the overall distributional impact of a switch to a flat tax very much.

It is also worth noting that special transition rules could have a major influence on the distributional effects of a flat tax. As discussed at length in Chapter 6, avoiding transition rules altogether will undoubtedly result in some redistributions among taxpayers, depending on a family's wealth and financial status, such as whether they own a house and have a mortgage; many of these redistributions seem arbitrary and unfair. But transitional provisions designed to minimize the capricious losses are costly, and inevitably force tax rates up. Perhaps the most important example would be transitional relief for depreciation deductions on existing capital. This could greatly reduce the revenues available from the business tax, forcing tax burdens to rise on wage earners, which would make the flat tax even less progressive.

What if you like the flat tax, but don't think that a single low rate with an exempt level of labor income provides enough progressivity for your tastes? Moreover, you are willing to sacrifice the extra efficiency cost of higher marginal tax rates to achieve that progressivity. Then you should consider the "graduated flat tax," which may sound as self-contradictory as jumbo shrimp. Such a tax has been championed by David Bradford of Princeton University as the "X-tax." Under the X-tax, the business and personal tax bases are exactly the same as the flat tax, but the business tax rate and the top personal rate on labor income are both set at a higher level, say 35 percent, and there are lower, graduated rates on labor income as well as a tax-exempt level. Such a system retains many of the efficiency and simplification advantages of a consumption tax, while raising revenue in a more progressive way; because it is more progressive, though, the incentive advantages of a lower marginal rate of tax are not achieved. The X-tax has not as yet garnered as much attention as the flat tax itself, undoubtedly because it does not have the attraction of a single low rate.

Up to this point the discussion has focused on how replacing the income tax with a flat or X-tax would affect the actual distribution of tax burdens across families of different levels of well-being. There is another fairness issue lurking here, that of *perceived* fairness, that might end up being even more decisive in the political fate of these plans. Many Americans, accustomed to a personal income tax system that subjects to tax not only wages and salaries but also interest, dividends, and capital gains, will think the personal tax base of the flat tax just doesn't smell right, and it will therefore fail the "sniff test" they apply to determine what's right and what isn't. This will probably happen in spite of the economic arguments that, because of the changes in the business tax, the flat tax is no better or worse than a retail sales tax. This state of affairs is a bit ironic because the *raison d'être* of the flat tax is to be a more progressive alternative to the RST or VAT, but its political prospects may founder because, although it in some ways looks like our current system, in other, possibly critical, dimensions, it does not at all.

Distributional Consequences of a Personal Consumption Tax

Supporters of the personal consumption tax approach prefer it to a sales tax or VAT in part because it can more easily accommodate a graduated rate structure, so that it can be made to achieve a more progressive distribution of the tax burden. The USA Tax has been explicitly designed to replicate the progressivity of the current income tax. Although it is unclear how close it would actually come to this goal, it's probably not too far off. But as just discussed, a Hall-Rabushka flat tax base could also support a graduated rate structure that would make it comparably progressive on a lifetime basis. Given the much greater complexity of the personal consumption tax base, this "X-tax" modification of the flat tax seems like a far preferable option if further progressivity of tax burdens is desired. Moreover, whatever the perception problems associated with the flat tax, there seems to be little public enthusiasm for a radical reform that could make the taxpaying process *more* complicated.

Economic Effects of Consumption Tax Plans

Chapter 4 considered all of the major channels through which tax reform could improve long-run economic prosperity. The proposals discussed in this chapter affect many of these channels. Each would remove taxation's negative impact on the incentive to save; more saving would lead to a larger and better capital stock, which in turn would make U.S. workers more productive and improve our long-run standard of living. They would eliminate capricious variation in tax rates on different types of investment, leading to a more efficient allocation of our capital stock; this is easier to achieve in a consumption tax than in an income tax. All of the consumption tax plans also promise to clean up the tax base to some degree, removing distortions among different types of consumption. To the extent that the consumption taxes shift tax burdens onto existing wealth and the elderly, they also provide an economic boost. The retail sales tax, VAT, and flat tax lower marginal tax rates by scaling back progressivity, which would reduce the tax system's drag on incentives to achieve success through hard work, initiative, innovation, and risk-taking.

The potential economic benefits of tax reform are very real. But how large would these benefits be? Ideally, we would want to quantify the impacts of each of the elements of the proposals, since they are separable, and then see how the economic impacts add up in various packages. But as seen in Chapter 4, the evidence on each of these effects is uncertain. In many cases, the best evidence suggests only a moderate effect.

Despite the uncertainty, bounds can be put on what kind of economic benefit is reasonable. It is clear that promises of miraculously higher growth rates forever are unjustified by the existing evidence. For instance, while some have claimed that switching to a flat-rate consumption tax could *double* our long-term rate of economic growth,[41] this is totally unsupported by the evidence, and no serious economist is making such claims. Nor would a consumption tax *permanently* increase our *rate* of growth. Rather, if it were successful at raising saving, growth would increase only for a while as we added to the economy's level of capital intensity, moving us to a *level* of income permanently higher than we would otherwise achieve. The growth reaches a limit because a higher level of saving will be needed just to maintain that greater degree of capital intensity. Those factors that could arguably induce a persistent increase in growth rates, such as investment in R&D or human capital, are not made much more attractive by a flat tax, and so are unlikely to noticeably increase.

Claims that massive tax cuts will cause the economy to grow so rapidly that no revenue will be lost are also outside the bounds of what is reasonable. For example, the July 1995 Armey-Shelby flat tax proposal, which has a 17 percent rate and an exemption of $31,400 for a family of four, is projected to lose $138 billion per year when fully phased-in after two years.[42] This represents a loss of about 18 percent of revenues currently raised by the taxes it would replace. It is true that if the tax plan induces faster economic growth than would otherwise occur, some of this revenue loss would eventually be offset. But this particular plan would require the economy to grow to be about 18 percent larger than it otherwise would before it raises as much revenue as the current system would. For example, if real GDP were to grow at an annual rate of 4.2 percent rather than 2.5 percent because of the tax reform, then it would become revenue-neutral ten years from enactment, with significant deficits until then. But even the most optimistic projections of economists do not suggest that such a large sustained increase in growth would be induced. The bill's sponsors promise unspecified spending cuts to offset some of the deficits. But any suggestion that stronger economic growth would quickly take care of such deficits is very misleading.

Putting aside such overly optimistic estimates, how can we get a sense of the size of economic benefits we can expect from reform proposals? One approach is to make an educated guess, considering all the types of evidence we discussed in Chapter 4. Based on such a review, Robert Hall and Alvin Rabushka, the fathers of the flat tax, claim their plan would increase real incomes by a total of 6 percent over seven years. As they point out, this is still a significant improvement: "By 2002, it would mean each American will have an income of about $1,900 higher, in 1995 dollars, as a consequence of tax reform."[43] Although there's no reason to believe the benefits of such economic growth would be shared equally, as this seems to imply, growth of this magnitude is at least conceivable.

A reading of the evidence presented in Chapter 4, however, could easily suggest a more modest economic impact. Based on historical experience, many important areas of economic behavior that we can measure, especially saving rates and hours worked, appear to be unresponsive to moderate changes in incentives. A stronger economic response cannot be ruled out, though, because some areas of economic behavior that might be responsive to incentives, such as entrepreneurial effort, are hard to measure. But there's no compelling evidence either way on these latter issues.

Some economists have taken a more ambitious approach to gauging the potential economic benefits of reform. They have put together stylized models of the economy that can be used to simulate the effects of adopting a new tax system. While these models produce very precise answers, these should not be taken to be anything more than what they really are, which is just a more sophisticated kind of educated guess. The results of any such modeling exercise depend heavily on the assumptions that are made about the responsiveness of economic behaviors, such as saving and labor supply, to incentives. And these assumptions can only be derived from a review of the same uncertain historical evidence we've discussed in this book. Moreover, both the tax system and economic behavior are incredibly complicated, so no feasible model can even come close to incorporating all the relevant features.

While the specific predictions of stylized models are merely suggestive, the models are useful for helping us think about how taxes affect the economy. Alan Auerbach, of the University of California at Berkeley, recently estimated the potential economic effects of each of the major consumption tax alternatives using such an approach.[44] He models the economy as consisting of multiple generations, each consisting of a single "representative consumer," and incorporates very stylized versions of the current tax code and its possible replacements.

As already discussed, two important ways that consumption tax proposals differ from each other are the progressivity of their rate structures and the degree to which they impose a one-time tax on wealth owners. Auerbach finds that these differences are critical to the likely economic benefits they would provide. According to his estimates, for example, under the USA Tax, which has the most progressive rate structure and significant transitional relief, output per capita grows very little, rising only 1.6 percent higher than it otherwise would after ten years. A flat tax with no transition relief fares better in its economic effects, primarily because it is less progressive than the USA Tax. Output per capita is 7 percent higher after ten years. As makes sense, granting transition relief reduces the growth, to about 5 percent.

A national sales tax or VAT with no measures to promote progressivity is projected to increase output per capita by a total of 9 percent after ten years.

In each of these simulations, the saving rate is projected to roughly double in the short run to achieve these economic gains.[45] While the model is based on a reasonable estimate for the parameter that determines the saving response, the fairly large increase in saving rates suggests that a smaller parameter or some other change in the model might also be reasonable. Auerbach examines the impact of allowing for some other factors, such as adjustment costs that make quick changes in the capital stock difficult, or lower responsiveness of work effort; these both would reduce the projected growth significantly.[46]

Other changes can have important impacts in these models as well. For example, Eric Engen of the Federal Reserve and William Gale of the Brookings Institution model a switch from an income tax system that lets much capital income go untaxed, which is what we have now, to a pure consumption tax, and also incorporate a precautionary motive for saving. This model suggests the saving rate would only increase by around one-tenth of its current level, leading to a correspondingly small impact on economic well-being.[47] Still other changes in modeling assumptions could lead to larger growth estimates. For example, neither of these models takes into account the potential gains from making the treatment of different types of investment more neutral or cleaning up the tax base, because incorporating these effects would be very complicated.

To this point, we've been focusing on projected increases in income or output, but this is not a good measure of how much better off people might be as a result of a tax change. For example, the higher output is achieved in part through a higher saving rate, which means that some consumption today must be sacrificed. Similarly, some of the increased output occurs because people are projected to work a greater number of hours. Working longer hours obviously has a cost in terms of lost leisure, so the increased output is an overestimate of the net benefit. "Welfare" is the economists' term for a measure of well-being that takes these factors into account. In these stylized models, increases in welfare from tax reform are considerably smaller than increases in output. For example, in Auerbach's model, welfare is estimated to increase by between .64 percent and 1.85 percent for future generations, depending on which consumption tax is adopted. Older generations alive today see little improvement or even a small drop in welfare, depending on the transitional provisions. Other studies have come to similar conclusions. For example, Jane Gravelle estimates the welfare gain to future generations of switching from an income to a consumption tax, abstracting from changes in progressivity, to be about 2 percent. Most of this gain comes from the transitional effects; compensating older generations for transitional losses reduces the gain to future generations to a fraction of 1 percent.[48]

What can be concluded from all this? It is possible that the shift to a flat-rate, clean-base consumption tax system could eventually cause incomes to increase by a few percentage points, with a somewhat smaller net increase in well-being. Many of the potential gains from the reform plans appear to come from scaling back progressivity or shifting burdens onto older generations. It is not clear how the economic gains would be distributed among the population, but they would probably go disproportionately to the same people who benefit most from the tax changes even without any economic response. There is an unavoidable trade-off here, as younger generations and higher-income people would be made better off at the expense of older generations and poorer people; it is extremely unlikely that economic growth would allow us to transcend these trade-offs entirely.[49] The gains from switching to a consumption base, abstracting from these other changes, do not necessarily have to come at the expense of low- and moderate-income people or older generations. But the gains here are uncertain and probably small, and need to be weighed against the transitional costs. Cleaning up the tax base could also produce important economic gains, but we have even less information on what these would be. In all cases, there is plenty of uncertainty.

After being frustrated by economists' forecasts that began "on the one hand if . . .," Harry Truman is reported to have said "bring me a one-armed economist!" The inability of economists to agree on precise answers to important questions is undoubtedly one reason their counsel is sometimes doubted. And whether to embark on radical tax reform is certainly an important question. If we could be sure that eliminating the income tax for, say, a flat tax would in short order usher in an era of undreamed-of prosperity, it would be a lot easier for many Americans to overlook the short-term disruption and increased tax burden on the low- and middle-income groups—those higher taxes would be offset soon enough by better jobs paying higher wages. Unfortunately, the fact is that we can't be sure. Any economists or politicians who say they can precisely predict the impact are either kidding themselves or kidding the rest of us. The intelligent citizen must be resigned to making choices in the face of imperfect information about the consequences of the alternatives.

Conclusion

Where does our discussion of radical alternatives to the income tax leave us? The retail sales tax is an unproven alternative, which is likely to be administratively infeasible at the rates necessary to replace the federal income tax. A VAT is probably doable, but it entails a radical shift in tax burden from the affluent to poor and middle-class families, and is for this reason likely to be unacceptable to most Americans, although this is a value judgment rather than a matter of economics. The personal consumption tax complicates rather than simplifies the personal tax system, and is unacceptable on these grounds. So the flat tax, or its more progressive version the X-tax, stands as the most attractive of the consumption tax alternatives to the income tax.

However, the policy choice is not between the flat tax and the system we have now. Many students of the tax system favor substantial reform, but reform that stays within the basic framework of an income tax. Recall from Chapter 6 the discussion of the characteristics of a generic flat tax—a clean base, a single rate, and a consumption base. The tax system can certainly be reformed in the direction of the first two, without moving toward a consumption base. We must distinguish between *the* flat tax, a reconstituted VAT, and other kinds of flatter, simpler *income* tax systems. Many, but not all, of the promised economic and simplification benefits ascribed to the consumption tax plans could also potentially be achieved through reform of the existing income tax structure. The next chapter will discuss the prospects and problems of building a better income tax.

8   Building a Better Income Tax

Dumping the income tax for a consumption tax promises economic and simplification gains, but can cause massive and capricious gains and losses, and perhaps, complexity in the transition. Many specific consumption tax proposals also involve a reshuffling of the tax burden toward those less able to bear it. Whether it is worth the leap depends on how one assesses the chance of significant economic gains, and also how one evaluates the regressive shift of tax burdens.

Not every economist thinks it's worth it. A 1994 poll of tax experts found 80 percent supported retaining a graduated income tax.[1] Not everyone else thinks it's worth it, either. An Associated Press poll of February 16–20, 1996, taken in the midst of a Republican presidential primary campaign that featured much discussion of tax reform, found that only 26 percent of Americans favored replacing the income tax system. However, only 17 percent wanted to keep the system just as it is. Of the three choices given, by far the highest percentage of respondents, 51 percent, favored "tinkering" with the current system.[2]

Tinkering. This is hardly the kind of word that excites even a wide-eyed academic, or galvanizes a political campaign. In a sense, we've been tinkering with the income tax ever since it began in 1913, although every so often the changes to the tax code deserve a nobler title, as in the Tax Reform Act of 1986.

Even if contemplating reform of the income tax is not as exhilarating as contemplating its abolition, we must do exactly that. We must because the radical alternatives should be compared not only to the system as it is today, but also to the system as it could be feasibly reformed. This is especially true because some of the purported advantages of the flat tax and other similar plans can be achieved without starting from scratch with a new tax system.

Income tax reform can proceed on a number of different, but not mutually exclusive, avenues. One avenue is the elimination of some or all of the itemized deductions and special preferences in both the personal and corporate codes. This type of base cleaning was a major element of the Tax Reform Act of 1986, and some income tax reform plans would take this approach at least a few steps further.

A second possible area for improvement involves eliminating certain structural flaws that make our income tax less like the idealized tax on all economic income discussed in Chapter 2. These are the kinds of issues that usually attract the interest only of hard-core tax system aficionados; for this reason, they tend to be a part of relatively obscure, often government-proposed, reforms rather than a part of politicians' stump speeches. Nevertheless, they address serious problems that impose costs, although not apparent ones, on all taxpayers. Examples of such structural reform are the elimination of the double taxation of corporate income, and the introduction of indexing to eliminate taxation of the inflationary portion of capital income.

A third area that engenders a great deal of public debate concerns efforts to promote saving and investment within the context of an income tax. Examples include preferential treatment of capital gains, and savings incentives such as IRAs and tax-deferred pension plans. Some would like to go further in these directions, while others would like to see them eliminated, so as to move closer to a more comprehensive income base.

A number of other changes could help to simplify the income tax. Some of these are structural changes, such as eliminating alternative minimum taxes and "phase-outs." Others are simplifying changes in the tax process, such as making tax filing easier, or making the system "return free" for a larger number of people.

Finally, there is the option that has been getting much more attention than usual lately—moving to a single, flat income tax rate, or at least making rates flatter than they are now. Are there advantages to a flat income tax, compared to a flat consumption tax?

This chapter will address each of these aspects of income tax reform; because we assume basic familiarity with the existing income tax, we can do this with more dispatch than in Chapter 7. A recent reform proposal that combines a number of these elements—the "10% Tax" put forward by House Minority Leader Richard Gephardt—will also be reviewed. Finally, this chapter will examine the option of replacing some, but not all, of income tax revenues with a VAT.

Base Cleaning

Most income tax reform plans adopt the principle of moving toward a cleaner tax base, and using the revenue raised thereby to lower tax rates. This involves eliminating many widely cherished deductions and preferences in both the personal and corporate codes. The arguments for and against many of the major deviations from a clean base were discussed in Chapter 6. Refer to our discussion there to evaluate income tax reform plans that eliminate the deductions for mortgage interest payments, charitable contributions, or state and local taxes and that subject fringe benefits such as health insurance payments to tax. However, there are other important aspects of "base cleaning" that are unique to the income tax, some examples of which will now be examined.

Integration: Eliminating the Double Taxation of Corporate Income

Chapter 4 discussed the distortions that arise because of the fact that income derived from investment in the corporate sector can be taxed twice under our current tax system—first as corporation income, and then again when the income is received by shareholders in the form of dividends or, to a lesser extent, capital gains. This tax treatment puts an inefficient penalty on business activity carried out in corporate form and distorts corporate financial structure toward debt finance. It makes investment in corporate stock particularly unattractive relative to investment in owner-occupied housing, causing too much high-priced housing to be built at the expense of more productive corporate investments.

On the surface, an obvious solution is to eliminate the corporate income tax altogether. This, however, would create tremendous problems. As noted before, much corporate income goes untaxed at the individual level. For example, at the personal level accrued capital gains are not taxed until they are realized, are not taxed at all if held until death and passed on to heirs, and even when realized are taxed at preferential rates.[3] Much corporate income is also left untaxed at the individual level because of evasion or sophisticated avoidance schemes. If there was no corporate income tax at all, there would be a strong incentive to keep as much income in corporations as possible, deferring or perhaps eliminating taxation on that income altogether.

As a practical matter, an income tax system such as ours requires some form of corporate tax to serve as a backstop to the personal taxation of capital income. At the very least, it is needed to serve as a way to withhold individual tax liability for shareholders.

Many other countries alleviate the problem of double taxation by reducing the total tax burden, corporate plus personal, on corporate earnings via what is called "integration" of the two tax systems. The most common approach is to grant corporate shareholders a credit against personal tax liability for a portion of the corporate tax attributable to the dividends they receive; it is typically not offered to foreign shareholders or to shareholders that are exempt from the individual income tax. The Treasury tax proposals of 1984 included an alternative approach to this issue. Under this plan, corporations would be able to deduct a portion of their dividend payments, just as they deduct interest payments. To mitigate the revenue loss from this plan, the proposal actually called for the deductibility of only one-half of dividends paid.

In 1992, the U.S. Treasury undertook a major study of the double taxation issue, and developed the "Comprehensive Business Income Tax" (CBIT) as an alternative to the current system.[4] This plan would eliminate all personal-level taxes on income from corporations—interest on corporate bonds, and dividends and capital gains on corporate stocks. Instead, all this income would be taxed, once, under the corporate tax at a single rate (the Treasury plan set it at 31 percent). Corporate interest deductions would be eliminated, ensuring that interest is taxed and eliminating the preference for debt over equity. In essence, CBIT would turn the corporate income tax into a withholding tax on corporate-source capital income, eliminating the need to tax it at the personal level. This plan shares some aspects in common with the flat tax, because corporate interest deductions are eliminated, as is personal-level taxation of corporate-source income. However, the CBIT would still be a type of income tax because the cost of business investment would continue to be depreciated, rather than expensed. Thus, the normal return to corporate investment would be taxed, albeit only at the firm level.

Integration plans of this sort would have significant benefits for the economy, by removing arbitrary differences in the tax rates on different types of investments. But they have not proven to be attractive to either the public or to politicians, perhaps in part because of a view that "corporate income" and "personal income received from corporations" are somehow different.[5] Another possible reason for the lack of interest is that the double tax on corporate income disproportionately affects higher-income people, so removing it would make the system less progressive. If this is the concern, the distributional effects could be offset on average by making the graduated rate structure more progressive. The same degree of progressivity could in this way be maintained, but the inefficient distortion between corporate and non-corporate investments would be mitigated or eliminated.

Inflation Indexing

The U.S. income tax ignores inflation in the measurement of capital income, interest deductions, and depreciation deductions. In some cases it overstates income, finding taxable income where no real income exists. In other cases, it understates income, by overstating deductions. It does all this in a capricious way, leading to distortions in capital investment.

The issue here is completely separate from the "bracket creep" caused by inflation. That phenomenon arises when the real value of tax brackets, exemption levels, and all other dollar figures are eroded over time as the price level rises. For example, in tax year 1995 a family of four taking the standard deduction pays no tax until their income reaches $16,550. If the standard deduction and exemption amounts were to stay the same, over time as prices rise that $16,550 would correspond to a lower and lower real income, and more and more families would find, by dint of inflation alone, that they had gone from nontaxable to taxable status. Other families would move from one tax bracket to the next. The problem of bracket creep has been eliminated from the U.S. income tax system since 1984; now all dollar figures for brackets, personal exemptions, standard deductions, and similar features are automatically increased by the rate of inflation.[6]

Eliminating bracket creep doesn't address the capital income mismeasurement problem, though. If you earn a 10 percent interest rate on your certificate of deposit, but half of that 10 percent reflects inflation, you still pay tax on the full 10 percent. For someone with a 40 percent marginal tax rate, this turns a 5 percent real return before tax (10 percent nominal return minus 5 percent inflation) into a 1 percent real return after tax (10 percent minus 4 percent in tax, minus 5 percent inflation), which is much more onerous than a 40 percent tax on the real return alone.[7]

At the current inflation rate of about 2 percent, the problems this mismeasurement causes are not that large, because nominal returns to capital largely reflect real, rather than inflationary, gains. If we could be sure inflation would go no higher, fixing this problem would probably not be worth the complications that would be involved. If inflation approaches double digits, it gets to be a serious problem, a big enough one that, in its 1984 tax reform proposal, the Treasury Department included a comprehensive scheme to "index" the measurement of capital income for inflation. This is by no means an easy task, and would surely complicate the taxpaying process. The Treasury proposed to index the basis (purchase price for tax purposes) of capital gains for the inflation that has occurred since the purchase of the asset, to inflation-index the basis of depreciable assets, to allow firms the option of using indexed first-in, first-out inventory accounting rules, and to index interest receipts and payments (other than on mortgages) by excluding a given fraction that depends on the previous year's inflation rate.[8] The indexing scheme did not survive the legislative process, and was not part of the Tax Reform Act of 1986, primarily because of its complexity.[9]

Making the entire income tax system inflation-neutral is clearly a tall order, but indexing only one piece and not the others has its own problems. For example, consider the consequences if only capital gains were indexed, by allowing the seller of appreciated assets to increase the reported buying price by the rise in the price level since the purchase. This would certainly improve the measurement of real capital gains. However, this would make investments in assets that yield capital gains more attractive than other investments. Moreover, in high-inflation environments it would give a tremendous tax-induced advantage to debt-financed purchases of capital assets, because the presumably high nominal interest rates on borrowing would remain completely deductible, even though most of the nominal interest rate represented an inflation premium, while any nominal capital gains would go tax-free. This is the recipe for a classic tax shelter, the economic cost of which is that investment would be drawn away from other outlets that, taxes aside, yield a higher return to their investors. There would also be a cost in complication, not only because the process of indexing itself is complicated, but also because it would encourage extra financial transactions, such as borrowing money to buy appreciating assets, for the sole purpose of reducing one's taxes.

"Corporate Welfare"

One frequent rhetorical target of politicians is "corporate welfare." When it comes to the current income tax, this is somewhat ironic, because much corporate-source income is actually taxed relatively heavily. However, there are certainly provisions in the tax code that provide preferences for investments done by certain types of corporations or businesses. The most obvious example is the generous depreciation deductions granted to oil, gas, and mining operations. Other industries that tend to be favored include rental housing, real estate, insurance, and financial services.

The main problem with these types of preferences is that they are inefficient. For example, the preference for oil drilling has caused investment funds to flow into that line of business at the expense of other, more productive investments. Whether it makes sense to eliminate these preferences in the name of equity is less clear-cut. People who owned oil-drilling operations when the preference was instituted certainly gained from the preference. But by now, the value of the preference is probably reflected in the price that people pay to buy shares in such a business. So people who buy into oil-drilling operations now probably gain little or nothing from the special depreciation allowances, but they would lose if the preference were removed. Still, getting rid of these preferences would certainly enhance the efficiency of our tax system.

Capital Gains

The treatment of capital gains is one of the most controversial and publicly debated issues regarding the income tax, with Republicans generally wanting to reduce rates on capital gains as much as possible, and Democrats wanting to keep them near rates on other income. It is a particularly divisive issue because realized capital gains are highly concentrated among high-income individuals. For example, in 1993, 53 percent of gains were received by households whose adjusted gross income (AGI) exceeded $200,000, and capital gains constituted 15 percent of the AGI of these taxpayers.[10] Because of this concentration, preferential tax treatment of capital gains is the archetypical example of "trickle-down economics," where the immediate benefits go to a small group of highly affluent people, and the extent of longer-term, more widely distributed, benefits is highly controversial.

According to the widely accepted conceptual definition of income—consumption plus the change in wealth—increases in the value of capital assets are certainly income. When a stock you own increases in value from $1,000 to $1,100, you are $100 wealthier just as you would be if you got lucky on a $100 lottery ticket or got paid $100 for overtime work.[11] By this logic all of capital gains should be included in taxable income as they accrue, with no preferences.

But it's not nearly as simple as that. For many capital assets it is extremely difficult to regularly obtain a market value that can be verified by the IRS or even be known to the owner. It's no problem for highly liquid securities such as shares of companies traded on the New York Stock Exchange. But it is a problem for closely held businesses, real estate, and other assets such as paintings. From an administrative standpoint, it would be very cumbersome to require taxpayers to value all their capital assets each year and report as income the increase in value, and for the IRS to monitor these reports.

Rather than requiring taxpayers to annually value all their capital assets, capital gains are taxed only upon "realization," which usually means when the asset is sold.[12] Postponing the taxation of the gain until the time of sale, rather than when the asset appreciated, confers on the taxpayer the time value of money—it is always better to pay the bill later rather than sooner. It's as if the IRS offers the asset holder an interest-free loan equal to the tax due at the time the asset appreciates, from the time when the gain is made until the time the asset is sold. This loan is more valuable the higher are interest rates, and the longer an asset is held. This provides an incentive to hold on to appreciated assets longer than otherwise, a phenomenon known as the "lock-in" effect. The lock-in effect is greatly exacerbated because of another feature of current law—no tax at all is due on capital gains if the asset is not sold during the holder's lifetime. If an appreciated asset is bequeathed, the recipient can upon any subsequent sale treat it for tax purposes as if it were purchased at the value when inherited.

The combination of the deferral of tax until sale, and the possibility that all the gain will be forgiven from tax, makes potentially appreciating assets much more attractive than assets, like taxable bonds, which pay out their return in a taxable form. This provides a purely tax-created advantage to those investments that more easily can provide returns to their investors in the form of appreciation, such as real estate. This was a key element of the rash of tax shelter investments of the early 1980s, which involved the purchase of appreciating assets coupled with loans offering fully deductible interest.

Tax preferences accorded to capital gains also create a tremendous incentive to repackage ordinary income into capital gains. People who buy fixer-upper houses take advantage of this feature, because their time and effort is not taxed as labor income; instead it is reflected in a higher sale price for their house, and hardly taxed at all due to generous rules about capital gains on owner-occupied housing. Other sophisticated taxpayers make use of stock options or "collapsible" corporations to convert labor compensation into capital gains. Some lawyers speculate that, before the Tax Reform Act of 1986 when the capital gains tax rate preference was especially large (a 30 percentage-point difference for top-bracket taxpayers), about half of all the transactional complexity of the tax law was due to this feature of the law.

The 1986 tax reform virtually eliminated the rate differential on capital gains, although the advantages of deferral and tax exemption at death remained. The rate differential has since crept back up, as taxpayers in the 36 percent and 39.6 percent brackets pay no more than 28 percent on their realized capital gains.

On grounds of allocational efficiency and simplicity, there seems to be a strong case for taxing capital gains like other income. But this still poses many problems, particularly given other features of the current tax code. For one thing, in inflationary periods much capital appreciation does not represent a real increase in income, only a catching up to higher prices. Second, the income that triggers capital gains on corporate shares is already taxed to some extent by the corporate income tax. Third, given the realization-based tax system, imposing higher rates of tax will inevitably provide some deterrent to efficient sales of capital assets, the "lock-in effect." Fourth, for structural reasons it is infeasible to allow full deductibility of capital losses, because it would allow investors with diversified portfolios to "cherrypick" their assets, selling only those with losses and holding those with gains, and thereby consistently generating losses for tax purposes. The asymmetrical treatment of losses and gains means that the terms of the government "partnership" are particularly favorable to the government—it gets a tax share of gains, but when there are losses, it kicks in only a limited amount. This makes the private investor's deal look less attractive—she pays a share to the government if the investment turns out well, but gets little help if it turns out badly. Such treatment can inefficiently deter risky investments.

Comprehensive integration and indexing, discussed earlier, could help solve many of these problems. Not only could double taxation and inflation-induced distortions be eliminated, but an integration plan like the CBIT could even eliminate the lock-in effect on corporate stocks, because capital gains on corporate shares would be untaxed at the personal level, and only the income underlying the gain would be taxed at the corporate level when earned. But integration and indexing seem to have little public support, and indexing would be complicated. Partial solutions have their own problems. As discussed earlier, indexing capital gains but not other capital income or deductions is problematic. Either taxing accrued capital gains at death, or requiring that tax basis be carried over to heirs, could help reduce the "lock-in effect," but neither idea has ever gained much political support.[13] Reducing capital gains rates below rates on other income is often defended as a means of reducing the lock-in effect, encouraging risk-taking, and reducing double taxation. But differential rates on different types of income lead to all the problems mentioned above. It is a very blunt instrument for attacking double taxation, because there are many appreciating assets besides corporate stock; sales of corporate stock account for a minority of realized capital gains.[14] And as we discussed in Chapter 4, the evidence on the lock-in effect and the impact on risk-taking is uncertain.

For all these reasons, the tax treatment of capital gains under an income tax involves a conceptually unsatisfying compromise between the desire to tax all income uniformly, so as to minimize distortions and complexity, and the difficulty of implementing a truly uniform regime. Whatever uneasy compromise is reached, one caveat regarding changes in capital gains taxation applies. Expanding the preferential treatment of past capital gains provides no incentive to buy new stock or new real estate, and instead just provides a windfall gain for past decisions. Any new preference should, if feasible, be restricted to new gains.

Savings Incentives in the Income Tax

Although the U.S. federal tax system is referred to as an income tax system, in fact, it is an awkward hybrid of income and consumption taxes. This is because there are a variety of provisions, including IRAs, Keogh plans, 401(k) and 403(c) pension plans, and other tax-preferred employer-provided pension plans, that to various degrees of effectiveness eliminate the tax on the return to savings. Employer or individual contributions to such plans are deductible, interest and other returns are exempt from tax as they accrue, and only when withdrawn or paid out at retirement are the proceeds subject to tax.

Notice that these plans mimic how a consumption tax would work, by postponing tax on income until it is consumed. As discussed earlier, one way of implementing a consumption tax would be to allow all net saving to be deductible, as if there were an unlimited, unrestricted IRA.

All of these saving incentive plans represent deviations from a pure income tax. They have nothing to do with "ability-to-pay" or externalities. So what rationale is there? One argument for such plans is that they provide a method of encouraging saving in a "limited" way, which, compared to simply abandoning all taxation of capital income, is not too expensive and does not provide a large windfall to very high-income people who have vast amounts of capital income.

Another justification for special incentives is that they institutionalize saving to some degree. People may be more likely to do the saving that they know is good for them if there is some structured plan in place. Of course, such a plan could still be instituted *without* the special tax treatment. Many economists are also uncomfortable with the idea that people are not fully rational about their saving decisions. But there is at least some evidence to support this idea. For example, when IRA eligibility was cut back for high-income people by the Tax Reform Act of 1986, contributions by low- and middle-income people who remained eligible also declined. One interpretation of this put forward by economist and current Deputy Secretary of the Treasury, Lawrence Summers, is that sharply reduced advertising of IRAs by banks was responsible.[15]

But are these plans really effective in raising saving? This is not clear at all, especially in the case of IRAs. One problem with IRAs as an inducement rather than a reward to saving is that there is an annual $2,000 limit to deductible contributions. This limit makes no difference to taxpayers who would not in any event want or be able to contribute as much as $2,000 in a year. However, for those taxpayers who would otherwise save more than that, and don't mind subjecting their funds to a penalty for early withdrawal, the IRA deduction is a nice gift, but at the margin it will have absolutely no influence on how much they save. If you're trying to decide whether to save $3,000 or $4,000, the IRA program is immaterial, as you get the maximum deduction in either case. Alas, most of the saving in this country is done by people who normally do save more than $2,000 a year, so that much of the revenue cost of the program is a reward, but not an inducement, for saving. As such, it adds to individuals' income and should therefore increase their consumption, reducing rather than increasing national saving.

IRAs illustrate a critical design issue for tax subsidies—make sure the subsidy is closely tied to the behavior to be induced. IRAs fail this commonsense criterion of a well-designed incentive system. They fail because they are supposed to encourage saving, but they subsidize deposits into an account, and deposits are not at all the same thing as saving. Consider the family that over the years has saved up $10,000, which is now invested in stocks and bonds. If they take $2,000 of this and deposit it into an IRA account, their saving has not increased or decreased, it's just been moved from one account to another. The same problem arises if someone borrows money to deposit into an IRA; no new saving has occurred, but a tax deduction is obtained.

Of course, if this family deposits $2,000 every year into their IRA account, and does no more new saving, after five years they will have transferred all of their wealth into their IRA account. At that time they face the decision that the IRA is designed to alter—in order to get any further deduction, they must do some saving. But even then, it is unclear whether the incentive is effective. In fact, an alternative explanation of the decline in IRA contributions after 1986 for those who continued to be eligible is that these people had already successfully transferred most of their other saving to IRAs by then.[16] Chapter 4 showed, moreover, the tenuous relationship between savings rates and the rate of return.

Our current savings incentives in general subsidize deposits rather than saving, because deposits are a lot easier to measure. Accurately measuring saving would require at a minimum every taxpayer keeping track of all additions to assets, subtracting out all withdrawals, and recording all borrowing. As discussed earlier, this procedure would be even more complicated than our current income tax system.

Eliminating Complex Provisions Aimed at the Perception of Fairness

There are a number of features in the current income tax that cause a great deal of complication for those who are subject to them, but are by no means inherent aspects of an income tax. The alternative minimum taxes (AMTs) in the personal and corporate codes are an important example. At the corporate level, the AMT requires many businesses to do a tremendous amount of extra accounting, without even knowing whether they will be subject to it. Many corporations cite this as one of the most complicated and burdensome aspects of the taxpaying process. It is also in many cases inefficient, because it mismeasures income and in some cases can force companies with real economic losses to pay tax. The personal AMT is very complicated as well. Moreover, the number of individuals sending AMT forms in to the IRS is over nine times as large as the number who are required to do so.[17] This doesn't even count those who fill it out, find out it doesn't affect them, and don't file the form.

Another complicating feature of the personal code is the "phase-out" of personal exemptions and itemized deductions for high-income taxpayers. As discussed in Chapter 5, these have essentially the same effect as raising marginal tax rates in certain income ranges, but are hidden and involve much more complicated calculations.

The AMTs and the phase-outs are intended to keep those with apparently high incomes from reducing their taxes "too much" through the use of deductions and other avoidance schemes. That adds complication on top of complication. A much simpler approach would be to eliminate the deductions that are considered unjustified. Even absent that, eliminating the AMTs and the phase-outs would have significant simplification benefits.

Process Improvements

Modernization of IRS operations promises continual, although gradual, improvement in the tax filing process. The most notable recent innovation is the ability to file one's tax returns electronically over the telephone lines. In 1994, about 14 million individual taxpayers took advantage of this innovation.[18]

Although electronic filing simplifies and expedites the filing process for those who qualify, it pales in comparison to the postcard return of the flat tax. But in the income tax systems of the United Kingdom and Japan, the ultimate simplification is achieved—no filing at all. They do so by having a very simple tax base and a sophisticated system of employer withholding (called PAYE, or Pay As You Earn, in the United Kingdom) that ensures that come year-end, exactly the appropriate amount of tax has been withheld by employers—no refund and no tax due. Most British taxpayers wouldn't recognize a tax form if they saw one.

The U.S. Treasury tax proposals of 1984 contained a similar scheme, called the "return-free" system, which was to be available for more than half of all taxpayers, but was never enacted because the system wasn't sufficiently simplified to make it feasible. In early 1996, Michigan governor John Engler proposed revamping his state's income tax along these lines, by allowing any taxpayer receiving less than $200 in interest and investment earnings to skip filing a state income tax return, and instead check off a "no file, no form" box on their W–2 forms: for these taxpayers, employers would automatically deduct 4 percent from wages, which is less than the statutory flat rate of 4.4 percent, reflecting the typical amount of state personal exemption. An estimated 500,000 Michigan taxpayers, out of a total of four million, would qualify for this no-file option.[19]

Establishing a return-free system for many taxpayers accomplishes what might be called "populist simplification," because it completely eliminates the hassle of tax filing for a large number of voters. But it does not address the difficult issues of complexity that would continue to affect businesses and many high-income households.

A Single-Rate Income Tax

Independently of base cleaning, structural reforms, or process improvements, the graduated rate structure can be made flatter, or made completely flat, by adopting a single rate. Even combined with eliminating most deductions, a single-rate system cannot, though, replicate the current distribution of tax burdens by income class, and would therefore shift the tax burden away from high-income taxpayers to other taxpayers. It would increase the incentive to work, but probably actually raise labor supply only modestly. A single rate facilitates accurate employer withholding and a return-free system. This is not an all-or-nothing proposition, either. Putting *most* taxpayers on a single rate, and reserving a higher rate for only the most affluent taxpayers, allows a return-free system for almost everyone, as in the United Kingdom.

The Gephardt "10% Tax"

Just about any income tax reform plan combines some set of the changes discussed above. In order to focus on a particular plan, we'll next take a look at a scheme put forward in July of 1995 by House Minority Leader Representative Richard A. Gephardt (D-MO). The plan, which he calls "The 10% Tax," is firmly in the income tax tradition. It moves toward, but certainly not all the way to, a comprehensive income tax base, but eschews both the single rate and a consumption base for taxation.

The 10% Tax cleans the tax base in several dimensions. It eliminates the tax exclusion for state and local bond interest and all current itemized deductions except the deduction for mortgage interest; it would end both the child-care and elderly credit. It also proposes to tax fringe benefits, especially health insurance. Finally, it would move the taxation of savings back toward pure income tax treatment by subjecting employer pension contributions to taxation when made (while eliminating the taxation of pension distributions to reflect the nonexclusion of contributions) and ending all special savings incentive programs such as IRAs and Keogh plans. The 10% Tax does not, though, address the structural problems of the double taxation of corporate income, or of capital income mismeasurement caused by inflation.

In contrast to the flat tax, taxable income at the personal level would include not only wages and salaries, but also interest, dividends, business income, capital gain or loss, and other items of capital income. The corporate tax structure is kept essentially in its current form, although "corporate welfare" is to be tightened in unspecified ways.

Broadening the tax base in this way raises substantial revenue. The reward to taxpayers for giving up many cherished preferences is that the basic rate of tax, now faced by 71 percent of all taxpayers, would be reduced from 15 percent to 10 percent—hence the name.[20] However, a graduated rate structure is retained; it features four rates beyond the 10 percent rate—20, 26, 32, and 34 percent; it is, in Gephardt's words, "unapologetically progressive." In fact, a table accompanying the proposal suggests that families with incomes below $130,000 would pay less tax under this scheme, and a family with $500,000 of income would pay $4,610 more in tax.[21]

Simplification is one objective of the 10% Tax; it claims to "drastically reduce" collection costs and to allow "dramatic cuts in the Internal Revenue Service." It is true that much progress is made toward a clean base, which would simplify the tax filing process. Mimicking the flat tax, personal tax forms for the 10% Tax would be printed on a small postcard. This claim is a bit of a stretch, because line 2 on the postcard is for "subtractions," which would presumably have to be totaled and itemized on a supplementary form. Perhaps the most intriguing aspect of all about the 10% Tax is the establishment of a return-free system for the majority of taxpayers, presumably operating in a manner similar to the British system, though perhaps on a voluntary basis.

Although Gephardt refers to the 10% Tax as an "overhaul" of the tax system rather than "toying or tinkering at the margins," it is clearly not nearly as radical as the consumption tax proposals discussed in Chapter 7. It firmly embraces the concept of a graduated income tax. Although it makes substantial movement toward a broader, cleaner personal tax base, it does not address some of the fundamental structural defects of the U.S. income tax system, such as inflation-induced distortions and double taxation of corporate income. Furthermore, some of the more innovative features, such as the return-free system, are only vaguely sketched out. Nevertheless, it illustrates that some extent of simplification and economic rationalization can be achieved short of dumping the income tax into the trash bin.

A Hybrid Approach: Combining a VAT with Income Taxation

The policy choice between income and consumption taxation is not really an either-or one. There is no reason not to consider a third way of simultaneously having an income tax and an impersonal consumption tax like a VAT. Many other industrialized countries do operate both, although most of these countries need to raise substantially more revenue, as a fraction of GDP, than the United States must raise.

The introduction of a large VAT could allow us to reduce both personal and corporate income tax rates substantially, and perhaps even exempt most people from personal income taxation altogether. Note, however, that it would *not* be a good idea to simply replace our corporate income tax with a VAT while retaining a personal income tax. As noted earlier, the corporate income tax is an important "backstop" to the personal income tax for taxing capital income. Replacing it entirely with a VAT would create many inefficient and complicating avoidance opportunities involving the sheltering of personal income in businesses.

A broad-based VAT levied at a 10 percent rate would raise close to $400 billion, allowing total revenue raised by personal and corporate income taxes to be cut by more than half.[22] This cut could be achieved in any number of ways, depending on the desired result. One obvious possibility is to cut back on all tax rates proportionally, so that the basic 15 percent rate becomes 7.5 percent, the 28 percent rate becomes 14 percent, and so forth. The standard corporation income tax rate could also be cut from 35 percent to 17.5 percent.

This would give the United States the lowest income tax rate structure of any major country. It would, though, also cause a regressive shift in tax burdens, because the VAT will be borne, over the long run, slightly less than proportionally to income, while the rate cuts will offer much more tax relief to those high-income families who are now in the top brackets. It would offer many of the economic advantages ascribed to the VAT, although the simplification gains would be mitigated due to having to maintain the infrastructure of an additional tax system. Although all of the inherent structural as well as man-made inefficiencies of the income tax would remain, they would be considerably less damaging because of the lower rates of tax.

Alternatively, the revenue raised by a VAT could be used to significantly increase the standard deduction of the income tax.[23] This is another example of populist simplification because, by raising the income threshold for filing, it relieves many taxpayers of filing at all,[24] and at the same time induces many others who still file to pass up itemizing their deductions. On the other hand, this plan retains the income tax infrastructure for just those people for whom the tax is most complicated. Although it would greatly reduce the number of income tax returns, it would not reduce by much the number of *complex* returns. The aggregate cost of compliance would not be significantly reduced, although millions of individual taxpayers would be relieved of the burden of filing tax returns.

Compared to a proportional decrease in tax rates, raising the standard deduction is a more progressive way to spread a given income tax reduction. Even so, the VAT would still be likely to increase tax burdens on low-income people who currently pay no income tax.

Increasing the exempt level of income could also be accomplished by upping the personal exemption allowances, but that would not reduce the number of itemizers. The trade-off here is that, to the extent that one thinks the deductions are legitimate adjustments to a measure of ability-to-pay, increasing the standard deduction achieves only approximate justice.

Such a proposal would face a major political roadblock, because in the current environment no politician could endorse something that could be characterized by opponents as a "new tax." It is certainly true that, if the *number* of tax systems is the principal indicator of simplicity, efficiency, and fairness, this plan rates a low score. But the number of separate taxes is by no means a sensible criterion by which to judge a tax system. There are fixed costs associated with each separate kind of tax, but these additional costs are likely to be small relative to the other potential simplification and economic advantages of a VAT plus income tax system like that described here.

Conclusion

The reform options discussed so far represent only a subset of the possible alternatives, and the political process may eventually focus on other possibilities. Any alternative, though, can be classified according to whether it has a single rate or multiple rates, how clean the tax base is, and the extent to which it relies on an income or consumption base.

Where does this leave the intelligent citizen who is convinced that the income tax system needs fixing, but is unsure about what should be done? One option is to pull the tax system out "by its roots," as Representative Archer has called for, and replace it with a clean-base, single-rate system based on consumption rather than income. Because the VAT version of this would starkly shift the burden of tax from affluent Americans to everyone else, we suspect that this will be rejected by most of us. That leaves the flat tax and "graduated flat tax" as the best candidates for radical reform. But these plans are untested, often still entail a regressive change in the distribution of tax burdens, could produce large windfall gains and losses, and the critical but potentially complex details about how to get from here to there are still to be fleshed out. Aside from the substantive issues of equity, efficiency, and simplicity, we sense that they will fail a simple "sniff test" of Americans accustomed to a personal tax on all income, who will find that a tax that appears to be on labor income only just doesn't smell right.

Contemplating this sort of change is not for the meek. We are reminded of a sketch from the old British television series *Monty Python's Flying Circus*. In it, an accountant comes to a job change counselor, complaining of his boring job and inquiring about the career possibilities of being a lion tamer. Once the counselor makes abundantly clear how ferocious a lion actually is (the accountant had thought it to be a more domesticated sort of animal), the accountant decides to settle for pursuing opportunities in banking.

Can the income tax be fixed up enough, so as to be worthy of saving? The base can certainly be thoroughly cleaned, eliminating substantial complexity and inefficiency. By so doing the tax rates can be lowered, which reduces the cost of those bugs that remain. And remain they will, because any system based on income contains inherent difficulties that have no simple solution.

A Voter's Guide to the Tax Policy Debate

Most people's views about tax policy can be boiled down to one question—which system will cost me the least? Most likely this person would decide about whether tax reform is a good idea by consulting a newspaper, magazine, or the Internet, all of which will, when the right time comes, feature articles about how much tax is due from "typical" families under the current system and the alternative of the moment. If you are that typical taxpayer, beware. These simple comparisons can be completely misleading, convincing you that reform would make you better-off when it would not, or vice versa.

If you've read this far, your interest in tax policy probably goes beyond discovering which plan offers you and your family the best deal. You are interested in learning what tax policy is best for the country, and considering what is an equitable distribution of the tax burden across all families. Coming to a reasoned judgment about tax policy requires clarifying your own values about fairness, sifting through some subtle conceptual issues and, perhaps hardest of all, evaluating conflicting claims about the economic impact of tax alternatives—if economists can't agree, how can you decide?

In this book, we have attempted to clearly explain the conceptual issues and have presented what is known, and what is not known, about economic impacts. You must supply your own value judgments. We have tried to narrow down the choices by ruling out systems that are infeasible, and have stated the terms of the choices as clearly as we could.

The public debate about tax reform will, though, be dominated by advocates whose purpose is not to educate, but to persuade. A citizen must learn how to ask the right questions. To help you do that, in what follows we offer a voter's guide to tax policy choices, to keep by your television as the issue is debated, in the same way that newspapers offer viewers' guides to the Super Bowl or the Academy Awards. But, unlike the Academy Awards, in this election you have a vote.

1. Make Sure the Numbers Add Up

It's easy to make tax reform look like a no-brainer if it raises hundreds of billions of dollars less than the current system. Raising less money obviously makes it easier for advocates of an alternative system to claim that most, or even all, taxpayers come out ahead. But that's an unfair advantage, because the revenue shortfall will certainly have further repercussions. Either the deficit will go up, some kinds of expenditures will be cut, or, most likely, the rates on the alternative system will have to be raised before it is passed into law. Besides, the current system could look more attractive if all the tax rates were slashed, and no other changes were made.

2. Beware of Hidden Taxes

Writing checks to the IRS is not the only way that you can take a hit from the tax system. Some reform options shift the burden of check-writing from individuals to businesses; some do so entirely, leaving individuals no role in remitting taxes to the government. Taxpayer, beware. Taxes remitted by business come out of the hide of individuals one way or the other, either through higher prices for what we buy or lower wages and dividends we receive from businesses, or some of each.

The importance of these first two guidelines is well illustrated by the flat tax championed by Steve Forbes in his 1996 run for the Republican presidential nomination, which featured a single 17 percent tax rate and an exempt income level of $35,750 for a family of four in 1996.

With these numbers, the flat tax can look very attractive, indeed. The problem is that such a system wouldn't come anywhere close to replacing the revenues of the current income tax system. In fact, according to a U.S. Treasury study,[1] this flat tax would leave the government short by a whopping $186 billion per year!

Most quick-and-dirty analyses of the winners and losers from the flat tax ignore both of these issues. Consider, for instance, the figures presented in an April 17, 1995, article in *Time* magazine, reproduced in Table 9.1. This was before Steve Forbes' run for the presidency, but it

Table 9.1
Make sure the numbers add up, and beware of hidden taxes: A misleading table from
Time magazine

	Tax on a family of four with income of $50,000	Tax on a family of four with income of $200,000
Existing system	$4,249	$46,323
Forbes plan	$2,244	$27,744
Treasury rates	$3,023	$37,370

Source: Goodgame (1995).

analyzed the plan he later was to support. According to this table, a middle-class family of four would do rather nicely under the Forbes flat tax, with a cut of just over $2,000. The family with $200,000 of wages and salaries would do even better, with a tax cut of nearly $20,000. But we've already mentioned that these rates would leave us almost $200 billion short per year, so it is no surprise that this plan can provide a generous tax cut for almost everyone now paying taxes.

A bit more surprising are the figures in the third row of the table, which show the taxes of these two families using the 22.9 percent tax rate that the Treasury estimated would be required to make up the revenue shortfall. They too show significant tax cuts for both families, although only about half as large as with the 17 percent rate.

How can a revenue-neutral tax change offer tax cuts, in some cases sizable tax cuts, to nearly everyone? The answer is that it cannot. What's missing in the numbers in the third row is the impact of taxes on business. According to the Treasury, business payments would rise, from $137 billion now to $315 billion.[2] A complete analysis of the winners and losers from switching to the flat tax would have to assign all of the increased $178 billion of revenue to some taxpayer or another, because these tax collections will certainly make someone worse off. The Treasury Department undertook just such an analysis of this plan, the results from which were shown in Tables 7.1 and 7.2.

3. The Devil Is in the Details

After eight decades, the U.S. income tax system has grown encrusted and Byzantine. In comparison, a two-page sketch of a replacement is bound to look breathtakingly simple. But be warned that, in taxation, the devil is in the details.

All tax systems have gray areas that require rules and regulations. All tax systems require an enforcement agency to see that the tax burden is shared equitably, and not unfairly shouldered by those who feel morally obligated to pay taxes. All tax systems will be subject to the same political pressures that have contributed to the current system's problems. Finally, a tax plan that includes transition rules or other aspects "to be fleshed out later" will later turn out to be a lot more complicated than it appears.

4. The Tax System Can't Encourage Everything

In defending a tax break, politicians always point out how it will encourage or reward some laudable activity, such as housing, charity, or saving. Every time you hear the word "encourage," remember that the break, by virtue of the higher tax rates it requires, discourages all other endeavors. Every time you hear the word "reward," remember that it penalizes other activities.

There may be cases when it makes sense to implement social or economic policy through the tax code. But these must clear a high hurdle. Tax preferences in the tax code are too easily hidden from plain view, leading to what is in effect a hidden industrial or distributional policy.

5. Simpler Isn't Necessarily Better, But It Helps

The IRS budget plus the time and money spent by Americans on tax matters add up to a substantial resource cost—on the order of ten cents per dollar raised. There are simpler tax systems that probably cut this number at least by half and can reduce your tax return to a postcard, or eliminate it altogether.

But simpler isn't necessarily better. Some of the simplification from tax reform comes at the cost of abandoning the personalization of tax burdens, some comes at the cost of abandoning progressivity, and some comes at the cost of abandoning the tax system as an instrument of social and economic policy.

6. Fairness Is a Slippery Concept. Make Up Your Own Mind

No politician, and no economist, has the one true answer to what is fair. That is an ethical judgment that each person must make. It is also an issue that cannot be avoided in deciding how to raise $700 billion plus in taxes. But keep in mind that it is too much to expect of a tax system to compensate for all the injustices of economic life.

7. Be Skeptical of Claims of Economic Nirvana

It is certainly true that high tax rates can stifle initiative and wrong-headed taxes can waste resources. To some degree, these problems can be reduced by tax reform. But another part is an unavoidable consequence of the desire for an equitable distribution of tax burden. The terms of this trade-off between justice and prosperity are uncertain.

The unresolvable differences about what is fair could be put aside if we could move to a tax system that is so good for the economy that everyone ends up better-off. But don't hold your breath. Vague promises of an economic nirvana are just that. Tax reform will not double the growth rate forever.

No one graph should convince you otherwise. The relationship between tax structure and the economy is complex and controversial. For every graph that purports to prove that high tax rates on the rich raise no revenue and are therefore counterproductive, there is another that purports to prove the opposite. Most economists believe that the potential economic benefits from tax reform are substantial, but many of these benefits could be obtained without a radical reshuffling of tax burdens.

8. The Tax System Can Be Improved

From a tactical point of view, there is much to be gained from Congress clearly separating the distinct aspects of tax reform we have discussed in the book and debating which aspects are *not* desirable, rather than considering what, if any, steps toward reform should be taken. Recall the plight of Hercules, who, as penance for having killed his wife and children in a fit of madness, was given 12 tasks of immense difficulty. The fifth of these tasks was one of the most daunting of all—to clean, in one day, thirty years of accumulated manure left by thousands of cattle in the stables of Augeas. (The analogy to the tax system is, we fear, obvious.) Hercules did not attempt to clean out the stables one shovelful at a time. Instead, Hercules diverted the rivers Alpheus and Peneus through the stables, ridding them of their filth at once. There is much to clean in the tax system, and contemplating a Herculean approach is an appropriate way to begin the great debate about tax reform.

But the best should not become the enemy of the good. If fundamental reform is not to be, then the debate ought to continue, because the tax system is too important for us to neglect.

The tax system can be made simpler. It can be made fairer. It can be made more conducive to economic growth. Some changes can accomplish all three, but in most cases difficult choices among these objectives must be made. We hope this book will help to clarify those choices, and guide us toward the best way to tax ourselves.

Notes

Chapter 1

1. An ABC News/*Washington Post* poll conducted June 12–24, 1993, found 60 percent said they favored "a smaller government with fewer services," while only 29 percent favored "a larger government with many services." In a December 1994 Gallup Poll, 66 percent of respondents said the amount of federal income tax they paid was "too high." Cited in Bowman (1995, p. 3).
2. We will, however, address some of the connections between government spending and taxes in Chapter 4.
3. IRS *Statistics of Income Bulletin*, Spring 1995, p. 118, and Blumenthal and Slemrod (1992, p. 189).
4. Blumenthal and Slemrod (1992, p. 185).
5. According to the 1991 IRS public-use database on individual income tax returns, 53.2 percent of all personal tax returns bore the signature of a paid preparer. Many of those who use a professional preparer apparently have very simple returns, including in 1992 3.9 percent of those who file a Form 1040EZ and 32.7 percent of those who file a Form 1040A. (Source: IRS *SOI Bulletin*, Summer 1993, p. 135 and Winter 1994–1995, p. 225) Presumably many of these taxpayers use a preparer not because their return is complex, but in the hope of speeding up their tax refund.
6. Herman (1995d) and Gephardt (1995).
7. Two of the largest compliance cost estimates in published studies are $202 billion for the entire federal tax system in 1995 (Arthur P. Hall, 1995), and $159 billion for the personal and corporate income taxes in 1985 (Payne, 1993). We'll explore this issue in greater depth in Chapter 5.
8. Projected outlays for IRS processing, assistance, management, and information systems are $7.97 billion for fiscal year 1996 (OMB 1995b, p. 430). A House bill passed in June, 1995 would cut that to $7.5 billion (Rogers, 1995).
9. Hershey (1993, p. D1).
10. See Chapter 2.
11. Shafer (1995a).
12. Survey by Advisory Commission on Intergovernmental Relations, cited in Bowman (1995).
13. Birnbaum and Murray (1987, p. 15).
14. Neubig and Joulfaian (1988).
15. The distributional impact of the Tax Reform Act of 1986 is analyzed in Joint Committee on Taxation (1987, pp. 17–18).

16. Newport (1990, pp. 6, 8).

17. Gray (1995, p. 18).

18. These tax systems collect all revenue from businesses, and would certainly require a tax collection and enforcement bureaucracy, perhaps under a name other than the IRS.

19. We defer to Chapter 7 the question of whether a 17 percent rate is high enough to raise the revenue now collected by the income tax.

20. Lugar (1995b, p. 3).

21. Hall and Rabushka (1995, p. vii)

22. Hall and Rabushka (1995, p. viii, 52).

23. Armey (1995, p. 1).

24. Hall and Rabushka (1995, p. vii).

25. Hall and Rabushka (1995, p. vii, 52).

26. Domenici (1995).

27. Domenici (1994, p. 320).

28. Domenici (1994, p. 304).

29. Birnbaum and Murray (1987, p. 52), Steuerle (1992, p. 94).

30. Slemrod (1995, p. 134).

31. Gray (1995, pp. 22–23).

32. Kuttner (1995).

33. McIntyre (1995b, p. 1).

34. Authors' calculation based on U.S. Department of Treasury, Office of Tax Analysis (1996, Table 2). Assumes a flat-tax plan with an exemption of $31,400 for a family of four in 1996, repeal of the earned-income tax credit and estate and gift taxation, and a revenue-neutral flat rate of 20.8 percent. The analysis assumes that the burden of taxes on wages and salaries falls on workers, and that the burden of business taxes falls on owners of capital.

Note that in a revenue-neutral tax change, the average percentage tax cut for the rich can be much larger than the average percentage tax increase on everyone else, because nonrich people greatly outnumber the rich.

35. Shafer (1995b).

36. Newport and Saad (1993, p. 19).

37. Fineman (1995, p. 36).

38. U.S. Department of Treasury, Office of Tax Analysis (1996, p. 1).

39. Gephardt (1995, p. 1).

40. Kirchheimer (1995, p. 136).

41. Lindsey (1990, p. 12).

Chapter 2

1. Certain nontax revenues, such as fees and fines, are included at both the federal and the state and local levels. Contributions to government employee pension plans are also counted as revenues. State and local revenues exclude federal grants-in-aid.

2. In 1993, the latest year for which detailed statistics are available, the Social Security payroll tax accounted for 80 percent of total contributions to federal social insurance (U.S. Bureau of Economic Analysis *Survey of Current Business*, July 1994). In 1995, the Social Security tax amounted to 15.3 percent of wages and salaries below $61,200, and 2.9 percent of wages and salaries above that, including both the employer and employee portions.

3. Some proposals do, though, change the federal income tax treatment of social insurance contributions, making them deductible or creditable against taxable income, or the tax treatment of benefits, making them fully taxable or exempt from tax.

4. The 24 OECD member nations, listed in descending order by their 1993 tax-to-GDP ratios, were: Sweden, Denmark, the Netherlands, Italy, Finland, Belgium, Norway, Luxembourg, France, Austria, Greece, Germany, Ireland, New Zealand, Canada, Spain, the United Kingdom, Switzerland, Portugal, Iceland, the United States, Japan, Australia, and Turkey. Statistics were not yet available for Mexico and the Czech Republic, which joined the OECD in 1994 and 1995, respectively, expanding it to 26 member nations. Revenue totals in the United States are slightly smaller in Table 2.2 than in Table 2.1 in part because the OECD calculations exclude certain "nontax" revenues, such as fees and fines. Source: OECD (1995a).

5. Real GDP was 1.86 times as large in 1994 as it was in 1969. Source: *Economic Report of the President* (1995, Table B–2).

6. The Supreme Court decision barring income taxation was in *Pollock vs. Farmers Loan and Trust Company* (1895). Its ruling was based on the clause in Article I, Section 9, stating: "No capitation, or other direct, tax shall be laid, unless in proportion to the census or enumeration herein before directed to be taken."

7. Histories of the U.S. personal income tax are provided in Witte (1985), Goode (1976), Pechman (1987), and Brownlee (1989).

8. Goode (1976) discusses the history of deductions and exclusions in the personal income tax base. Later additions include the standard deduction (1941), the deduction for medical expenses (1942), and a deduction for child and dependent care expenses (1954) that was later turned into a tax credit.

9. Historical information on the number of tax returns filed is available in U.S. Bureau of the Census (1975).

10. Brownlee (1989, p. 1615) notes the special Civil War tax on corporations. Pechman (1987, p. 135) discusses the Constitutional questions surrounding the 1909 corporate income tax.

11. U.S. Bureau of Economic Analysis, *Survey of Current Business* (July 1994) and *National Income and Product Accounts of the U.S.* (1992).

12. U.S. Bureau of Economic Analysis, *Survey of Current Business* (July 1994) and *National Income and Product Accounts of the U.S.* (1992). Steuerle (1992, p. 28) discusses this issue in more detail.

13. Rates below 50 percent were reduced by 10 percent in each of 1982 and 1983, and by an additional 5 percent in 1984. Tax rates in 1984 equaled (90 percent x 90 percent x 95 percent) = 76.95 percent of their 1981 levels, so the total tax cut was 23.05 percent.

14. This is sometimes referred to as the "Haig-Simons" definition of income, after economists Robert M. Haig and Henry C. Simons, who helped develop it.

15. In 1992, 90.8 percent of the total number of businesses were taxed solely under the personal code, where "total number of businesses" includes C corporations, S corporations, partnerships, and nonfarm sole proprietorships. Source: IRS *Statistics of Income Bulletin* (Spring 1995, pp. 82, 182–183, and 184–185).

16. A few adjustments need to be made to GDP to get the net amount of income actually counted as going to persons. The most notable subtractions are depreciation and indirect business taxes (such as sales and excise taxes).

17. IRS *Statistics of Income Bulletin* (Fall 1995, p. 143). Income tax after credits was 20.4 percent of aggregate taxable income in 1993.

18. This category includes investment income in all life insurance plans, including those that are not provided by employers.

19. Other families can set up an IRA with nondeductible contributions, the earnings of which are exempt from taxation.

20. Specifically, the miscellaneous accounting differences include: imputed income for things such as the rental value of owner-occupied homes; investment income received by nonprofit institutions or retained by fiduciaries; and net differences in accounting

treatment (National Income and Product Accounts versus IRS). It subtracts out certain items that are part of AGI but not personal income, such as: net capital gain less loss from sales of property; S corporation income less loss; and other taxable income less loss. All of these are line items in Table 4 of "Selected Historical and Other Data" in the appendix of the IRS *Statistics of Income Bulletin* (Fall 1995, p. 199).

21. IRS *Statistics of Income Bulletin* (Spring 1995, pp. 21 and 25).

22. IRS *Statistics of Income Bulletin* (Fall 1995, p. 143). Numbers do not include the effect of the itemized deduction phase-out for high-income taxpayers, since it is not allocated among individual deductions.

23. Above an AGI threshold ($172,050 for a joint return in 1995), 2 percent of the value of exemptions is phased out for every additional $2,500 of AGI. Similarly, itemized deductions are reduced in value by 3 percent of the amount by which AGI exceeds $117,950, until only 20 percent of itemized deductions are left. For example, consider a family of four in the 36 percent tax bracket, with $200,000 in AGI. Earning one more dollar of income causes them to lose 3 cents of itemized deductions and 8 cents worth of personal exemptions. At a 36 percent tax rate, this increases their tax bill by 3.96 cents, in effect increasing their marginal rate by 3.96 percentage points to 39.96 percent.

24. IRS *Statistics of Income Bulletin* (Spring 1995, pp. 20–26).

25. IRS *Statistics of Income Bulletin* (Spring 1995, p. 120).

26. U.S. House of Representatives Committee on Ways and Means *Green Book* (1994).

27. Parameters of the EITC for 1996 are from Forman (1996, p. 944).

28. Examples of items added back into the AMT tax base are tax-exempt interest from private activity bonds issued after August 7, 1986, accelerated depreciation allowances on real or leased property placed in service before 1987, intangible drilling costs, medical and dental expense deductions, miscellaneous itemized deductions, and state and local taxes, among others.

29. IRS *Statistics of Income Bulletin* (Fall 1995, p. 143), and Herman (1995a).

30. In 1992, 9.2 percent of total businesses were C corporations, where "total businesses" includes C corporations, S corporations, partnerships, and nonfarm sole proprietorships. C corporations received 58.2 percent of business income, defined as net income less deficit. Source: IRS *Statistics of Income Bulletin* (Spring 1995, pp. 82, 182–183, and 184–185).

31. The benefits of low rates in the lower brackets are phased out in certain income ranges, effectively leading to higher marginal tax rates in those ranges. In 1994, the marginal rate was effectively 39 percent on income between $100,000 and $335,000, and 38 percent on income between $15,000,000 and $18,333,333. Source: Gravelle (1994a, p. 262). In 1992, total tax payments by C corporations equaled 34.7 percent of taxable income. Since the top rate in 1992 was 34 percent, this suggests that most C corporation income was taxed at or above 34 percent. Source: IRS *Statistics of Income Bulletin* (Spring 1995, p. 185).

32. In an attempt to combat tax shelters, the TRA introduced a restriction on the deductibility of losses from "passive" investments, that is, investments in which the taxpayer does not materially participate.

Chapter 3

1. Whitney (1990) describes the protesting and rioting over the U.K. poll tax. Smith (1991) offers an analysis of its failure.

2. McHardy (1992, p. xxiv). Accounts of the peasant revolt of 1381 are also given in McKissack (1959) and Powell (1894).

3. Fisher (1996, p. 37).

4. Although in this illustration we use income as the tax base, the definition would apply to any alternative measure of well-being.

5. A tax system can be progressive over some income ranges and not others. Similarly, when comparing two tax systems, one might be more progressive over some income ranges and not others.

6. Clinton (1992, pp. 644–645).

7. From an April 13 CNN interview, quoted in "Clinton Voices Reservations About Flat-Tax Proposals" *The Wall Street Journal*, April 14, 1995, p. A10.

8. Safire (1995). Safire advocated an income tax with fewer deductions, a large exempt level of income, a rate of 25 percent on income above the exempt level but less than $150,000, and a rate of 30 percent on income above $150,000.

9. Armey (1995, p. 1)

10. Hall and Rabushka (1995, p. 26). Both Armey as well as Hall and Rabushka advocate a large exempt level of income, which would add some progressivity to their flat rate taxes. But they oppose having multiple tax rates, which almost certainly means their systems would levy less tax on high-income families than the current income tax. These issues are discussed in more detail in Chapter 7.

11. Higgins (1995).

12. Davies (1995).

13. Simons (1938, p. 24).

14. Source: U.S. House of Representatives Committee on Ways and Means (1993, pp. 1502 and 1486), based on CBO analysis. In order to adjust for differences in well-being caused by differing family sizes, families are ranked by "adjusted family income" (AFI) in the CBO analysis. This involves dividing family income by the poverty threshold for that size family; poverty thresholds are designed to adjust for the living expenses of different size families. The CBO arranges quintiles to contain an equal number of people, not families. The CBO definition of income is given below in note 38.

15. Kennickell and Woodburn (1992) based on a study of the 1983 and 1989 Survey of Consumer Finances. Cited in U.S. House of Representatives Committee on Ways and Means (1993, p. 1551).

16. Sawhill and Condon (1992) analyzed a sample of 4,829 individuals from the Panel Study of Income Dynamics who were aged 25 to 54 at the beginning of the sample period. A similar study put out by the Treasury Department at the same time suggested a bit more mobility. However, it suffered from a number of problems. Its sample consisted only of taxpayers who had filed a tax return in every year between 1979 and 1988, which caused them to omit the vast majority of poor people. Moreover, in the Treasury study, the average age of people in the lowest quintile in 1979 was just 21. Nasar (1992) discusses both of these studies.

17. Gottschalk and Moffitt (1994, p. 223) examine white males in the Panel Study of Income Dynamics, and find that the variance of average earnings in 1979–1987 was 41 percent higher than it was in 1970–1978.

18. More generally, why incomes are unequal plays a role in the arguments about what, if anything, the tax system ought to do about it. For example, if the predominant factor is luck, then the disincentive effects of a progressive tax system are less worrisome, and may even provide some social insurance against bad outcomes. If, alternatively, a principal source of inequality is variations in the willingness to work hard, then the case for highly progressive taxes is less compelling, as it is differentially taxing on the basis of tastes rather than on the basis of endowments of skills, over which individuals have little control. In fact, both luck (including the inheritance of money and other advantages) and hard work are factors in determining incomes.

19. Newport and Saad (1993). A February 1993 *Boston Globe* poll found 83 percent support for increasing the tax rate from 31 percent to 35 percent for people with annual

incomes over $140,000. A January 1993 NBC poll found 77 percent thought upper-income Americans did not pay their "fair share" in taxes (both cited in Fisher and Temple, 1995).

20. Cited in Fisher and Temple (1995).

21. Gallup and Newport (1990).

22. Roper poll, June 1986, cited in Bowman (1995, p. 6). The poll asked respondents to estimate the tax bill for a married couple with two children.

23. We estimated the actual tax rates using the IRS's public-use database of individual tax returns for tax year 1986. The average personal income tax rate on married couples with two children and incomes between $45,000 and $55,000 was 11.8 percent in 1986. The average personal income tax rate on such families with incomes between $180,000 and $220,000 was 21.1 percent. Tax is defined as income tax after credits. We define income here in a way that poll respondents would be likely to think of it. Income is defined as adjusted gross income plus the excluded portions of capital gains, dividends, unemployment benefits, and Social Security benefits. All statutory adjustments, such as deductible IRA and Keogh contributions and the two-earner couple deduction, are also added back into income.

24. McKee and Gerbing (1989), cited in Roberts, Hite, and Bradley (1994).

25. Shafer (1995a and 1995b).

26. Thirty-two percent of respondents preferred "a flat tax of about 20 percent, with deductions for home mortgages and charitable contributions," while 29 percent preferred "a flat tax of about 17 percent with no deductions, credits, or exemptions." Fineman (1995, p. 36).

27. Survey by Luntz Research Companies, January 4–5, 1995. Cited in Bowman (1995, p. 6).

28. Wessel (1995a).

29. A later survey by Roberts, Hite, and Bradley (1994) examined people's understandings of concepts such as "marginal," "average," "proportional," and "progressive" as applied to taxes, and found that even when these concepts are defined for respondents, they often become confused or give inconsistent responses.

30. To be precise, one pays the difference between tax liability and withheld taxes *plus* estimated tax payments.

31. With heavily advertised goods like Coke and Pepsi, even if all consumers could not distinguish them in a blind taste test, many still might strongly prefer to buy one or the other. This example presumes that consumers think the two products are identical, except possibly for price.

32. U.S. Bureau of Economic Analysis, *Survey of Current Business*, June, 1995, Tables 3.2 and 3.3.

33. This was also a feature of the Tax Reform Act of 1986, which was designed to be revenue-neutral overall, but accomplished this by reducing individual income tax payments by about $25 billion per year and increasing corporation income taxes by a similar amount (Feldstein, 1988, p. 37). Analyses that ignored the latter often showed that the great majority of taxpayers would benefit from a tax cut. In fact, because the corporation income tax increases would be passed on to individuals in some way, the reform was not nearly as generous.

34. Martin Feldstein of Harvard University has argued that, although there is certainly foreign investment over short periods, over the long term a country's investment is limited by its own citizens' saving. If this is true, the link between domestic savings and domestic investment is restored. See Feldstein (1994).

35. Discussed in Gravelle (1994b).

36. Bastiat (1964, p. 1).

37. Customs duties and estate and gift taxes are not included, but they raise relatively little revenue.

38. The CBO definition of income includes: the sum of wages, salaries, self-employment income, personal rents, interest, and dividends; employer contributions to Social Security; government cash transfer payments; cash pension benefits; the imputed federal corporate tax burden borne by a family; and realized capital gains. Source: Kasten, Sammartino, and Toder (1994, p. 13).

The Treasury definition of income adds several things that are excluded by the CBO definition, such as: employer-provided fringe benefits; imputed rent on owner-occupied housing; and accumulated interest on pensions, IRAs, Keoghs, and life insurance. Capital gains are counted on an accrual rather than a realization basis. Capital income and losses are adjusted for inflation. An adjustment is also made for accelerated depreciation allowances given to certain noncorporate businesses. Source: U.S. Department of Treasury, Office of Tax Analysis (1996).

The other major difference is that to adjust for family size, the CBO ranks families by "adjusted family income," which is family income divided by poverty thresholds. Treasury ranks families by economic income, without any adjustment for family size. Note that single individuals are counted as families.

39. See, for example, Kasten, Sammartino, and Toder (1994).

40. Note that the average tax rate for 1994 includes the fully phased-in (1996) version of the earned income tax credit.

41. Compare horizontal equity to the concept introduced earlier of vertical equity, which concerns the appropriate relation of tax burden of families at *different* levels of well-being.

42. At present the federal government doesn't levy a special tax on movies. But in 1990, it did impose a new "luxury" tax of 10 percent of the purchase price over $10,000 for furs and jewelry, over $30,000 for autos, over $100,000 for boats, and over $250,000 for airplanes. The luxury tax on everything but automobiles was repealed in 1993.

43. For this reason, the deduction for medical expenses is limited to "involuntary" expenses, and specifically excludes such things as elective cosmetic surgery.

44. Note that an application of the benefit principle might suggest that larger families should have *higher* tax liabilities, reflecting the fact that many tax-funded benefits, like public education, increase with family size. This argument is made by Kaplow (1994).

45. See Feenberg and Rosen (1995) for details on the magnitude of the tax penalty (or reward) to marriage under the current tax system.

46. One reason for abandoning the earlier system of taxing each spouse separately was that spouses in community property states could claim to earn half of family income, thus lowering the couple's total taxes. Many states adopted community property laws, apparently so their residents could receive this benefit.

Chapter 4

1. National Commission on Economic Growth and Tax Reform (1996, p. 5).

2. Murray (1996).

3. Hall and Rabushka (1995, p. 89).

4. Gale (1995, p. 22). Note that Gale refers here to gain in welfare, not income. In other words, it is the gain net of costs of foregone leisure, foregone current consumption, and the like. See Chapter 7 for more discussion of this issue.

5. Net interest payments accounted for 15 percent of the federal budget in fiscal year 1995. Source: OMB (1995b, Table 6.2).

6. It is also possible that a deficit could increase investment in the short run if there is a recession. Business investment is determined in part by firms' confidence in consumer demand, and if a deficit helps alleviate a recession, it could boost this confidence.

7. This judgment applies to deficits created by reducing taxes collected, holding constant government expenditure on consumption. It may not apply to deficits created by increasing government-funded investment in infrastructure or education, which provide current and future benefits.

8. See Steuerle and Bakija (1994, p. 60) for a discussion of this issue.

9. See Bakija and Steuerle (1991) for a discussion of this issue.

10. See Slemrod (1995a).

11. For the rest of this chapter, we will be referring to taxes other than lump-sum, or poll, taxes.

12. Compensation of employees was 73 percent of national income in 1994. Source: *Economic Report of the President* (1996, p. 306).

13. This argument applies even more directly when the base broadening refers to eliminating the deductibility of state and local income taxes. This may allow a lowering of the federal tax rate, but does not permit an overall reduction in the combined rate of tax from local, state, and federal levels.

14. As discussed earlier, this is but one example where our country's (and every other country's) national income statistics will mismeasure the economic cost from tax disincentives. The statistics will record the $200 decrease due to lost labor income but, because the value of leisure is not included in national income, ignore the $150 worth of extra leisure that Roger enjoys when taxed. It should only take a moment's reflection to convince yourself that national income measured without considering the value of leisure does not accurately reflect national prosperity. If it did, then a law forcing everyone to work, regardless of whether they wanted to or not, would make us better off. National income would rise, but we would in fact be worse off.

15. It also depends on how sensitive labor demand is to changes in the cost of hiring workers. To the extent it is not, taxes on labor income increase the equilibrium pretax wage rate, offsetting the decline in labor supply.

16. Only the responsiveness due to the substitution effect of taxes is relevant to this argument.

17. Killingsworth (1983) and Heckman (1993) provide surveys of this literature.

18. Eissa (1995a and 1995b).

19. Mariger (1995).

20. Bosworth and Burtless (1992) illustrate this on p. 14 of their study, based on wage data from the Census Bureau's Current Population Survey.

21. Seib (1996).

22. Lindbeck (1993).

23. Triest (1990).

24. To be precise, what offsets the incentive effect of lower taxes on saving is an income effect. The lower taxes on saving make the taxpayer better off, and we should expect the taxpayer to respond by consuming more both today and tomorrow. Higher consumption today means a lower saving rate.

25. See Gravelle (1994a) for details. The real after-tax rate of return is based on the yield on Baa corporate bonds. A fixed premium for holding equity of 2.67 percentage points is added in all years. This is based on an assumption of a 4 percent premium for holding equity, multiplied by the typical share of corporate investments financed by equity, which Gravelle puts at two-thirds. The tax rate used is the average marginal individual tax rate on interest income. We extend her series from 1989 to 1994 using the following sources. Tax rates are taken from CBO (1994, p. 7). We estimate the expected inflation

rate based on annual forecasts by the U.S. Office of Management and Budget in the *Budget of the U.S. Government* (OMB, various years). The nominal yield on Baa bonds is taken from the *Economic Report of the President* (1995, Table B–72).

26. Poterba, Venti, and Wise (1995, Table 4.1) show that personal saving rates also declined during the 1980s under both the *National Income and Product Accounts* measure (used here), and the alternative *Flow of Funds* measure of the Federal Reserve. The one measure that shows an increase in saving during the 1980s is the total private saving rate derived from changes in the "net worth" estimates of the Federal Reserve. The main difference between this and other measures of saving is that it includes purely financial capital gains (as opposed to capital gains reflecting retained earnings of corporations). A major cause of such gains is probably improved expectations about the future state of the economy, which may have contributed to the stock market boom of the 1980s. However, it is probably inappropriate for this purpose to count these gains as an increase in saving, because it does not reflect any increase in the amount of loanable funds made available for business investment, nor does it indicate a response of individuals to higher rates of return. It may, however, have caused individuals to reduce their saving rates (measured in other ways) because it made them feel wealthier. Bradford (1991) discusses some of these issues.

The rates of return depicted here are calculated using the average marginal tax rate on interest income. They thus do not reflect the impact of higher capital gains tax rates and reduced IRA eligibility after 1986. Adjusting for either of these factors would make the rate of return slightly lower after 1986, but still much higher than in the period prior to the 1980s.

27. For a recent review of these studies, see Bernheim (1996). Ironically, one influential study suggesting a very low responsiveness of saving was authored by Robert E. Hall, who is also one of the designers of the flat tax, among the selling points of which is that it reduces the tax on saving. See Hall (1988).

28. OMB (1995b, pp. 64–65).

29. Gravelle (1994a, p. 109).

30. The most sophisticated study of this issue to date, by Leonard Burman of CBO and William Randolph of the Treasury Department (1994), concludes that the long-run responsiveness of capital gains realizations to changes in marginal tax rates is probably low, but there is a wide confidence interval around their estimate.

31. See Poterba (1989) for a discussion of this issue.

32. Hall and Rabushka (1995, p. 87) make this case.

33. For an expansion of this view, see Krugman (1994) or Slemrod (1992).

34. We leave aside the controversial employment effect of minimum wage legislation.

35. See Davies and Whalley (1991) for a review of this issue.

36. We focus on the subject of tax evasion in Chapter 5.

37. Burman, Clausing, and O'Hare (1994).

38. Source: Authors' calculations based on IRS *Statistics of Income: Corporation Income Tax Returns* (various years).

39. See Auerbach and Slemrod (forthcoming) for examples.

40. Mitchell (1996).

41. Steuerle (1992, p. 186).

42. See Auerbach (1996b) for a discussion of the pros and cons of dynamic revenue estimation.

43. See Feenberg and Poterba (1993). The figures reported there were biased because they failed to adjust for changes in the definition of adjusted gross income. The text cites the corrected numbers presented in Slemrod (1996b).

44. See Feldstein (1995a) and Auten and Carroll (1994).

45. See Rosen (1981) and Frank and Cook (1995).

46. Feldstein and Feenberg (1995).

47. Fastis (1992) and Peers and Tannenbaum (1992).

48. *Economic Report of the President* (1996, p. 92).

49. See Parcell (1996).

50. One heroic, although now dated, attempt to measure the total welfare cost of all taxes—federal, state, and local—came up with a range of estimates from 13 to 24 cents per dollar of revenue. See Ballard, Shoven, and Whalley (1985).

Chapter 5

1. Tritch (1993, p. 98).

2. Tritch and Lohse (1992, p. 92).

3. West Publishing Co. (1995a and 1995b).

4. Hall, Arthur P. (1955, p. 4).

5. IRS budget is for fiscal year 1995. Total revenues collected by the IRS were approximately $1.27 trillion in fiscal year 1995. This includes not only the federal individual and corporate income taxes, but also Social Security and federal unemployment insurance payroll taxes, estate and gift taxes, and excise taxes. Source: OMB (1995b)

6. Blumenthal and Slemrod (1992).

7. Slemrod and Sorum (1984).

8. Tabulations from the IRS public-use data indicate 53.2 percent of all personal tax returns bore the signature of a paid preparer in 1991. In the Blumenthal/Slemrod study, 51.3 percent of respondents paid for professional help with their tax returns. The average expenditure on professional help for all taxpayers was $66 in 1989 dollars, or $81 in 1995 dollars. The average for those who use preparers is thus (81/.513) = $158.

9. These expenses average $11.20 per taxpayer, or $13.80 in 1995 dollars, in the Blumenthal/Slemrod survey.

10. See Slemrod (1996a) for more details.

11. These estimates, and those that follow, are discussed in detail in Slemrod (1996a).

12. IRS *Statistics of Income Bulletin* (Fall 1995, p. 217).

13. Slemrod and Blumenthal (1996).

14. See, for example, Slemrod and Blumenthal (1996); Arthur P. Hall (1995, Table 2); and Sandford (1995).

15. The Blumenthal/Slemrod study asked about compliance with the personal income tax, and did not specify how businesses taxed under the personal code should be treated. It appears that self-employed people (sole proprietors) generally reported the costs of compliance for their businesses. Owners of partnerships and S corporations probably reported only a small fraction of the costs. While income from these latter types of firms is taxed under the personal code, most of the difficult parts of the taxpaying process, such as calculating depreciation deductions, are performed on a separate business tax form.

16. Arthur D. Little (1988, pp. I–7).

17. The Arthur D. Little study calculated that, in 1983, the average firm spent about 115 hours on compliance. There were 4.73 million firms, implying that businesses spent a total of 546.7 million hours complying with income taxation. But instead of using this figure, the study constructs a forecasting model that predicts an aggregate figure of 2.75 billion hours for 1983, about five times higher than their own survey averages suggest. The flaws in their procedures are discussed in more detail in Slemrod (1996a).

18. Payne used Arthur Anderson, and Hall used Price Waterhouse.

19. Herman (1995d).

20. Gephardt (1995).
21. Richman (1995, p. 38).
22. Blumenthal and Slemrod (1992, Table 1).
23. There have been studies of the compliance cost of income taxation in other countries, but differences in methodology make comparisons very tenuous. That being said, a careful study of the U.K.'s tax system provided an estimate of 4.7 cents on the dollar of collection cost. See Sandford (1995). One reason for the lower cost is the special nature of the British individual income tax system, under which most taxpayers need not even fill out and file a return.
24. We consider what makes any given tax structure complex, but it is also certainly true that continuous change in the tax system is itself complex, as it takes time and effort for the taxpayers to learn and adjust to the new environment. This raises the classic problem of policy reform—should the movement to a better policy be put off because of the costs of getting there?
25. As we discussed in Chapter 3, a poll tax would likely also be difficult to enforce.
26. The British are, however, moving away from this system. Starting in April of 1996, nine million residents with more than a modicum of income from rents, dividends, interest, or capital gains will have to file an eight-page tax return, plus related schedules. See Johnston (1996).
27. On the other hand, the tax system is not a particularly effective way to deliver subsidies to families whose income is below the threshold level of income for filing a return. It also postpones the receipt of the tax credit to when the return is filed, unless the subsidy can be integrated into the employer withholding system.
28. Of all personal returns in 1993, 28 percent used the itemized deduction for state and local taxes paid. Source: IRS *Statistics of Income Bulletin* (Fall 1995, p. 143).
29. There is no reason that the tax system could not provide a subsidy that was a constant rate for all taxpayers. If this is desired, it should be a refundable credit, rather than an itemized deduction.
30. Doernberg (1988, p. 967).
31. Recent legislation has placed limitations on what members of Congress can accept from lobbyists. Under the new rules, members of Congress can still accept a dinner invitation, but cannot accept payment for meals or gifts totaling more than $100 from any one source per year.
32. This point is illustrated in note 21 of Chapter 2.
33. In some ways, the very existence of the corporate income tax is just such a policy; it acts as a backstop to the personal income tax, to keep income earned through corporations from escaping tax entirely. We address this issue in Chapter 8.
34. See Moore (1987).
35. We consider devolving to the states the responsibility for collecting taxes an example of renaming the IRS.
36. Lambert (1989).
37. Vecsey (1994).
38. The dependent exemption episode is chronicled in Lewin (1991) and Szilagyi (1990). There is a similar story regarding the child-care credit. Beginning in tax year 1989, in order to claim a child-care credit a taxpayer had to report the name of the care provider, plus either the provider's Social Security number or, if the provider was a business rather than an individual, the employer identification number. As in the dependent exemption case, the results were immediate and striking. The number of taxpayers claiming child-care credits dropped from 8.7 million in 1988 to 6 million in 1989, reversing a nine-year trend of annual increases; the dollar amount claimed fell from $3.7 billion to $2.4 billion. Even more incredible, the number of taxpayers reporting self-employment income from child-care services rose from 261,000 in 1988 to 431,000 in 1989, a 65 percent increase!

The combination of the decrease in child care credit taken and increase in income reported by self-employed child care providers resulted in a $1.5 billion increase in tax revenues. See O'Neil and Lanese (1993).

39. The principal purpose of the Taxpayer Compliance Measurement Program is to gather information that enables the IRS to come up with a formula based on the information provided on tax returns, for determining which returns it is cost-effective to audit. The latest round of this program, scheduled for 1996, was canceled in 1995 due to impending cuts in the IRS budget.

40. The tax gap estimates for 1987 were based largely on the 1982 TCMP. See IRS Research Division (1988).

41. Total revenues for the personal and corporate income taxes in 1987 were $495.7 billion (U.S. Bureau of Economic Analysis *National Income and Product Accounts* 1992, Table 3.2), and 84.9/(495.7 + 84.9) = 0.146.

42. This figure was given in a November 1993 appearance before Congress by IRS commissioner Margaret Milner Richardson, cited in Hershey (1993).

43. Our simple extrapolation from 1992 to 1995 assumes the tax gap grows at the same rate as revenues.

44. U.S. General Accounting Office (1988, p. 9) notes that the tax gap estimate for 1987 did not include unreported income from illegal sources, such as illegal gambling, drug trafficking, and prostitution. There was also no estimate of revenue loss from certain remittance problems, such as employers who underdeposit employee income tax withheld from salaries. Other hard-to-uncover evasion, such as unreported income from tips and moonlighting, was estimated on the basis of special studies.

45. Federal personal income tax revenues for fiscal year 1995 are estimated at $588.5 billion (OMB 1995b, p. 29).

46. Reported in Roth, Scholz, and Witte (1989, p. 51). Based on the 1979 TCMP.

47. Roth, Scholz, and Witte (1989, p. 55).

48. Roth, Scholz, and Witte (1989, p. 60), based on the 1982 TCMP.

49. Alm (1985).

50. Tritch (1995, p. 121).

51. Payne (1993, p. 38).

52. The original goal was to double the audit rate to 2.2 percent (Tritch, 1995, p. 126). However, this is likely to be scaled back a bit by budget cuts; the IRS Assistant Commissioner for Examination said on August 15, 1995, that the number of audits was expected to increase by 45 percent in fiscal 1995 compared to fiscal 1994 (Marvin, 1995, p. G–2).

53. Income is here defined as total positive income, which sums all these components of income that are positive, and does not subtract items that are negative. Source: IRS 1992 *Annual Report* (1993, p. 34).

54. IRS 1992 *Annual Report* (1993, p. 4).

55. The 70 percent figure is for fiscal year 1994, and equals total withheld collections less refunds divided by total net individual income tax revenues. Source: OMB (1995, p. 29).

56. IRS 1992 *Annual Report* (1993, p. 4).

57. Steuerle (1986, p. 27).

58. Burnham (1989) and Payne (1993) provide abundant examples.

59. Willette (1996).

60. See Yitzhaki (1974).

61. Sheffrin and Triest (1992) offer a literature review as well as some new evidence on this subject.

62. Hessing et al. (1992, p. 298).

Chapter 6

1. In calculating the revenue-neutral tax rate, we ignore any taxpayer response to the new rate schedule.

2. The single rate that would be required to raise the same revenue from *all* taxpayers is lower than that reported here, because four-person families have a larger than proportional share of itemized deductions. Also note that if all personal exemptions and standard deductions are increased by the same proportion, this shifts some of the tax burden away from four-person families and onto smaller families and single people. To maintain the balanced-budget character of this exercise, we use the rate that would be necessary to raise a fixed amount of revenue from married couples with two children as a group.

3. The $4,000 is $750 billion in personal and corporate income taxes divided by a population of 187 million people aged 20 or over.

4. If the consumption tax were levied on the net-of-tax price it would have to be set at a 25 percent rate to be equivalent to a 20 percent tax on wage income.

5. This may not be true for people who are already fairly old when the consumption or wage tax is adopted, since their saving won't benefit from many years of higher after-tax returns. However, this just matters in the transition to a consumption tax. Once it is in place, a consumption tax that raises the same revenue as an income tax need not provide a greater disincentive to working.

6. See Sabelhaus (1993) for an examination of consumption and saving rates by income level.

7. The precise statement is that the present discounted value of consumption must equal the present discounted value of labor earnings and inherited wealth.

8. Economists Henry Aaron and Harvey Galper take this position in their 1985 book *Assessing Tax Reform.*

9. The total private net worth held by U.S. households, as estimated by the Federal Reserve, was $23 trillion in 1993 (*Economic Report of the President*, 1995, Table B-114). We extrapolate to 1996 to come up with about $25 trillion.

10. Whether in fact consumer prices would rise in the event of tax reform depends on the monetary policy set by the Federal Reserve Board.

11. Whether eliminating the tax on dividends would increase the value of corporate stock depends on whether these taxes have been capitalized (negatively) into the value of shares, or whether firms can find ways to distribute funds to shareholders in ways that avoid the dividend tax, say through share repurchases. This is a controversial topic among economists, although the evidence points to at least some capitalization. See Bradford (1981) or Auerbach (1979) for discussion of this issue.

12. As noted in Chapter 3, according to a study by Kennickell and Woodburn (1992), 37.1 percent of all wealth in the United States was held by the richest 1 percent of households. A study by the U.S. Bureau of the Census (1990) found that in 1988, the median wealth of households whose head was over age 65 was $73,471, compared to $35,752 for the population as a whole. Both are cited in U.S. House of Representatives Committee on Ways and Means (1993, pp. 1551–1559)

13. Steuerle and Bakija (1994) provide estimates of the subsidies received by members of current elderly generations, above and beyond their lifetime contributions to Social Security and Medicare.

14. Fullerton and Rogers (1996) argue that a wage tax could actually increase saving by *more* than a consumption tax, because it leaves more wealth in the hands of the very wealthy, who have a much higher propensity to save than everyone else.

15. Gordon and Slemrod (1988) estimated that replacing the 1983 corporate and personal taxes on capital income with a consumption tax at the same rates would *increase* revenue. They also estimated that, even if businesses were allowed to continue taking

deductions for depreciation on existing capital, the present value of revenues would rise. The Tax Reform Act of 1986 made taxation of capital income considerably more uniform. Combined with lower inflation rates, this greatly reduced arbitrage and tax shelter opportunities, so that these results may not be as applicable to today's income tax.

16. OMB (1995b). Personal income tax revenues are estimated at $623 billion for fiscal year 1996.

17. The best argument may be that a federal preference offsets a bias against housing due to the heavy reliance of local governments on property taxes. However, many economists argue that property taxes on housing act not as a disincentive to purchase housing, but rather as the price for obtaining local public services, predominantly elementary and secondary education. To the extent that local property taxes are a user charge for public services, they do not act as a disincentive to purchase housing, and the argument for offsetting preferences in the federal income tax does not apply.

18. Messere (1993, p. 234) notes that 12 European countries tax the imputed rental value of owner-occupied houses. These countries generally estimate the rent by applying a low, fixed percentage rate to an estimate of the value of the home.

19. Messere (1993, p. 234).

20. The study was carried out by the economic consulting firm, Data Resources Incorporated. See Sullivan (1996, p. 341).

21. See Feldstein (1995b) and Hall and Rabushka (1995, pp. 94–95).

22. Poterba (1990) finds that single-family housing starts showed similar patterns in the United States and Canada after 1986, despite the fact that Canada did not have a tax reform that made owner-occupied housing less attractive. Moreover, in the 1970s and 1980s movements in the real price of single-family homes in the United States were only partially consistent with tax-induced changes in the cost of housing.

23. Canada's homeownership rate for 1992 was 63 percent, compared to 64 percent for the United States. Source: Bartlett (1995), based on data from the International Housing Association and the OECD.

24. Hall and Rabushka (1995) suggest that, in the transition to a flat tax, holders of existing mortgages could continue to deduct a portion of the interest as long as the lender continues to pay tax on the interest. This, they argue, would give an incentive to refinance the loan, converting it into a "new" mortgage subject to the new rules.

25. OMB (1995b).

26. Randolph (1995) performs a sophisticated econometric analysis examining how charitable contributions of individuals responded to changes in marginal tax rates over the 1980s. He concludes that, in the long run, giving is not very sensitive to tax incentives, although the *timing* of giving is.

27. If a uniform rate of subsidy is desired, it could in theory be administered not through the tax system, but by direct government grants to qualifying charitable organizations. Many resist this idea as inappropriate government intrusiveness; others fear it because once the rate of subsidy is decoupled from marginal income tax rates, it could be arbitrarily reduced when budget cutting fever breaks out.

28. OMB (1995b). Both figures are for fiscal year 1996.

29. In other words, the combined federal and state tax rate would be the same either way.

30. In its current form, it also provides an encouragement for subfederal governments to use income and property taxes, which are deductible, instead of sales taxes, which since 1986 are not deductible. The federal tax bias against sales taxes has not, though, resulted in a post-1986 movement away from sales taxes. On the contrary, if anything there has been a trend *toward* greater reliance by states on sales taxes.

Chapter 7

1. Due and Mikesell (1994, pp. 52–54) catalog numerous examples of states that charge different rates for different goods, such as preferential lower rates on automobile purchases. They discuss refund programs for the elderly and the poor on pages 80–84. These refund schemes are generally administered through personal income tax forms.
2. If sales of investment goods were taxable under the VAT, but were not deductible at all for the firms that purchased them, then the tax base would include *gross* investment, making the base broader than an income tax. Alternatively, if investment goods were deducted gradually as they depreciated, this would turn the VAT into an income tax. Immediate expensing of capital goods, or the equivalent, exemption of sales of investment goods from tax, is necessary to make the VAT a consumption tax.
3. A VAT may be levied either on the price inclusive of the tax, or the price before-tax, as with a retail sales tax. A tax that raises a given amount of revenue will have a lower rate if levied on the after-tax price than on the before-tax price, but the two are really equivalent. For example, a 10 percent tax on the before-tax price is equal to a 9.09 percent tax on the after-tax price. According to Tait (1988, p. 8), Finland and Sweden are the only countries that have persistently charged the VAT on the after-tax price.
4. As noted above, a credit-invoice method VAT need not necessarily visibly charge the tax as a percentage of the before-tax price, but nearly every country that has one does.
5. In an invoice-credit type of VAT, there is a distinction between an "exemption" and "zero-rating." "Exemption" generally applies to small firms, and is explained in the section on simplicity and enforceability of a VAT. Zero-rating in a VAT means that credits are allowed for purchased inputs, although sales are not taxed. This method frees the entire final purchase price of the good from taxation. In general, zero-rating is used for goods accorded preferential treatment, such as food or, in most countries that use a VAT, exports.
6. Laurence Kotlikoff of Boston University has proposed using an electronic debit card system that would automatically record consumers' transactions and calculate their tax liability. A brief description is offered in Kotlikoff (1995, p. 17). This would share many of the administrative difficulties associated with a retail sales tax (discussed later in this chapter). It would also require either that all transactions use this electronic payment method, or that individuals keep records of and voluntarily report all cash transactions. Banning all other means of payment, including cash, would probably be necessary.
7. They promise to gradually reduce the rates in the USA Tax to 8, 19, and 40 percent by the year 2000.
8. Pearlman (1996) argues that our political system would be very unlikely to adopt any kind of consumption tax without major transition relief for old assets.
9. The U.S. Treasury Department estimates that the corporate and personal income taxes (net of all EITC payments) will raise $729.4 billion in 1996 (U.S. Department of Treasury, Office of Tax Analysis, 1996). We estimate personal consumption expenditures for 1996 by taking the average of 2nd and 3rd quarter personal consumption expenditures for 1995, which is $4,874 billion (from U.S. Bureau of Economic Analysis *Survey of Current Business*, Oct. 1995, Table 1.1), and increasing it by 4.6 percent (growth in nominal GDP forecast in CBO, 1995a, Table 4). This yields a 1996 figure for personal consumption expenditures of $5,084 billion, and a tax rate of 14.3 percent.
10. See Chapter 5's discussion on the extent of tax evasion.
11. We calculate the 23.6 percent figure as follows. According to Due and Mikesell (1994, pp. 21–22), the average state's retail sales tax base is equal to 0.49 percent of personal income. We estimate personal income for 1996 at $6,301 billion (average of 2nd and 3rd quarters of 1995 multiplied by 1.043, projected growth in nominal GDP from CBO 1995,

Table 4). This suggests a sales tax base of $3,088 billion for 1996 if the U.S. adopted a base typical of the states. Raising revenue of $729.4 billion (see note 9 above) would thus require a 23.6 percent rate.

12. According to Due and Mikesell, leaving aside Hawaii, the five states with the broadest sales tax coverage are Arizona, Arkansas, New Mexico, South Dakota, and Wyoming. These five have a sales tax base equal to 70 percent of personal income. This implies a national sales tax base of $4,411 billion in 1996, and a rate of 16.5 percent. Hawaii is an outlier, with an RST base equal to 126 percent of personal income, which must imply very heavy taxation of business inputs.

13. Of the five states listed with broad sales tax coverage, all but Arizona fully subject food to sales tax. Due and Mikesell (1995, p. 75) estimate that a food exemption costs a state between 20 and 25 percent of sales tax revenue.

14. Ring (1989, Table 1). For the five states with broad coverage mentioned above, Ring estimated consumer purchases represented only 45 percent of retail sales tax revenues. Due and Mikesell (1994, pp. 72–73) note that other studies are consistent with this finding. For instance, a 1979 Texas survey estimated that 58 percent of RST revenues came from business purchases, and a recent Iowa study by KPMG Peat Marwick found that 39 percent of RST revenues came from business purchases.

15. CBO (1992, Table 8) estimated that the broadest possible VAT base for 1988 would be $2,823 billion, or $2,681 billion assuming a 95 percent compliance rate. Personal consumption expenditures (PCE) in 1988 were $3,296.1 billion, so the VAT base would be 81.3 percent of PCE (*Economic Report of the President*, 1995, Table B–1). Multiplying this by PCE of $5,084 billion for 1996 implies a tax base of $4,133 billion. Replacing income taxation (including EITC) would take $729.4 billion, suggesting a rate of 17.6 percent would be required. Among the personal consumption expenditures that CBO assumes would not be taxed are: food produced and consumed on farms; food furnished to employees; business meals; tips; employee compensation for small businesses; rental value of the existing housing stock; employer contributions to group health insurance and federal expenditures under Medicare and Medicaid; services furnished without payment by financial institutions and the expense of handling life insurance; personal use of business automobiles; pari-mutuel net receipts; educational and research expenditures other than tuition and fees; employee compensation in religious organizations; unreimbursed medical care expenses; and purchases of federal government services by state and local governments. The CBO uses this tax base to estimate the amount of revenue that could be raised by the adoption of a 5 percent VAT on top of the existing tax structure, and adjusts its revenue estimates downward significantly to reflect reduced revenues from other taxes. This last adjustment is not relevant to the rate required for a VAT that would provide a revenue-neutral *replacement* for the personal and corporate income taxes.

16. The rate for a flat tax appears lower than the rate for a comparable VAT or retail sales tax. The VAT and retail sales tax are levied on the before-tax price of goods and services, while the flat tax is levied on a base that includes the tax payments themselves.

17. Hall and Rabushka (1995) propose a personal allowance of $16,500 for a married couple filing jointly, $9,500 for a single filer, and $14,000 for a single head of household. In addition, there would be an exemption of $4,500 per dependent for 1995. Exemptions in the Armey-Shelby and Forbes plans follow a similar pattern.

18. Hall and Rabushka (1995, Table 3.1) estimate the revenues raised by their flat tax by starting from GDP for 1993, and subtracting out items from the National Income and Product Accounts that would be excluded from their tax base. One item they subtract out is "income included in GDP but not in the tax base," which in the appendix they note is imputed rent from owner-occupied homes. However, they copied the number from the wrong table in the *Economic Report of the President*, and as a result measure it in

1987 dollars rather than 1993 dollars. A second error is that, when they subtract out "wages, salaries, and pensions," they actually only subtract out wages and salaries—they forget to count pension contributions, even though they are deductible from the flat tax base. Finally, all of their tax base data is for calendar year 1993, but the revenues they say they need to replace are from fiscal year 1993. Since the federal fiscal year starts three months before the calendar year, this underestimates the amount of revenue they need to raise. All of these factors would cause them to underestimate the revenue-neutral tax rate. On the other hand, they correctly note that they probably overestimated the aggregate revenue cost of their family allowances.

19. U.S. Department of Treasury, Office of Tax Analysis (1996).

20. U.S. Department of Treasury, Office of Tax Analysis (1995a).

21. Sullivan (1996a, p. 490). Gale (1996, p. 721) comes up with a similar estimate.

22. Due and Mikesell (1994) report that in 1991–1993 the administrative cost as a percentage of revenue, for a sample of eight states, ranged from 0.41 to 1.0. Over a much larger sample of states in 1979–1981, the average ratio was 0.73 percent. A study by Peat Marwick, Mitchell and Company (1982) studied seven states and concluded that private compliance costs ranged from 2.0 to 3.75 percent of revenue. A more recent survey in *Tax Administrator News* (1993) reported an overall average compliance cost of 3.18 percent. This puts the range of enforcement and private compliance costs at 2.4 to 4.8 percent of revenue raised.

23. Tait (1988, p. 18).

24. Tait (1988, p. 18) notes that Iceland, Norway, South Africa, Sweden, and Zimbabwe all at one time had retail sales taxes with rates over 10 percent; Sweden and Norway switched to VATs many years ago; and Iceland switched to a VAT in 1990 (OECD 1995a, p. 116).

25. Tanzi (1995, pp. 50–51).

26. U.S. Department of Treasury (1984, Vol. 3, p. 124). The figure was $700 billion in 1984 dollars.

27. U.S. General Accounting Office (1993). The GAO figure in 1993 dollars was $1.8 billion.

28. CBO (1992, p. 72). Amounts are adjusted by the authors to 1996 income levels. Cnossen (1994) provides an excellent summary of the cost estimates done by CBO and others.

29. Authors' calculations based on OECD (1995a). Figures are for 1993.

30. The corporation income tax was the lowest of the three at 2.7 percent of revenue, comprised of 0.5 percent administration and 2.2 percent compliance costs. See Godwin (1995, p. 75).

31. The income tax cost was 1 percent for administrative cost, 1.7 percent for taxpayer cost. For VAT, it was .6 percent for administrative cost, and 2.5 percent for taxpayer cost. See Malmer (1995, p. 258).

32. Tait (1988, p. 304).

33. It may be possible to construct a system where the full VAT, including the labor cost component, is charged on each transaction, but the wages and salaries of each worker still appear on workers' paychecks net-of-tax. This would require firms to file for credits not only for tax paid to other firms, but also for the tax value of the exemption amounts for its workers. Such a system would retain many of the enforcement and simplification benefits of a credit-invoice VAT.

34. McLure (1993, pp. 349–350) discusses how a subtraction-method VAT can be made to achieve the same result as a credit-method VAT for exemptions of small business at both the retail and pretail stages.

35. Feld (1995) discusses some examples of "game-playing" that could occur under a flat tax.

36. U.S. Department of Treasury (1984, Vol. 1, p. 203).

37. See Ginsburg (1995, p. 21). Another lawyer, Clifton Fleming, Jr., concluded that the USA Tax would be simpler than the current system, but nevertheless "significantly intricate." See Fleming (1995).

38. Assuming the burden falls on individuals or families according to their consumption would make the flat tax look more regressive in the Treasury analysis, if ability-to-pay continued to be measured by income and people continued to be ranked by income.

39. The Treasury uses a broad definition of income that approximates the economic income concept described in Chapter 2. See Chapter 3, note 38 for details of the Treasury income definition.

40. Note that the Treasury does not include the burden of estate and gift taxes in its estimates for the current system or alternative (3), but does include the cost of replacing them in alternatives (1) and (2). This does not have an important impact on the results—it mainly just makes average tax rates on high-income people look slightly lower under the current system and alternative (3).

41. This is the claim made in the Kemp Commission report on tax reform.

42. U.S. Department of Treasury, Office of Tax Analysis (1996).

43. Hall and Rabushka (1995, p. 89).

44. Auerbach (1996a).

45. The doubling of the saving rate is only temporary. After jumping up initially, it declines very gradually over time, so that the rate in the distant future is generally only a bit higher than it is now. This saving rate can sustain the larger capital stock because incomes are higher.

46. Kotlikoff (1995) uses a similar model to simulate the replacement of a proportional income tax with a retail sales tax, and estimates that such a change would increase output per capita by about 6 percent after ten years, and by a total of 8 percent ultimately. His model implies that the savings rate nearly quadruples, which seems implausible given historical experience. He notes that switching from a more progressive income tax would yield an increase in output per capita topping off at 18 percent several decades into the future, although he doesn't specify what kind of increase in the saving rate that implies.

47. Engen and Gale (1996).

48. Gravelle (1991). Auerbach and Kotlikoff (1987) find a consumption tax would make future generations better off by 2.32 percent, but most of this gain is from intergenerational redistribution rather than improvements in efficiency. Gravelle (1994a) provides a survey of these types of models and their results.

49. A model developed by Fullerton and Rogers (1996), which incorporates people of different income levels within each generation, suggests that moving to a stylized version of a flat tax could make people at all income levels better off in future generations, although some people in current generations are made worse off. Their model, however, assumes a very large responsiveness of saving and labor supply to incentives, so it probably overstates the economic benefits of fundamental tax reform. For example, switching to a VAT is predicted to immediately increase the level of saving to four-and-a-half times its former level, which seems to be implausible.

Chapter 8

1. Poll of members of the National Tax Association, in Slemrod (1995b, p. 134)

2. Associated Press (1996).

3. Offsetting this favorable treatment is the failure to limit the tax to real, inflation-adjusted, capital gains. We address this issue in the next section.

4. See U.S. Department of Treasury (1992). Gravelle (1994a, pp. 92–93) discusses this proposal in more detail.

5. Even representatives of corporations have been lukewarm, perhaps also distinguishing between the corporation's income and the shareholders' stake in that income (and preferring the former), and perhaps fearing increased pressure from shareholders for dividend payments once the apparent tax penalty attached to such payouts is eliminated.

6. Other examples of indexing in the current system include the thresholds for phasing in and phasing out the EITC, and the thresholds for itemized deduction and personal exemption phase-outs.

7. At the same time, the lender can deduct all of the nominal interest, even though the real, inflation-adjusted, payment is lower; thus, the market interest rate is probably higher than under an indexed tax system.

8. See Halperin and Steuerle (1988) for an insightful discussion of the issues concerning indexing of capital income taxation for inflation.

9. Another reason for its demise was the exception made for home mortgage interest, which would have continued to be fully deductible. This provision would have exacerbated the tax bias toward owner-occupied housing, and opened up tax arbitrage opportunities tied to home equity loans.

10. IRS *Statistics of Income Bulletin* (Spring 1995, pp. 21–22).

11. For this example, we ignore inflation.

12. For example, if you bought a share of Pfizer stock at $100, you would owe no tax until you sold it. If you sold it five years later at $300, $200 of capital gains would be taxable in the year of sale, no matter if the $200 increase all occurred in the first year that you held the stock.

13. Carryover basis was passed as part of the 1978 tax bill, to take effect one year hence. It was, though, repealed in the year before it was to take effect.

14. Clark and Paris (1986) estimated that corporate stock sales accounted for only 28 percent of realized capital gains in 1981.

15. Summers (1989). See also Bernheim (1996) for a defense of savings incentive plans based on the assumption of less-than-fully-rational taxpayers and the importance of institutionalized savings schemes.

16. Hendershott (1990, p. 87) makes this point.

17. Herman (1995a).

18. Source: IRS *Statistics of Income Bulletin* (Fall 1995, p. 217).

19. The total number of filers for Michigan (federal returns, which should be close to the state number) is from the IRS *Statistics of Income Bulletin* (Spring 1995, p. 143). Hornbeck (1996) discusses the Engler plan.

20. According to the IRS *Statistics of Income: Individual Income Tax Returns 1991* (Table 3.4), 66.3 million returns faced a marginal rate of 15 percent, out of a total of 92.6 million with taxable income.

21. The increase is undoubtedly partly due to the proposal that eliminates the maximum 28 percent rate on capital gains, and thus subjects them to rates as high as 34 percent. We have no way to evaluate the incidence assumptions behind this distributional analysis; for example, we do not know how, if at all, the unspecified cuts in "corporate welfare" are assumed to be passed on to individuals. Nor can we confirm that the tax plan is revenue-neutral.

22. See note 15 of Chapter 7 for the basis of this estimate.

23. This is the essence of the Bush Administration Treasury Department's proposal floated in December 1992, which included a single-rate subtraction method VAT, the revenue from which financed a standard deduction increase to $33,800 for married tax-

payers filing jointly. The Treasury Department estimated that this plan would reduce the number of itemizers by 94 percent and take 52 percent of individual taxpayers with positive tax liabilities entirely off the tax rolls. Source: Brady (1992).

24. This begs the question of how to administer the refundable earned income tax credit.

Chapter 9

1. U.S. Department of Treasury, Office of Tax Analysis (1995).

2. U.S. Department of Treasury, Office of Tax Analysis (1995). Revenue numbers are calculated at 1995 income levels here.

References

Aaron, Henry J., and Harvey Galper. 1985. *Assessing Tax Reform*. Washington, D.C.: The Brookings Institution.

Alm, James. 1985. "The Welfare Cost of the Underground Economy." *Economic Inquiry* Vol. 23, No. 2 (April): 243–63.

Armey, Richard. 1995. "Testimony Before the Senate Finance Committee on the Flat Tax," Washington, D.C., April 5.

Armey, Richard, and Richard Shelby. 1995. *The Freedom and Fairness Restoration Act: A Comprehensive Plan to Shrink the Government and Grow the Economy*. Washington, D.C., July.

Arthur D. Little, Inc. 1988. *Development of Methodology for Estimating the Taxpayer Paperwork Burden*. Final Report to the Department of the Treasury, Internal Revenue Service, Washington, D.C., June.

Associated Press. 1996. "Poll Shows Few Want Total Tax Overhaul." *Ann Arbor News*. February 26: 3.

Auerbach, Alan J. 1996a. "Tax Reform, Capital Allocation, Efficiency and Growth." In Henry Aaron and William Gale, eds. *The Economic Effects of Fundamental Tax Reform*. Washington, D.C.: The Brookings Institution (forthcoming).

Auerbach, Alan J. 1996b. "Dynamic Revenue Estimation." *Journal of Economic Perspectives* Vol. 10, No. 1 (Winter): 141–57.

Auerbach, Alan J. 1979. "Wealth Maximization and the Cost of Capital." *Quarterly Journal of Economics* Vol. 93, No. 3 (August): 433–46.

Auerbach, Alan J., and Laurence J. Kotlikoff. 1987. *Dynamic Fiscal Policy*. Cambridge: Cambridge University Press.

Auerbach, Alan J., and Joel Slemrod. Forthcoming. "The Economic Effects of the Tax Reform Act of 1986." *Journal of Economic Literature*.

Auten, Gerald, and Robert Carroll. 1994. "Behavior of the Affluent and the 1986 Tax Reform Act: The Role of Demand-Side Characteristics." Paper presented at the National Tax Association Meetings, Charleston, SC, November.

Bakija, Jon M., and C. Eugene Steuerle. 1991. "Individual Income Taxation Since 1948." *National Tax Journal* Vol. 44, No. 4, Part 1 (December): 451–75.

Ballard, Charles L., John B. Shoven, and John Whalley. 1985. "The Total Welfare Cost of the United States Tax System: A General Equilibrium Approach." *National Tax Journal* Vol. 38, No. 2 (June): 125–40.

Bartlett, Bruce. 1995. "Will the Flat Tax KO Housing?" *The Wall Street Journal*. August 2.

Bastiat, Frédéric. 1964. *Selected Essays on Political Economy.* 1850. Reprint. Irvington-on-Hudson, NY: The Foundation for Economic Education.

Bernheim, Douglas. 1996. "Rethinking Saving Incentives." In Alan Auerbach, ed., *Fiscal Policy: Lessons from Economic Research.* Cambridge, MA: MIT Press (forthcoming).

Birnbaum, Jeffrey H., and Alan S. Murray. 1987. *Showdown at Gucci Gulch.* New York: Random House.

Blumenthal, Marsha, and Joel Slemrod. 1992. "The Compliance Cost of the U.S. Individual Income Tax System: A Second Look after Tax Reform." *National Tax Journal* Vol. 45, No. 2 (June): 185–202.

Bosworth, Barry, and Gary Burtless. 1992. "Effects of Tax Reform on Labor Supply, Investment, and Saving." *Journal of Economic Perspectives* Vol. 6, No. 1 (Winter): 3–25.

Bowman, Karlyn. 1995. "AEI Poll Watch: Taxes." Paper presented at the American Enterprise Institute Conference, The Flat Tax: An Alternative to the Current Income Tax? Washington, D.C., January 27.

Bradford, David F. 1995. "Consumption Tax Alternatives: Implementation and Transition Issues." Paper presented at the Hoover Institution Conference on Frontiers of Tax Reform, Washington D.C., May 11.

Bradford, David F. 1991. "Market Value versus Financial Accounting Measures of National Saving." In Douglas Bernheim and John B. Shoven, eds. *National Saving and Economic Performance.* Chicago: National Bureau of Economic Research and University of Chicago Press.

Bradford, David F. 1986. *Untangling the Income Tax.* Cambridge, MA: Harvard University Press.

Bradford, David F. 1981. "The Incidence and Allocation Effects of a Tax on Corporate Distributions." *Journal of Public Economics* Vol. 15, No. 1 (February): 1–22.

Brady, Nicholas. 1992. Speech given at Columbia University Graduate School of Business, New York, December 10.

Brownlee, W. Elliot. 1989. "Taxation for a Strong and Virtuous Republic: A Bicentennial Retrospective," *Tax Notes* Vol. 45, No. 13 (December 25): 1613–21.

Burman, Leonard E., Kimberly A. Clausing, and John F. O'Hare. 1994. "Tax Reform and Realizations of Capital Gains in 1986." *National Tax Journal* Vol. 47, No. 1 (March): 1–18.

Burman, Leonard E., and William C. Randolph. 1994. "Measuring Permanent Responses to Capital Gains Tax Changes in Panel Data." *American Economic Review* Vol. 84, No. 4 (September): 794–809.

Burnham, David. 1989. *A Law Unto Itself: Power, Politics, and the IRS.* New York: Random House.

CBO (Congressional Budget Office). 1995. *The Economic and Budget Outlook: An Update.* (August). Washington, D.C.: GPO.

CBO. 1994. "An Economic Analysis of the Revenue Provisions of OBRA-93." Working paper. (January). Washington, D.C.: CBO.

CBO. 1992. *Effects of Adopting a Value-Added Tax.* (February) Washington, D.C.: CBO.

Christian, Charles W. 1994. "Voluntary Compliance with the Individual Income

Tax: Results from the 1988 TCMP Study." *IRS Research Bulletin, 1993/1994*. Publication 1500 (August). Washington, D.C.: Internal Revenue Service.

Christian, Ernest S., and George J. Schutzer. 1995. "USA Tax System: Description and Explanation of the Unlimited Savings Allowance Income Tax System." *Tax Notes* Vol. 66, No. 11 (March 10): 1483–1575.

Clark, Robert, and David Paris. 1986. "Sales of Capital Assets, 1981 and 1982." *IRS Statistics of Income Bulletin* (Winter 1985/86): 65–89.

Clinton, William. 1992. "Acceptance Address: Democratic Nominee for President." Delivered at the Democratic National Convention, New York, July 16, 1992. *Vital Speeches of the Day* Vol. 58, No. 21 (August 15).

Cnossen, Sijbren. 1994. "Administrative and Compliance Costs of the VAT: A Review of the Evidence." Tax Analysts Special Report No. 94, *Tax Notes Today* (June 23): 121–35.

Davies, A. J. 1995. "Only One Name for It: Bureaucratic Theft." *The Wall Street Journal*. April 5: A11.

Davies, James, and John Whalley. 1991. "Taxes and Capital Formation: How Important is Human Capital?" In Douglas Bernheim and John Shoven, eds. *National Saving and Economic Performance.* Chicago: National Bureau of Economic Research and University of Chicago Press.

Doernberg, Richard L. 1988. "The Market for Tax Reform: Public Pain for Private Gain." *Tax Notes* 33 (November 28): 965–69.

Domenici, Pete. 1995. "Testimony Before the Committee on Ways and Means on S. 722—The USA Tax," Washington, D.C., June 7.

Domenici, Pete. 1994. "The Unamerican Spirit of the Federal Income Tax." *Harvard Journal on Legislation* Vol. 31, No. 2 (Summer): 273–320.

Due, John F., and John L. Mikesell. 1994. *Sales Taxation: State and Local Structure and Administration.* Washington, D.C.: The Urban Institute Press.

Economic Report of the President. (Various years). Washington, D.C.: GPO.

Eissa, Nada. 1995a. "Tax Reforms and Labor Supply." Working paper. University of California at Berkeley, October.

Eissa, Nada. 1995b. "Taxation and Labor Supply of Married Women: The Tax Reform Act of 1986 as a Natural Experiment." NBER Working Paper 5023. Cambridge, MA: National Bureau of Economic Research.

Engen, Eric, and William Gale. 1996. "The Effects of Fundamental Tax Reform on Saving." In Henry Aaron and William Gale, eds. *The Economic Effects of Fundamental Tax Reform.* Washington, D.C.: The Brookings Institution (forthcoming).

Fastis, Stefan. 1992. "Big Earners Cash in Early to Beat Tax Bite" Associated Press wire story in *The San Francisco Chronicle.* December 29: C1.

Feenberg, Daniel R., and James M. Poterba. 1993. "Income Inequality and the Incomes of Very High-Income Taxpayers: Evidence from Tax Returns." *Tax Policy and the Economy* No. 7. Cambridge, MA: National Bureau of Economic Research and MIT Press.

Feenberg, Daniel R., and Harvey S. Rosen. 1995. "Recent Developments in the Marriage Tax." *National Tax Journal* Vol. 48, No. 1 (March): 91–101.

Feld, Alan. 1995. "Living with the Flat Tax." *National Tax Journal* Vol. 48, No. 4 (December): 603–18.

Feldstein, Martin. 1995a. "The Effect of Marginal Tax Rates on Taxable Income: A Panel Study of the 1986 Tax Reform Act." *Journal of Political Economy* Vol. 103, No. 3 (June): 551–72.

Feldstein, Martin. 1995b. "The Effect of a Consumption Tax on the Rate of Interest." NBER Working Paper No. 5397. Cambridge, MA: National Bureau of Economic Research.

Feldstein, Martin. 1994. "Tax Policy and International Capital Flows." NBER Working Paper No. 4851. Cambridge, MA: National Bureau of Economic Research.

Feldstein, Martin. 1988. "Imputing Corporate Tax Liabilities to Individual Taxpayers." *National Tax Journal* Vol. 41, No. 1 (March): 37–59.

Feldstein, Martin, and Daniel Feenberg. 1995. "The Effect of Increased Tax Rates on Taxable Income and Economic Efficiency: A Preliminary Analysis of the 1993 Tax Rate Increases." NBER Working Paper No. 5370. Cambridge, MA: National Bureau of Economic Research.

Fineman, Howard. 1995. "The Trouble With Taxes." *Newsweek* (April 17): 36–38.

Fisher, Glenn W. 1996. *The Worst Tax? A History of the Property Tax in America.* Lawrence: The University Press of Kansas.

Fisher, Ronald C., and Judy A. Temple. 1995. "Comparing Economists' Views and Popular Opinions about Tax Policy: Implications for Education." Presented at the National Tax Association Annual Meetings, San Diego, CA, October 9.

Fleming, J. Clifton, Jr. 1995. "Scoping Out the Uncertain Simplification (Complication?) Effects of VATs, BATs and Consumed Income Taxes." *Florida Tax Review* Vol. 2, No. 7: 390–443.

Forman, Jonathan Barry. 1996. "Poverty Levels and Federal Tax Thresholds: 1996." *Tax Notes* Vol. 71, No. 7 (May 13): 943–46.

Frank, Robert H., and Philip J. Cook. 1995. *The Winner-Take-All Society.* New York: The Free Press.

Fullerton, Don, and Diane Lim Rogers. 1996. "Lifetime Effects of Fundamental Tax Reform." In Henry Aaron and William Gale, eds. *The Economic Effects of Fundamental Tax Reform.* Washington, D.C.: The Brookings Institution (forthcoming).

Fullerton, Don, and Diane Lim Rogers. 1993. *Who Bears the Lifetime Tax Burden?* Washington, D.C.: The Brookings Institution.

Gale, William. 1996. "The Kemp Commission and the Future of Tax Reform." *Tax Notes* Vol. 70 (February 5): 717–29.

Gale, William. 1995. "Building a Better Tax System: Can a Consumption Tax Deliver the Goods?" *Brookings Review* Vol. 13 (Fall): 18–23.

Gallup, George, Jr., and Frank Newport. 1990. "Americans Widely Disagree on What Constitutes 'Rich'." *The Gallup Poll Monthly* (July): 28–36.

Gephardt, Richard. 1995. "A Democratic Plan for America's Economy: Toward a Fairer, Simpler Tax Code." Remarks Before the Center for National Policy, Washington, D.C., July 6.

Gibbons, Sam M. 1995. "A Revenue System for America's Future." Testimony Before the Committee on Ways and Means, Washington, D.C., June 7.

Ginsburg, Martin. 1995. "Life Under a Personal Consumption Tax: Some Thoughts on Working, Saving, and Consuming in Nunn-Domenici's Tax World." *National Tax Journal* Vol. 48, No. 4 (December): 585–602.

Godwin, Michael. 1995. "The Compliance Costs of the United Kingdom Tax System." In Cedric Sandford, ed. *Tax Compliance Costs Measurement and Policy.* Bath, UK: Fiscal Publications.

Goode, Richard. 1976. *The Individual Income Tax.* Washington, D.C.: The Brookings Institution.

Goodgame, Dan. 1995. "The Point of No Return." *Time* (April 17): 27–32.

Gordon, Roger H., and Joel Slemrod. 1988. "Do We Collect Any Revenue from Taxing Capital Income?" In Lawrence Summers, ed. *Tax Policy and the Economy,* No. 2. Cambridge, MA: National Bureau of Economic Research.

Gottschalk, Peter, and Robert Moffitt. 1994. "The Growth of Earnings Instability in the U.S. Labor Market." *Brookings Papers on Economic Activity* No. 2: 217–72.

Gravelle, Jane. 1995. "The Flat Tax and Other Proposals: Who Will Bear the Tax Burden?" *Tax Notes* Vol. 69 (December 18): 1517–27.

Gravelle, Jane. 1994a. *The Economic Effects of Taxing Capital Income.* Cambridge, MA: MIT Press.

Gravelle, Jane. 1994b. "Corporate Tax Incidence in an Open Economy." In *Proceedings of the 86th Annual Conference on Taxation.* Columbus: National Tax Association—Tax Institute of America.

Gravelle, Jane. 1991. "Income, Consumption and Wage Taxation in a Life Cycle Model: Separating Efficiency from Redistribution." *American Economic Review* Vol. 81, No. 4 (September): 985–95.

Gray, Robert T. 1995. "Blockbuster Tax Reform." *Nation's Business* Vol. 83 (April): 18–24.

Hall, Arthur P. 1995. "Compliance Costs of Alternative Tax Systems: Ways and Means Testimony." Tax Foundation *Special Brief* (June).

Hall, Robert E. 1988. "Intertemporal Substitution in Consumption." *Journal of Political Economy* Vol. 96, No. 2 (April): 339–57.

Hall, Robert E., and Alvin Rabushka. 1995. *The Flat Tax* 2d ed. Stanford, CA: The Hoover Institution Press.

Hall, Robert E., and Alvin Rabushka. 1983. *Low Tax, Simple Tax, Flat Tax.* New York: McGraw-Hill.

Halperin, Daniel, and Eugene Steuerle. 1988. "Indexing the Tax System for Inflation." In Henry J. Aaron, Harvey Galper, and Joseph A. Pechman, eds. *Uneasy Compromise: Problems of a Hybrid Income-Consumption Tax.* Washington, D.C.: The Brookings Institution.

Heckman, James. 1993. "What Has Been Learned About Labor Supply in the United States in the Past Twenty Years?" *American Economic Review* Vol. 83, No. 2 (May): 116–21.

Hendershott, Patric. 1990. "Comment on 'The Impact of the 1986 Tax Reform on Personal Saving'." In Joel Slemrod, ed. *Do Taxes Matter?: The Impact of the Tax Reform Act of 1986.* Cambridge, MA: MIT Press.

Herman, Tom. 1995a. "The Treasury Vows to Simplify the Rules on the Alternative Minimum Tax." *The Wall Street Journal.* November 29: A1.

Herman, Tom. 1995b. "Many Crooks Had a Rough Year in 1994." *The Wall Street Journal.* July 26: A1.

Herman, Tom. 1995c. "Tax Cheating Doesn't Sound So Bad to Many Men." *The Wall Street Journal.* June 14: A1.

Herman, Tom. 1995d. "Tax Complexity Weighs Increasingly Heavily on the Economy." *The Wall Street Journal.* June 7: A1.

Herman, Tom. 1994. "Persuading Tax Dodgers to Start Filing Returns Isn't Easy, the IRS Finds." *The Wall Street Journal.* February 23: A1.

Hershey, Robert D. 1993. "IRS Raises Its Estimate of Tax Cheating." *New York Times.* December 29: D6.

Hessing, Dick J., Hank Elffers, Henry S. J. Robben, and Paul Webley. 1992. "Does Deterrence Deter? Measuring the Effect of Deterrence on Tax Compliance in Field Studies and Experimental Studies." In Joel Slemrod, ed., *Why People Pay Taxes: Tax Compliance and Enforcement.* Ann Arbor: University of Michigan Press.

Higgins, Heather Richardson. 1995. "Tax Fairness: Treat All Dollars Equally." *The Wall Street Journal.* April 5: A11.

Hite, Peggy A., and Michael L. Roberts. 1991. "An Experimental Investigation of Taxpayer Judgments on Rate Structure in the Individual Income Tax System." *Journal of the American Taxation Association* Vol. 13: 47–63.

Hornbeck, Mark. 1996. "Engler Plan Won't Cut Tax for Poor." *The Detroit News.* January 22.

Internal Revenue Service. 1993. *Annual Report 1992.* Washington, D.C.: GPO.

Internal Revenue Service. IRS Research Division. 1988. *Income Tax Compliance Research: Gross Tax Gap Estimates and Projections for 1973–1992.* Publication 7285 (March). Washington, D.C.: GPO.

Internal Revenue Service. Statistics of Income Division. Various years. *Corporation Income Tax Returns.* Washington, D.C.: GPO.

Internal Revenue Service. Statistics of Income Division. Various years. *Individual Income Tax Returns.* Washington, D.C.: GPO.

Internal Revenue Service. Statistics of Income Division. Various years. *Statistics of Income Bulletin.* Washington, D.C.: GPO.

Johnston, David Cay. 1996. "British to Adopt American-Style Tax Filing." *New York Times.* February 15: D6.

Joint Committee on Taxation. 1987. *General Explanation of the Tax Reform Act of 1986.* Washington, D.C.: GPO.

Kaplow, Louis. 1996. "How Tax Complexity and Enforcement Affect the Equity and Efficiency of the Income Tax." *National Tax Journal* Vol. 49, No. 1 (March): 135–50.

Kaplow, Louis. 1994. Tax Treatment of Families." Working paper. (October). Cambridge, MA: Harvard Law School.

Kasten, Richard, Frank Sammartino, and Eric Toder. 1994. "Trends in Federal Tax Progressivity, 1980–93." In Joel Slemrod, ed. *Tax Progressivity and Income Inequality.* Cambridge: Cambridge University Press.

Kennickell, Arthur B., and R. Louise Woodburn. 1992. "Estimation of Household Net Worth Using Model-Based and Design-Based Weights: Evidence from the 1989 Survey of Consumer Finances." Working paper. Washington, D.C.: Board of Governors of the Federal Reserve System.

Killingsworth, Mark. 1983. *Labor Supply.* Cambridge: Cambridge University Press.

Kirchheimer, Barbara. 1995. "Gephardt Introduces 10 Percent Tax for Most, Four Brackets for Others." *Tax Notes* Vol. 68 (July 10): 135–36.

Kotlikoff, Laurence J. 1995. "Saving and Consumption Taxation: The Federal Retail Sales Tax Example." Paper presented at the Hoover Institution Conference on Frontiers of Tax Reform, Washington D.C., May 11.

Krugman, Paul. 1994. *Peddling Prosperity.* New York: W. W. Norton.

Kuttner, Robert. 1995. "Instead, Close Loopholes." *New York Times.* February 8.

Lambert, Wade. 1989. "Leona Helmsley Fined $7.2 Million, Sentenced to Prison." *The Wall Street Journal.* December 13: A3.

Lewin, Tamar. 1991. "Data Show Wide Tax Cheating on Child Care, IRS Says." *New York Times.* Section 1. (January 6): 14.

Lindbeck, Assar. 1993. *The Welfare State: Selected Essays of Assar Lindbeck* Vol. II. Aldershot, UK: Edward Elgar Publishing.

Lindsey, Lawrence B. 1990. *The Growth Experiment: How the New Tax Policy is Transforming the U.S. Economy.* New York: Basic Books.

Lugar, Dick. 1995a. "Republican Candidate for President." *Vital Speeches of the Day* Vol. 61, No. 15 (May 15): 454–56.

Lugar, Dick. 1995b, "The Lugar Plan to End the Income Tax." Statement delivered to the Cato Institute in Washington, D.C., April 5.

McHardy, A. K. 1992. *Clerical Poll-Taxes of the Diocese of Lincoln, 1377–1381.* Woodbridge, Suffolk, UK: The Boydell Press.

McIntyre, Robert S. 1995a. "Statement Concerning Proposals for a Flat-Rate Consumption Tax before the Joint Economic Committee," Washington, D.C., May 17.

McIntyre, Robert S. 1995b. "Taxing the Poor." *The New Republic* (January 30): 15–16.

McKee, T. C., and M. D. Gerbing. 1989. "Taxpayer Perceptions of Fairness: The TRA of 1986." Paper presented at the Internal Revenue Service Research Conference, Washington, D.C.

McKissack, May. 1959. *The Fourteenth Century, 1307–1399. The Oxford History of England,* Vol. 5. Oxford: Clarendon Press.

McLure, Charles E., Jr. 1993. "Economic, Administrative, and Political Factors in Choosing a General Consumption Tax." *National Tax Journal* Vol. 46, No. 3 (September): 345–58.

Malmer, Hakan. 1995. "The Swedish Tax Reform in 1990–1991 and Tax Compliance Costs in Sweden." In Cedric Sandford, ed. *Tax Compliance Costs: Measurement and Policy.* Bath, UK: Fiscal Publications.

Mariger, Randall P. 1995. "Labor Supply and the Tax Reform Act of 1986: Evidence from Panel Data." Working paper. Washington D.C.: Board of Governors of Federal Reserve System.

Marvin, Rob. 1995. "IRS Examinations Chief Says Audits Will Be Up by 45 Percent Over Last Year." *Bureau of National Affairs Tax Reporter* (August 16): G-2.

Messere, Ken C. 1993. *Tax Policy in OECD Countries: Choices and Conflicts.* Amsterdam: IBFD Publications.

Mitchell, Daniel J. 1996. "Supply Side 'Alchemy' at Work." *The Wall Street Journal.* January 17.

Moore, Schuyler M. 1987. "A Proposal to Reduce the Complexity of Tax Regulations." *Tax Notes* Vol. 37 (December 14): 1167.

Murray, Alan. 1996. "GOP Adherents Study Merits of a Flat Tax." *The Wall Street Journal*. January 29: A1.

Nasar, Sylvia. 1992. "One Study's Riches, Another Study's Rags." *New York Times*. June 17: D1.

National Commission on Economic Growth and Tax Reform. 1996. *Unleashing America's Potential: A Pro-Growth, Pro-Family Tax System for the 21st Century*. Washington, D.C.: Author.

Neubig, Thomas, and David Joulfaian. 1988. *The Tax Expenditure Budget Before and After the Tax Reform Act of 1986*. U.S. Department of Treasury, Office of Tax Analysis Paper 60. Washington, D.C.: GPO.

Newport, Frank. 1990. "Tax Reform Fails to Achieve Its Goals." *The Gallup Poll Monthly* (March): 6–10.

Newport, Frank, and Lydia Saad. 1993. "Americans Still Feel They Pay Too Much on April 15th." *The Gallup Poll Monthly* (April): 18–21.

OECD (Organisation for Economic Co-operation and Development). 1995a. *Revenue Statistics of OECD Member Countries, 1965–1994*. Paris: OECD.

OECD. 1995b. *National Accounts. Vol. 1: Main Aggregates*. Paris: OECD.

OMB (Office of Management and Budget). 1995a. *The Budget of the United States Government, Fiscal Year 1996*. Washington, D.C.: GPO.

OMB. 1995b. *The Budget of the United States Government, Fiscal Year 1996: Analytical Perspectives*. Washington, D.C.: GPO.

O'Neil, Cherie J., and Karen B. Lanese. 1993. "T.I.N. Requirements and the Child Care Credit: Impact on Taxpayer Behavior." Working paper. Tampa: University of South Florida.

Parcell, Ann D. 1996. "Income Shifting in Response to Higher Tax Rates: The Effects of OBRA 93." Paper presented at the Allied Social Science Associations Meetings, San Francisco, January 5–7.

Passell, Peter. 1995. "Do Tax Cuts Raise Revenue? The Supply-Side War Continues." *New York Times*. November 16: C2.

Payne, James L. 1993. *Costly Returns: The Burdens of the U.S. Tax System*. San Francisco: Institute for Contemporary Studies.

Pearlman, Ronald. 1996. "Transition Issues in Moving to a Consumption Tax: A Tax Lawyer's Perspective." In Henry Aaron and William Gale, eds. *The Economic Effects of Fundamental Tax Reform*. Washington, D.C.: The Brookings Institution (forthcoming).

Peat Marwick, Mitchell, and Company. 1982. *Report to the American Retail Federation on Costs to Retailers of Sales Use Tax Compliance*. New York: Author.

Pechman, Joseph A. 1987. *Federal Tax Policy*. 5th ed. Washington, D.C.: The Brookings Institution.

Peers, Alexandra, and Jeffrey A. Tannebaum. 1992 "Insiders Race to Exercise Stock Options." *The Wall Street Journal*. December 16: C1.

Poterba, James M. 1990. "Taxation and Housing Markets: Preliminary Evidence on the Effects of Recent Tax Reforms." In Joel Slemrod, ed. *Do Taxes Matter?: The Impact of the Tax Reform Act of 1986*. Cambridge, MA: MIT Press.

Poterba, James M. 1989. "Capital Gains Tax Policy toward Entrepreneurship." *National Tax Journal*. Vol. 47, No. 3 (June): 375–89.

Poterba, James M., Steven F. Venti, and David A. Wise. 1995. "The Effects of Special Saving Programs on Saving and Wealth." NBER Working Paper No. 5287. Cambridge, MA: National Bureau of Economic Research.

Powell, Edgar. 1894. "An Account of the Proceedings in Suffolk During the Peasants' Rising in 1381." *Transactions of the Royal Historical Society* Vol. 8., 203–49. London: Longmans, Green, and Co.

Quigley, John M., and Eugene Smolensky. 1990. "Improving Efficiency in the Tax Treatment of Training and Educational Expenditures." In Laurie J. Bassi and David L. Crawford, eds. *Research in Labor Economics: Labor Economics and Public Policy,* Vol. 11. Greenwich, CT: JAI Press.

Randolph, William C. 1995. "Dynamic Income, Progressive Taxes, and the Timing of Charitable Contributions." *Journal of Political Economy* Vol. 103 (August): 709–38.

Richman, Louis S. 1995. "The Flat Tax: It's Hot, It's Now, It Could Change the Way You Live." *Fortune* Vol. 131 (June 12): 36–51.

Ring, Raymond J., Jr. 1989. "The Proportion of Consumers' and Producers' Goods in the General Sales Tax." *National Tax Journal* Vol. 42, No. 2 (June): 167–69.

Roberts, Michael L., Peggy A. Hite, and Cassie F. Bradley. 1994. "Understanding Attitudes Toward Progressive Taxation." *Public Opinion Quarterly* Vol. 58 (Summer): 165–90.

Rogers, David. 1995. "House GOP Seeks Deep Cuts in Labor, Education, Threatening Clinton's Gains." *The Wall Street Journal.* June 12: A3.

Rosen, Harvey S. 1995. *Public Finance.* 4th ed. Homewood, IL: Richard D. Irwin, Inc.

Rosen, Sherwin. 1981. "The Economics of Superstars." *American Economic Review* Vol. 71, No. 5 (December): 845–58.

Roth, Jeffrey A., John T. Scholz, and Ann Dryden Witte. 1989. *Taxpayer Compliance, Volume 1: An Agenda for Research.* Philadelphia: University of Pennsylvania Press.

Sabelhaus, John. 1993. "What is the Distributional Burden of Taxing Consumption?" *National Tax Journal* Vol. 46, No. 3 (September): 331–43.

Safire, William. 1995. "The 25% Solution" *New York Times.* April 20: A19.

Samuels, Leslie. 1995. "Testimony Before the House Ways and Means Committee on Tax Reform," Washington, D.C., June 7.

Sandford, Cedric, ed. 1995. *Tax Compliance Costs: Measurement and Policy.* Bath, UK: Fiscal Publications.

Sarkar, Shounak, and George R. Zodrow. 1993. "Transitional Issues in Moving to a Direct Consumption Tax." *National Tax Journal* Vol. 46, No. 3 (September): 359–76.

Sawhill, Isabel V., and Mark Condon. 1992. "Is U.S. Income Inequality Really Growing? Sorting Out the Fairness Question." *Policy Bites.* (June). Washington D.C.: The Urban Institute.

Seib, Gerald F. 1996. "Clinton's Coming Move Beyond Budget Politics." *The Wall Street Journal.* January 24: A16.

Shafer, Ronald G. 1995a. "Tax Overhaul? Yes. Flat Tax? Not So Fast." *The Wall Street Journal.* April 28: A1 .

Shafer, Ronald G. 1995b. "Falling Flat?" *The Wall Street Journal.* September 22: A1.

Sheffrin, Steven M. 1994. "Perceptions of Fairness in the Crucible of Tax Policy." In Joel Slemrod, ed. *Tax Progressivity and Income Inequality.* Cambridge: Cambridge University Press.

Sheffrin, Steven M., and Robert K. Triest. 1992. "Can Brute Deterrence Backfire? Perceptions and Attitudes in Taxpayer Compliance." In Joel Slemrod, ed. *Why People Pay Taxes: Tax Compliance and Enforcement*. Ann Arbor: University of Michigan Press.

Shoven, John. 1991. "Using the Corporate Cash Flow Tax to Integrate Corporate and Personal Taxes." In *Proceedings of the 84th Annual Conference on Taxation*, 19–27. Columbus: National Tax Association—Tax Institute of America.

Simons, Henry. 1938. *Personal Income Taxation*. Chicago: University of Chicago Press.

Skinner, Jonathan, and Daniel Feenberg. 1990. "The Impact of the 1986 Tax Reform on Personal Saving." In Joel Slemrod, ed. *Do Taxes Matter?: The Impact of the Tax Reform Act of 1986*. Cambridge, MA: MIT Press.

Slemrod, Joel. 1996a. "Which is the Simplest Tax System of Them All?" In Henry Aaron and William Gale, eds. *The Economic Effects of Fundamental Tax Reform*. Washington, D.C.: The Brookings Institution (forthcoming).

Slemrod, Joel. 1996b. "High-Income Families and the Tax Changes of the 1980s: The Anatomy of Behavioral Response." In Martin Feldstein and James Poterba, eds. *Empirical Foundations of Household Taxation*. Chicago: National Bureau of Economic Research and Chicago Press (forthcoming).

Slemrod, Joel. 1995a. "What Do Cross-Country Studies Teach About Government Involvement, Prosperity, and Economic Growth?" *Brookings Papers on Economic Activity* No. 2: 373–431.

Slemrod, Joel. 1995b. "Professional Opinions About Tax Policy: 1994 and 1934." *National Tax Journal* Vol. 48, No. 1 (March): 121–47.

Slemrod, Joel. 1994. "The Simplification Potential of Alternatives to the Income Tax." Testimony before the Bipartisan Commission on Entitlement and Tax Reform, Washington, D.C., October 6.

Slemrod, Joel. 1992. "What Makes a Nation Prosperous, What Makes it Competitive, and Which Goal Should We Strive For?" *Australian Tax Forum* Vol. 9, No. 4: 373–86.

Slemrod, Joel, and Marsha Blumenthal. 1996. "The Income Tax Compliance Cost of Big Business." *Public Finance Quarterly* (forthcoming).

Slemrod, Joel, and Nikki Sorum. 1984. "The Compliance Cost of the U.S. Individual Income Tax System." *National Tax Journal* Vol. 37, No. 4 (December): 461–74.

Smith, Peter. 1991. "Lessons from the British Poll Tax Disaster." *National Tax Journal* Vol. 44, No. 4, Part 2 (December): 421–36.

Specter, Arlen. 1995. "Testimony before the House Ways and Means Committee Flat Tax Hearing," Washington, D.C., June 8.

Steuerle, C. Eugene. 1992. *The Tax Decade: How Taxes Came to Dominate the Public Agenda*. Washington, D.C.: The Urban Institute Press.

Steuerle, C. Eugene. 1986. *Who Should Pay for Collecting Taxes? Financing the IRS*. Washington, D.C.: American Enterprise Institute.

Steuerle, C. Eugene, and Jon M. Bakija. 1994. *Retooling Social Security for the 21st Century*. Washington, D.C.: The Urban Institute Press.

Stiglitz, Joseph. 1988. *Economics of the Public Sector*. New York: W. W. Norton.

Sullivan, Martin. 1996a. "What Rate for the Flat Tax?" *Tax Notes* Vol. 70 (January 29): 490.

Sullivan, Martin. 1996b. "Housing and the Flat Tax: Visible Pain, Subtle Benefits." *Tax Notes* Vol. 70 (January 22): 340–45.

Summers, Lawrence H. 1989. "How Best to Give Tax Incentives for Saving and Investment?" Testimony before Senate Finance Committee, Washington, D.C., September 29.

Summers, Robert, and Alan Heston. 1991. "The Penn World Table (Mark 5): An Expanded Set of International Comparisons, 1950–1988." *Quarterly Journal of Economics* Vol. 106, No. 2 (May): 327–68.

Szilagyi, John A. 1990. "Where Have All the Dependents Gone?" *Internal Revenue Service Trend Analyses and Related Statistics—1990 Update*. Publication 1500 (August). Washington, D.C.: Internal Revenue Service.

Tait, Alan A. 1988. *Value Added Tax: International Practice and Problems*. Washington, D.C.: International Monetary Fund.

Tanzi, Vito. 1995. *Taxation in an Integrating World*. Washington, D.C.: The Brookings Institution.

Tax Administrator News. 1993. "Vendor Collection of State Sales and Use Tax" Vol. 57 (August): 88.

Triest, Robert K. 1994. "The Efficiency Cost of Increased Progressivity." In Joel Slemrod, ed. *Tax Progressivity and Income Inequality*. Cambridge: Cambridge University Press.

Triest, Robert K. 1990. "The Effect of Income Taxation on Labor Supply in the United States." *The Journal of Human Resources* Vol. 25, No. 3 (Summer): 491–516.

Tritch, Teresa. 1995. "The $150 Billion Tax Cheats." *Money* Vol. 24 (April): 118–27.

Tritch, Teresa. 1993. "Keep an Eye on Your Tax Pro." *Money* Vol. 22 (March): 98–109.

Tritch, Teresa, and Deborah Lohse. 1992. "Tax Payers, Start Worrying!" *Money* Vol. 21 (March): 88–96.

U.S. Bureau of the Census. 1990. *Household Wealth and Asset Ownership: 1988*. Current Population Reports, Ser. P-60, No. 22. Washington, D.C.: GPO.

U.S. Bureau of the Census. 1975. *Historical Statistics of the United States, Colonial Times to 1970, Bicentennial Edition*. Washington, D.C.: GPO.

U.S. Bureau of Economic Analysis. Various years. *Survey of Current Business*. Washington, D.C.: GPO.

U.S. Bureau of Economic Analysis. 1992. *National Income and Product Accounts of the U.S., 1929–1988*. Washington, D.C.: GPO.

U.S. Department of Treasury. Office of Tax Analysis. 1996. "'New' Armey-Shelby Flat Tax Would Still Lose Money, Treasury Finds." *Tax Notes* Vol. (January 22): 451–61.

U.S. Department of Treasury. Office of Tax Analysis. 1995. "A Preliminary Analysis of a Flat Rate Consumption Tax," Washington, D.C., March 7.

U.S. Department of Treasury. 1992. *Report on Integration of the Individual and Corporate Tax Systems*. Washington, D.C.: GPO.

U.S. Department of Treasury. 1984. *Tax Reform for Fairness, Simplicity and Economic Growth*. Washington, D.C.: GPO.

U.S. Department of Treasury. 1977. *Blueprints for Basic Tax Reform*. Washington, D.C.: GPO.

U.S. General Accounting Office. 1993. *Value-Added Tax: Administrative Costs Vary with Complexity and Number of Businesses*. Study No. GAO/GGD-93-78. Washington, D.C.: GPO.

U.S. General Accounting Office. 1988. *Tax Administration: IRS' Tax Gap Studies.* (March). Washington, D.C.: GPO.

U.S. House of Representatives, Committee on Ways and Means. 1993. *Overview of Entitlement Programs: 1993 Green Book.* Washington, D.C.: GPO.

Vescey, George. 1994. "Players Weren't the Only Ones Holding Paper Bags." *New York Times.* December 11: S5.

Wessel, David. 1995a. "What Should Be Taxed Will Be the Key Issue." *The Wall Street Journal.* May 1: A1.

Wessel, David. 1995b. "Clinton Faces Pressure on Tax-Reform Issue." *The Wall Street Journal.* August 28: A1.

West Publishing Company. 1995a. *Internal Revenue Code 1995.* St. Paul, MN: Author.

West Publishing Company. 1995b. *Federal Tax Regulations 1995.* St. Paul, MN: Author.

Whitney, Craig R. 1990. "London's Tax Riot is Called the Work of a Violent Minority." *New York Times.* April 2.

Willette, Anne. 1996. "IRS Adopts Taxpayers' Bill of Rights." *USA Today.* January 5–7: 1A.

Witte, John F. 1985. *The Politics and Development of the Federal Income Tax.* Madison, WI: The University of Wisconsin Press.

Yitzhaki, Shlomo. 1974. "A Note on 'Income Tax Evasion: A Theoretical Analysis'." *Journal of Public Economics* Vol. 3, No. 2 (May): 201–02.

Index

Tax base (*cont.*)
  and charitable contributions, 189–190
  and education, 192–193
  and health care, 187–189
  and home mortgage interest, 182–187
  and standard deduction, 193–194
  and state and local taxes, 190–192
  complexity of, 139–142, 235
  consumption, 167–180
  corporate, 42
Tax evasion, 122–124, 143–156
  classification of, 147f, 147–148, 150,
    150t
  effects of, 148–152
  extent of, 146–148
  methods of detection, 152–154
  and vertical equity, 150–151, 151t
Tax-exempt threshold, 38
Tax forms, preparation of, time spent on.
  See Compliance costs
Tax gap, 146–147, 154
Tax incidence, 62–69
Taxpayer Compliance Measurement
  Program (TCMP), 146, 151, 154
Tax reform, 13–14
  competing plans for. *See* Alternative tax
  systems
  of existing income tax, 233–251
  capital gains and, 239–242
  corporate welfare and, 239
  deductions and, 29
  double taxation and, 235–237
  fairness and, 244–245
  inflation and, 237–238
  public opinion and, 233
  rate structure and, 186, 246
  savings and, 242–244
  tax base and, 235
  value-added tax and, 248–250
  history of, 27–30
  objections to, 10–13
  public debate over, 124–128, 253–258
  rhetoric of, 14–15, 253–258
Tax Reform Act (1986), 1, 5–6, 13–14, 29,
  72–73, 126, 131, 233
  and capital gains, 123, 241
  depreciation and, 43, 115
  and IRAs, 243
  and rate structure, 123, 138, 190
  repeal of investment tax credit, 44
  and tax base, 234

Tax revenue
  distribution of, 17
    by source, 18t
  federal, 18t
  historical aspects of, 21f, 21–22
  local, 18t
  as percentage of GDP, 17, 18t, 125
    comparison by country, 19–21, 20t, 100f,
      101f, 213–214
    economic impact of, 99–100, 100f, 101f
    historical trends in, 21f, 21–28, 24f, 26f,
      30, 96–97
  social insurance and, 18, 18t
  state, 18t
Tax shelters, 28–29
Tax shifting, 64–65
Tax system(s), alternative, 7–9, 14–16,
  195–232. *See also* Consumption tax; Flat
  tax; Poll tax; Sales tax; Value-added
  tax; Wage tax
  base of, 180–194
  consumption, 167–180
  and education, 192–193
  and health care, 187–189
  and home mortgage interest, 182–187
  and standard deduction, 193–194
  and state and local taxes, 190–192
  benefits of, 176–179
  capital gains in, 174–175, 179
  complexity and, 138–139, 179–180,
    208–219
  credits in, 9
  enforcement of, 208–219
  labor costs in, 8–9
  objections to, 10–13
  principles of, 161–194
  rate structure of, 162–167, 205–208
  transition to, 11–12, 173–176, 204–205
  work incentives and, 171
TCMP. *See* Taxpayer Compliance Measurement Program
1040A form, 133–134
1040EZ form, 2, 133–134
Thatcher, Margaret, 47
Time, 254–255, 255t
TRA. *See* Tax Reform Act (1986)
Training, effect of taxes on, 120–122
Transitional equity, 81–83
Treasury Department, 125–126, 147, 246
  analysis
    of double taxation, 236